OPERATIONS MANAGEMENT FOR SERVICE INDUSTRIES

OPERATIONS MANAGEMENT FOR SERVICE INDUSTRIES

COMPETING IN THE SERVICE ERA

Glenn Bassett

QUORUM BOOKS
WESTPORT, CONNECTICUT • LONDON

Library of Congress Cataloging-in-Publication Data

Bassett, Glenn.
    Operations management for service industries : competing in the
service era / Glenn Bassett.
      p. cm.
    Includes bibliographical references.
    ISBN 0–89930–746–9
    1. Service industries—Management. I. Title.
HD9980.5.B37   1993
658—dc20   92–19835

British Library Cataloguing in Publication Data is available.

Library of Congress Catalog Card Number: 92–19835
ISBN: 0–89930–746–9

First published in 1992

Quorum Books, 88 Post Road West, Westport, CT 06881
An imprint of Greenwood Publishing Group, Inc.

Printed in the United States of America

The paper used in this book complies with the
Permanent Paper Standard issued by the National
Information Standards Organization (Z39.48–1984).

10 9 8 7 6 5 4 3 2 1

for
Lolly

Contents

Contents

Preface

The Western world is on the threshold of an economic revolution—the long-foretold and -awaited service revolution. Already the labor force of the United States is 70% and more applied to service occupations. Soon it will be 90% plus. The mind-numbing routine of dirty factory work disappears daily, replaced by increasing customer contact and personal service. For those accustomed to vigorous human interplay, it is the dawn of a workplace Eden. To others less skilled at social give and take with strangers, it is a stressful if not terrifying journey into uncertainty and confusion. Some will be lifted up, others crushed by this juggernaut of change.

In the interest of accuracy, perhaps, it should be observed that the world is on the threshold of *another* economic revolution. Revolution in social and economic structure is hardly new or unusual. History records an endless parade of change in these dimensions. The most recent revolution was the industrial revolution, the same revolution that introduced the routine of factory and repetitive assembly-line work. It is, indeed, this very industrial revolution that has now run its course and is giving way to a dominant service economy. The lengthy reign of predictable stability in the industrial revolution's supporting social structure has habituated Western man to the 8:00 AM to 5:00 PM routine of isolated labor wherein social exchange was dismissed as wasteful and inefficient. The ideal factory worker was mute, perfect of hearing, but incapable of anything better than a nod or hand sign to acknowledge the boss' instructions. The preferred worker of the service era will be skilled socially, adept at small talk and attentive first to people rather than to things. A lot of human retrofitting is likely to be required.

The industrial revolution fulfilled its course of change on Western society approximately during the period between the American Civil War and World War I. Society was transformed from rural agricultural to urban industrial in a span of about a half-century. The experience of that transformation is beyond memory in the present-day world, accessible only through historical study and analysis. The scope of change that will be introduced in a transition to full-scale service economy is beyond ordinary commonsense knowledge, wholly outside the realm of shared social experience. Nothing in the collective social memory of present-day society prepares us for the crisis of this adjustment. We can only study, analyze and plan for this novel future by accessing the best available knowledge of the past. As a test of what is needed, we may we may apply that knowledge critically to an assessment of those institutions that at present exhibit stress or breakdown in the face of change to a service economy. One of the more profitable places to look for signs of stress and breakdown is in the management of service operations. Operations methods that fail because they cannot transfer over from mass commodity to service operations management methods are potential indicators of the scope of the transformation required.

This book will examine service operations to identify those transformations that are needed to manage service operations effectively in the new era. The major expected policy changes in service operations management have to do with sharply reduced standards of capacity utilization in plant and equipment, greatly expanded range and variety of skill in service-workers and assignment of top priority to forecasting, locating and managing transient bottlenecks in service processes. Those basic changes require that operations managers overcome more than a century of standard operations policy and method that worked well with mass commodity operations but have only limited utility in a commodity corner of the new services market. They are the same policy imperatives on which the emerging project economy structure of short-run and one-of-a-kind manufacturing processes must also be rebuilt. The common theme of twenty-first-century operations management policy and method will be the need to replace mass commodity operations methods with new service and project shop approaches, better suited to emerging cost and quality control requirements. From these changes will flow the broader transformations of social fabric needed to support the service revolution.

The chronic low quality of volume-oriented commodity production is the most visible current vulnerability of the old way. The new quality imperative is, to some extent, a demand for increased customization of services and products. But the problems of American industry in meeting the quality challenge of foreign competition are partly, at least, the result of overdependence on those "efficient" production methods that place quantity of output ahead of quality. Quality is a troublesome enough issue to define under the best of circumstances. The new era of higher quality begins with recognition that modern operations management policies can shape quality at its very foundation. Over and beyond that reality, definition and measurement of quality requires a prodigious effort that must typically be custom fitted to the industry, product and service. It is no accident and should be no surprise that more than one-quarter of the pages of this book are dedicated to examination of ways to support improved quality in service operations management.

The changes that the new service age introduces, though, go beyond new emphasis on quality and service. The extent of change anticipated in the management of service operations is only a rough analog of the magnitude of change that must come about in the whole of society and its social/legal/economic structure. Characteristic ways in which we relate to one another socially are about to undergo explosive revision. The polite amenities of the recent past will no longer do in a service business exchange. Customers are fast becoming individual, unique persons who want their individuality and uniqueness recognized.

Government—today a pervasive, costly and controversial service—requires change and revision on a magnitude unknown for more than a century. Government legislation must in many instances help pave the way to the service revolution by recognizing the new economic realities of the emerging service economy. And it must also lead the way by revolutionizing the quality of service delivered to its citizen customers. In an earlier industrial age, government evolved to serve in softening the harsher consequences of a competitive, concentrated mass commodity production system. It was a service adjunct to production, not a central element of the production economy. In a full-scale service economy, government emerges as one of the largest service suppliers. Its failure to supply quality, cost-effective services is partially if not largely a function of old commodity operations management methods and policies, inappropriately applied to service needs. The coming service revolution thus will inevitably be catalyzed *and* guided by government policy and action. Government reform is both metaphor and model for the coming service revolution.

Whether planned or unplanned, the service revolution will happen. The degree of foresight and planning applied to transforming our economy will determine how harsh and costly the transition must be for those human beings caught up in it. Thoughtful, rational preplanning of the revolution is an early service requirement of society. It is not yet one recognized for its service potential. Nor are the underlying principles of how to arrange an orderly transformation of an industrialized society—and perhaps even a world economy—yet adequately articulated. Maybe this book will provide a useful beginning.

OPERATIONS MANAGEMENT FOR SERVICE INDUSTRIES

Chapter 1

Service: The Customization Imperative

"In the final analysis, service, alone, establishes value."

Humankind has a long-term love affair with things. Like a flock of fluttering magpies, we accumulate things. Some are bright, some are dull; some are hard, some soft; all are tangible, real, substantial. We carry them in our pockets, on our backs, drag them on wheels or sleds and, if relatively immobile, set them down in a special place and put a fence around them. We work and scheme, make love and make war to retain or accumulate them. The physical universe is made up of things. They are a constant of our lives.

Some things are useful. A blanket warms us; a stick of wood serves as a club or fuel for the fire; a sharpened edge of iron splits wood or kills prey for food. Other things are merely decorative. A transparent bead catches the sun's beams; a small papier-maché palm tree on a wooden stand evokes the spirit of a warm summer's beach sand. The things we pursue and collect are things that serve our purposes and bring us enjoyment. To hold our attention, things must be useful. The universe, indeed, is full of things that we ignore completely. Some, noxious to our senses, we avoid. Only a fraction of all the things that exist merit our interest. We gather and retain only those that serve our purposes and pleasures.

Man is special in his love affair with things. He fashions things out of raw material in continually changing and unique ways. He polishes beads, smelts metals, carves wood, stacks stones for a wall and builds houses. But the things of humankind are not limited to the natural product of this world; we can conceive things that do not yet exist or copy things that do so as to expand the abundance of interesting things available for collection.

The largest part of the history of the species homo sapiens has been a history of toolmaking. Functional, purposeful tools that served the needs of warming, clothing, feeding and housing humankind exist in anthropological digs dating back tens of thousands of years. It is the intelligence demonstrated in the purposeful creation of tools that distinguishes man from earlier ancestors. Production of useful tools is an integral aspect of the place of humans in nature.

There is another important consequence of our intelligence that can easily be overlooked; we not only make tools, we also make icons. Pictures, representations, ornaments of every kind abound in our world. Earliest, preliterate man depicted significant events of life in crude paint on cave walls. We decorate our world, often for religious or spiritual purposes, and always to celebrate our highest pleasures and purposes. Some decorations serve as training devices, some as memory aids, some as messages to others. These are real even though intangible human possessions.

Those things we call plans and dreams come to exist in our imaginations as we expand our ability to use representations. The capacity to produce tools and ornamentations that bring us warmth, health, security and pleasure expands toward infinity as humans discover and rediscover their intelligence for fabricating ever new and different things. But things are now no longer exclusively physical things. Things are ideas and representations as often as not. They have substance only in the intelligence and in the mind of humankind. All of the things that we produce, tangible or intangible, are of value, fundamentally, because they serve our physical, metaphysical and psychological needs. It is, indeed, only in their utility for service that value is created in things.

SERVICEABILITY = VALUE

Tools that are not useful are not serviceable and are abandoned if they cannot be turned to alternative use. Physical things obtain their value out of their serviceability. Whether a product performs as intended or not is central to measurement of its quality. Performance to expectation is pure serviceability. Quality and service are closely related. But quality may also make reference to the aesthetically decorative aspects of a product. A large scratch on the white porcelain door of the new refrigerator will in no way impair its capacity for refrigerating the food inside. It may nonetheless destroy the ornamental simplicity of the clean, smooth surface, thereby impairing quality. Ornamental simplicity is a valued service—psychological in quality to be sure—but a service all the same. It is the serviceability of all dimensions of the "thing" under scrutiny that establishes its value.

The beads that a magpie collects don't appear to offer any real serviceability to the collector. They do not enhance physical well-being and don't seem to have any exchange value. We might reasonably surmise, though, that the glitter of light on the polished surface must evoke some pleasure response on a neural level that demands repetition. The bird must find enjoyment in the beads that makes it want to possess them. In that regard, humankind in the current age is not very different from magpies. People do seem to collect things that have no other utility for them other than the pleasure of owning them. Human beings, too, may possess some primitive neural response to color or glitter. That, too, we may accept as serviceability. We might also ascribe it to a crass materialism borne of fear, want or greed. Service need not always be noble or glamorous. As the psychological foundations of fear, want and greed diminish in the experience of plenty, though, we may reasonably expect that our fascination with tangible things may also relent. Mass-produced items drop in value as a direct function of their abundance. The serviceability of mere physical baubles will inevitably abate. We are not magpies. Ultimately, we demand serviceability that goes beyond mere glitter. Tangible things have no value in themselves until they serve their owner. Ideas and icons often serve more powerfully than mere physical things. Serviceability confers value. Intangibles that serve are as valuable as tangible ones. Service is the ultimate measure of economic value.

Given the ubiquitousness of service to the creation of value, we might reasonably ask if it is possible or even necessary to differentiate between things and services. Perhaps we should at least discriminate tangible from intangible. But value is so often obtained from a clever blend of the real and ideal. The physical and the psychological go hand in hand much of the time. Something more is needed if we are to usefully differentiate services from products in our conventional usage of these terms.

The notion of commodity is useful here. A standard product that is serviceable in many situations, that is mass supplied at minimum cost using highly specialized production equipment, is usefully classified as a commodity product. An electric steam iron or a pail of white paint would fit nicely into this class. Everything beyond that stage, customized and specialized to fit the individual customer's variation in preference, now becomes service. Indeed, the more individualized it is, the more serviceable it becomes.

It is this definition of service as the fitting of tangible and intangible offerings to the unique personal requirements of the individual that will be applied in these pages. Service is that which fits products and services to the special needs of individuals or limited groups of customers. Service celebrates our individuality. Commodity product demonstrates our alikeness. Conformity and sameness diminish in value as commodities proliferate. The greater value now inheres in uniqueness.

Part of the problem of defining service is in the fact that much of what we colloquially refer to as service in conventional terms is a package that combines individualized service with commodity product efficiencies. The typical American amusement park, clearly an intangible service— Disney World, for instance—is a commodity offering on nearly all terms. Some minimal special service may be offered the handicapped, the elderly or the ill who may happen on the premises, but the experiences available within the park are highly standardized offerings, mass promoted by a range of media, tightly organized and managed to assure the most cost-effective delivery of a thoroughly standardized and prepackaged offering. It is the total absence of any surprises among the "thrills" offered at the park that appeals. Customers know exactly what to expect and are seldom disappointed. Long queues of visitors wait in front of nearly every attraction, assuring maximized capacity utilization. Attendants are as fully preprogrammed in their roles as any assembly-line worker and are equally subject to the ills of mind-numbing routine. Supervision is close and continual. Work and equipment schedules are forecast with a high degree of precision to assure that personnel and "attractions" are fully and efficiently utilized. Efficiency and cost control are the hallmarks of commodity offerings. Disney World has both down to a science.

A scheduled airline—United, American, Delta and the rest—is largely a commodity service offering. Flights are scheduled to attract the numbers of passengers needed to break even, given the capacity of the equipment and the cost of its operation. A profitable flight is a full one whereon individualized service is necessarily reduced to a minimum. Some limited choice as to beverages, meals or magazines may be offered; wheelchairs may be available for the infirm; mothers with children may be permitted early boarding; but the commodity nature of the offering remains unmistakable. Volume traffic supported by maximized utilization of aircraft through a hub and spokes system of routes is indispensable to cost-effective operations. A scheduled airline is the most cost-efficient, seat-mile method of transporting passengers on lengthy, 500-plus-mile trips. Out-of-pocket ticket cost for a bus ticket may be lower, but the added cost of meals and personal time committed to the road make bus travel uneconomic for even ordinary business travel. Long-distance train travel is largely an exercise in nostalgia—a commodity offering in its own right. Auto travel requires that full passenger capacity be utilized to come near equaling the cost of air travel. Where driving is viewed as an entertainment in its own right, the value of an auto trip may outweigh air travel. There is very little, otherwise, that can compete cost- and convenience-wise with commodity air travel.

Distinguishing commodity service from noncommodity service in this manner is essential for purposes of proper organization and management of service. Commodity service offerings demand an operating approach that yields efficiency and cost minimization. Some degree of standardization and dependency on high volume are indispensable to cost control. Emphasis on cost control can limit the level of quality possible (we will examine this phenomenon in Chapter 12). Emphasis on intensive scheduling to utilize plant or equipment at near maximum capacity and thereby raise return on investment will often reduce quality markedly.

A simple experiment will illustrate the difference between volume and customized operations as they affect quality. Place a pail of dry beans on a waist-high surface. Set an empty pail fifteen feet away at the same level and spread some sheets between. Assume that you must pay rent on the two cups at the rate of one cent per second per cup (plant capital investment by analogy). The sales value upon transfer of each bean from one pail to the other is five cents. The cost of each bean awaiting transfer is one cent. Your goal is to transfer beans from one pail to the other using an ordinary teaspoon that rents at one cent per second (an unskilled laborer by analogy) and to maximize your profit. On one trial, transfer beans as fast as you can without undue concern for spilling them on the sheets, but avoiding spills as much as you can. Concentrate on speed and volume of production. On a second trial, transfer beans carefully, taking care not to spill, working as quickly as you can. This is a project that can be carried out with standard grocery store kidney beans and kitchen pots. The results of an actual demonstration of this experiment on one occasion are illustrated by Exhibit 1–1.

As is apparent from Exhibit 1–1, the profit derived from the sloppy transfer of beans is more than three times greater than with careful transfer because the cost of production resources is high. Some 35% of transfers must be defective before careful transfer becomes the profitable alternative. Given existing demand for payoff on capital, it is rational in bottom-line profit terms to risk waste of some beans (i.e., to produce poor quality) by moving as quickly as possible making transfers between pails (i.e., focusing on volume). If the cost of capital (rental of pails and spoon) were

Exhibit 1-1

The Dominant Effect of Capital Cost and the Payoff from Sloppy Work on "Moving Beans"

```
Specifications:
    Pails are set on tables at ends of 15-ft. transfer corridor.
    Pails are rented at $0.01 (one cent) per second.
    Beans cost @ $0.01 each.
    Teaspoon rents for $0.01 per second.
    Each fast transfer trip requires 7.5 seconds.
        12 beans are transferred with a spill rate of 15%.
    Each careful transfer trip requires 10 seconds.
        9 beans are transferred without spilling any.
    Transfer of beans is accomplished in a 5-minute work period.


Resultant financial position of "careful" 9-bean transfer trips:
    Transfer of 270 beans is complete at 300 seconds (5 min.).
    Value of beans transferred is $0.05 x 270 = $13.50.
    Cost of cup rental is $6.00.
    Cost of spoon rental is $3.00.
    Cost of material (beans) is $2.70.
    Total cost is $2.70 + $6.00 + $3.00 = $11.70.
    Net Profit is $1.80.


Resultant financial position of "fast" 12-bean transfer trips:
    Transfer of 408 beans is complete in 300 seconds (5 mins).
    15% or 72 are spilled in transit.
    Value of beans transferred is $.05 x 408 = $20.40.
    Cost of cup rental is $6.00.
    Cost of spoon rental is $3.00.
    Cost of material (beans) is $4.80.
    Total cost is $4.80 + $6.00 + $3.00 = $13.80.
    Net Profit is $6.60.
```

substantially reduced, it would no longer be economic to waste resources in the race for short-term payoff.

In the broader economy, inattention to quality is a direct function of the impatience of its controllers of capital wealth to further increase their holdings through investment in quick-payoff production capacity. That is essentially the dilemma of the commodity operation. Cost-effectiveness based on maximization of equipment or plant utilization can defeat quality goals and, if you assume that some bad beans get through to an individual customer, create major service problems for the operation.

COMMODITY VERSUS CUSTOMIZATION: THE PROJECT SHOP

In terms that I have defined elsewhere (Bassett 1991), customized, individualized service is, inherently, a matter of managing project shop operations—short-run or one-of-a-kind output, as opposed to managing commodity production operations. In operations management terms, customized service is the antithesis of commodity production. The qualities that distinguish a well-managed project shop are surplus capacity of plant and equipment to minimize waiting time for service, broadly skilled workers who can shift from one task to another as customer need dictates, assignment of responsibility for quality fully to those delivering the service, focusing attention on bottlenecks in the system wherever and whenever they occur and developing an ongoing dynamic simulation or model of the operation that predicts the impact of every added demand made upon it in terms of capacity usage and work skill application. These same operating methods are essential to effective delivery of high-quality service. They are examined more fully in subsequent chapters.

The project shop is a customizing device that fits physical production and service projects alike. Operating methods for project shop management depart maximally from those applicable to commodity shop operations. Service industries must blend the operating methods of a project shop and a commodity operation effectively to be successful. In many ways, this is a tougher job than merely redesigning operations in a project shop mode, a major transition in management style by any measure. There is potential for confusion and conflict of purpose in combining commodity operations with project shop operation methods in a service setting. We must therefore look first at the junctures of service where they meet. It is at these points that many of the major challenges of service industry operations management will be encountered.

Chapter 2

Commodity and Service
Aspects of Some Common
Services Contrasted

"Manage commodities with methods that are cost-efficient."

At this juncture of our analysis, we will examine a variety of common services to identify the commodity versus the unique offerings inherent in them. Managing service operations will rarely be a pure, simple matter of meeting individual needs. The part of the offering that can be cost-effectively obtained in a commodity mode must be identified and handled appropriately. The custom service part of the offering will draw as needed on commodity elements to supply the best value to the customer. Each, though, requires a different operations management approach. It is essential to identify which is which in order to avoid current-day confusion as to the most effective approach to managing service offerings.

The "easy" approach to managing operations is to reduce everything to the level of commodity and compete on price. The price of admission to Disney World is quite low given the technological elegance and cleanliness of the attractions offered, but the offsetting cost to the consumer is long waiting lines and the near total lack of personal exchange between patrons and employees. Anonymous actors in costumes of Mickey, Minnie, Pluto and Donald Duck represent well the strict circumscription of employee roles required for efficient delivery of this commodity product.

On the other end of the spectrum, we might identify the personal tutor who sits with the student, eliciting interest through human contact, identifying learning needs and adapting teaching methods to the level and ability of the learner. We might point to the seamstress or tailor who begins with a tape measure and bolt of material to produce custom-fitted clothing for the client. Even here, in this advanced age, we are likely to encounter some very basic commodities at the foundation of the offering. The tutor will employ printed text or, at least, mass-produced paper and pencils. The tailor's cloth and equipment may be commodity items. In a restaurant where everything is cooked to order, and the menu merely a guide to ordering, service can be at the maximum. Most restaurants, however, will fall somewhere between McDonald's or Pizza Hut—dominantly commodity offerings of food—and the familiar diner where 500 menu items are available with modest limitation on substitutions. The major distinction between commodity and service will be found in whether customer-requested variations or substitutions are permitted with standard menu items.

It is useful to examine the service-commodity distinction in a selected variety of service industries. Exhibit 2–1 is offered as a starting point for this purpose. We can begin to appreciate the complexity of managing operations in service industries more fully by looking at the range of service offerings that can be considered. For present purposes, the devices and techniques that are useful in blending commodity with service offering will be more easily grasped.

A hospital, for instance, would seem to be a clear example of service. In this age, many hospitals are poorly managed simply because there is so much opportunity for confusion over whether the health industry's offerings must be customized to the individual patient or rendered efficient so that the largest number of patients can be treated at the lowest cost.

Bed, room and meals in a hospital are typically commodity items at the extreme. There are two or three kinds of rooms, one kind of bed and a handful of different kinds of meals, mostly bland and uninteresting. The kitchen is almost always consolidated and centralized. Most food is hand-trucked to the patients' rooms, cooling in transport so that patients without taste cannot burn their gullets. It is often impossible to change a menu order with less than several hours' notice. Antiseptic cleanliness is pursued throughout as a commodity item.

Most hospitals today physically tag the patient upon entry so that identification is simplified, especially if the person becomes disoriented or unconscious. Treatment is, theoretically, individualized, but every disease has certain standards of treatment and many hospitals are departmentalized by types of disease to increase efficiency in delivery of standardized, commodity medical treatment. Patients are more often "cases" than they are people. Individualization comes mostly from the acts

Exhibit 2-1
Respresentative Listing of Service Industries

```
Financial Service:              Personal Service:
  Insurance                       Health Clubs
  Banks                           Recreation
                                  Beauticians
Health Service:                   Barbers
  Hospitals                       Tailors
  HMOs, etc.                      Seamstresses
                                  Realtors
Professionals:                    Hotels/Motels
  Physicians
  Pharmacists                   Public Service
  Dentists                        Police/Security
  Lawyers                         Fire Fighters
  Architects                      Refuse Removal
  Civil Engineers
                                Education
Business Service:                 Schools/Univ.
  Advertising                     Libraries
  Stockbrokerage
  Recruiting                    Restaurants
  Training                        Fast Food
  Corporate Staff                 Family/Diners
                                  Tray Service
Counselors:
  Weight Loss                   Service
  Marriage                        Churches
  Addiction                       Lodges/
  Career Planning                 Fraternities
  Pastoral                        Social Clubs
  Psychiatric                     Service Clubs

Communications:                 Maintenance Service
  Telephone                       Automobile
  Postal Service                  Appliance
  Information/MIS                  Household
                                    Plumbing
Entertainment:                    Electrical
  Television                      General
  Movies                          Landscaping
  Theater
  Amusement Park
  Ship

Public Transport:
  Railroads
  Airlines
  Buses
  Taxis/Limos
```

of visiting friends and relatives who often import specific food or equipment for the patient, and in the choice of the attending physician who, if chosen well, may be skillful and caring enough to apply the right kind of individualized, customized treatment.

The hospital itself is a commodity offering in almost every manner imaginable, but it is typically managed as though it were a personal service offering. Small, high-cost lots of any of thousands of items in inventory add cost but are justified as if each were for an individual customer. Inventory is seldom managed cost-effectively. The customer's choice—of room, of food, of personal schedule—is either limited or wholly made by physician or staff. Nurses are expected to follow the preferences of doctors first, patients later. If doctor and patient conflict, nurse must defer to doctor or risk professional censure. Patients are seldom treated as people. They are themselves commodities that are processed at a price through the system. The typical hospital thinks of itself as a service, charges patients as if it were a service, manages operations as if it were a commodity and is generally confused as to its economic identity. It should be no surprise that most hospital service is overpriced and severely disparaged.

Physicians sometimes seem confused as to whether it is they or the patient who is to be catered to. The exalted status of MDs can lead to arrogance and insensitivity that defeats service at its very roots. Doctors are rated more often on the technical skill of their surgery or diagnosis than on their concern for the whole patient. Displays of genuine caring are rare enough to be the topic of conversation among neighbors and the topic of Hollywood movies. Arm's length treatment, excessive fees and encouragement of naive patient expectation for painless restoration of full health inevitably lead to costly malpractice suits. The medical profession urgently needs to restore genuinely caring *and* realistic service as the center of its product offering. The doctor who delivers assembly-line medicine to patients scheduled to maximize utilization of his service delivery capacity is a contradiction in terms. He or she is to be avoided if service is the patient's objective.

Insurance companies face a dilemma similar to that of hospitals and physicians. The idea behind insurance is to collect money from customers in advance as a contingency against later loss due to chance events. On the face of it, this is a service. In an earlier age and, rarely, even today in special crises, loss through accident or crisis was handled by friends and neighbors in one's church or community. Everyone dipped into common or shared reserves to cover the loss. Excess resources of the wealthy community leader were considered part of those reserves.

In the age of megabusiness, it is hard for insurance company executives to think in terms of holding money in trust for its policyholders. Large funds must be invested. Investments may be risky with high potential return or safe with modest return. Which is the greater service to policyholders? The issue of service, here, may be lost. The executive ego or competitive pressures may, more likely, drive the final investment decision and, in consequence, insurance costs.

It is the business of an insurance company, of course, to take risk and expect loss. When loss occurs, insurance faces a new service question. To what extent should the policyholder be asked to produce clear proof of loss? What reasonable steps should be taken to reduce the cost of the loss? Many insurance companies adopt a policy of paying the maximum value of a loss so as to better service their policyholders. Is this fair to policy purchasers who do not have a loss but must pay a larger premium to cover the losses of others? Does it reward fraud and insurance claims padding at cost to honest policyholders?

Insurance has become a commodity in the present age, striving to manage investments and costs efficiently, but defining service in terms of generous, no-questions-asked payment, thereby mutating insurance from a contingency against loss into a lottery that pays off on accidents. Many of these purported losses represent no real loss in worth or serviceability of the insured item at all. A ten-year-old car with a damaged fender may be fully as reliable transport as one in good condition. Expecting insurance to restore it to original condition is likely to be ridiculous. A reasonable payoff would be the difference between the value of the vehicle as damaged and its value without damage.

Perhaps a lottery arrangement is as much a service as insurance against real loss is. Mutating insurance to a lottery commodity, however, defeats the intended service objectives of insurance. Real loss is sometimes hard to establish. Where the lottery is too generous, an insurance company can go broke, wiping out the value of all service from its policies.

The management option is to manage the insurance operation as a commodity or to redefine it as a genuine service that deals with the needs of individuals within a community. Group insurance policies offered through employers come as close as anything to this solution today. If medical insurance policies were sold by the same doctors or hospitals that honored them, the service aspect of medicine and insurance alike might be restored in both fields. Were auto damage policies sold by body repair shops, the costs of accident repairs and the policies supporting them might be more realistic. A basic service relationship between the parties to the contract may be essential, ultimately, to restore the service character to insurance.

Banks and financial institutions can easily lose sight of their customers. The emphasis on control and documentation of money transactions is a clear commodity operations imperative. Major credit card companies put great emphasis on their person-to-person service in supplying extra credit when the customer encounters an emergency, or permitting a payment to be skipped without penalty (though not without interest payment). Service in banks or with respect to credit cards is mostly a matter of ease and quickness of transactions. Machines and especially computers supply the necessary money commodity control and documentation cheaply and accurately, though without much personal contact between banker and customer. The opportunity exists for bankers to treat customers as individuals, addressing them by name, supplying useful information without being asked, smiling and offering pleasant comments. Loan officers may be given greater latitude in departing from standard procedure in approving loans to permit special, individual circumstances to be accommodated more often. Where it genuinely satisfies customer need, special "niche" services—including anything from child sitting and parking to securities brokerage—may be offered. Banking, at core, though, is a commodity offering. A bank can reduce cost by making customers stand in line longer or it can improve speed of service by opening more tellers' windows. It can offer a wide range of expensive services or a narrow range of cost-efficient basic ones. Service goes beyond cost, of course, and a bank can be self-consciously more friendly. It makes profit, though, only through efficient control of its operating costs. Banking is a classic commodity offering. Any "frills" add cost.

Entertainment is certainly a service, or is it? Many of the offerings we think of as service address mass markets and deal with customers as a class rather than as individuals. Major-league football and baseball are every bit as much commodity offerings as is Disney World. TV and movies also fit the commodity category in large measure. To the extent that mass entertainment markets are segmented by taste preference, there is some movement toward a service orientation. That is equally true of segmentation in automobile sales. The budget for movies aimed at smaller markets is correspondingly reduced to fit the forecast revenue, just as the design cost of an auto aimed at a limited segment is appropriately constrained. Cable TV offers multiple choice of viewing segmented to the variety of markets identified by advertisers and customer demand. Offering variety in choice is a manner of service. The greater the variety, the less the appropriateness of managing the industry in a commodity operations mode. The birthday party clown or belly dancer offers specific entertainment for the individual celebrated. The greater the entertainer's adaptation of the performance to the preferences and tastes of the target party, the closer we come to true service. The reality of a commodity offering modified in small measure to the immediate circumstance remains. Friends who gather to exchange stories or jokes over dinner and a card game come about as close as is possible to achieving a true service orientation in entertainment.

Dinner at a restaurant that features waiter or waitress service might also best be classified as entertainment. To be served as one passively sits at the table is the mark of wealth or royalty. The more elegant or unusual the dinner fare, the greater the status conferred on the customer by the event. Dining out, aside from being a convenience for those without food preparation capacity, is potentially an entertainment that permits the pretense of high personal status to be enacted from the occasion. Service must be found in the adaptation of menu or timing of food presentation or personal knowledge of customer preference to be accommodated. The maitre d' at Club 21 who greets customers by name and escorts them to their personal tables offers maximum service in this entertainment. He is usually well paid for the performance. Tips (an acronym for "to insure proper service") are a device for rewarding the deference demanded to create the status differential between server and customer required by the entertainment. The standard percentage—once 10%, now 15% or more—is merely the price of the deference offered. The increase in standard percent in recent times represents the reduced willingness of servers to play a lesser status role. True obsequiousness in service is vastly more expensive than mere standard pleasantness. The average waitress delivers a commodity product of food and service. Her tip is only part of the price. Increasingly, it is removed from the realm of customer discretion and added directly to the check. That is exactly what would be expected of a commodity offering.

Government service is considered by some an oxymoron—a contradiction in terms. For those who need it in an emergency, police or fire protection is an invaluable service. In the not-too-distant past, police protection was highly customized to individual circumstance. Those without credentials or visible means of self-support were treated as potentially dangerous until they demonstrated otherwise. Solid citizens and taxpayers who complained to the police could often get immediate redress. The rowdy or abusive were set straight, abusively if necessary, and the criminal caught in the act was subject to instant punishment.

Some years ago on a lonely Texas road, for instance, I was briefly harassed by a trio of young men. In my legitimate role as a young Air Force lieutenant, I called on the local sheriff for protection. These cowboy drifters were easily judged to be troublemakers by the officer, required to make restitution for the small monetary loss they had caused me, then detained briefly while I proceeded down the highway far enough to leave them many miles behind. It was a service of inestimable value to me.

In the interim, society has (mistakenly, in my view) made a commodity out of police protection, equally available to all, responsible citizen and penniless drifter alike. Service is no longer available from the police, at least not in these terms. Today I would have to be assaulted and bloodied before I could ask and get police intervention. Officers who effected redress in the fashion of my Texas lawman would be subject to complaint and discipline. Dealing with people simply and directly in terms of their relative behaviors and characters, a service of great value in maintaining social stability and community security, has been lost to the police. They may offer service today only under specified conditions and only to a specified extent. That has limited some past abuses of those without status or means, but it has also vastly diminished the value and efficacy of police services to the stable citizens of the community.

Government service has fallen victim to the commodity management age. Everything must be classified and handled in standard fashion. Even firemen seem to have less flexibility in handling problems than they once had. Technology has improved their performance in fighting fires, but bureaucracy has probably reduced their flexibility in offering service. In the cleanup of a fire site, for instance, regulations may specify exactly how far they can go. Simple remedy for smoke or heat damage that they might once have offered the unlucky citizen is now prohibited by regulation. That's classified as a problem for the insurance company.

The enforcement and confiscatory powers of some government agencies (such as assessors, tax collectors, zoning boards, health officers, probation officers, welfare officials, public housing officers and others) has made policemen—in the new, even-handedly bureaucratic sense—of many. Government as service to its citizens has been replaced by government as enforcer of rules and warden of the general populace. That may be efficient and relatively just. But it is hardly the kind of high-value service that government once offered its citizens. In an earlier age, social welfare was administered by government on a citizen-by-citizen basis, frequently for a small added fee to the individual government agent. Corruption and gross inequality in the delivery of service may have been partially redressed in the new era of government, but the quality of service offered has certainly diminished.

Indeed, it is not so much that taxes have escalated as that services have been lost that generates taxpayer revolution in the current era. Insistence by some on greater efficiency of service or reduction in service to decrease taxes only emphasizes government service as a commodity offering. The value of government to the average taxpayer has diminished as efficiency and equity of treatment have been added. The major government services offered today often come from elected officials who assist their constituents in overcoming the rigidities of bureaucratic regulation. The coin of current politics is often found in assistance offered to finding the exceptions and loopholes that can be exploited to individual advantage. Elected officials can be effective servants of their electors if they are so minded and skilled. Those who do can generally depend on enduring support for reelection. The service offered is valuable enough to garner and hold the most skeptical of votes.

The intention of government to provide service in matching people with open jobs in the private economy is a noble and impressive thrust in the direction of real service. The effective matching of talent, temperament and work opportunity is an individualized service of major economic significance. Present-day methods for accomplishing this noble aim are, unfortunately, only rudimentary at best. The attempt fails in the bureaucratic proceduralism thought necessary to treat all job seekers equally. Equality inevitably generates conditions that require a commodity operations management design. It is the uniquenesses of people that make for success in particular jobs. If only on a superficial level, private employment agencies can search for the right match. Often, where successful, private placement firms have negotiated the shape of the job with the employers and simultaneously mentored the candidate to file off any sharp edges that would impair the fit, thereby engineering a mutual adaptation to the needed match. It is a valuable service.

Unemployed citizens, anxious and demanding of employment, can see such measures as unfair only if applied by a government agency. Few workers appreciate the delicacy of job fit that typically and realistically prevails in complex organizations. Government is of service to them only if it can put them to work earning a good paycheck. The requirement of a reciprocal service in the form of effective work performance is easily overlooked here. This is an attempt at service by government that fails because it must be offered inappropriately in a commodity operations mode. To be offered as a service it must be radically redesigned. Otherwise it should be abandoned.

Some government services like road repair or trash collection began as devices that offer employment to political supporters from large voter blocks or in times of economic crisis. The inherent difficulty of maintaining commodity operations standards of high efficiency and low cost in these services usually defeats their utility to the taxpaying public. The service aspect of employment in municipal services is more likely to be supplying jobs. It is the government's intent to provide an alternative to private employment as a form of social service that must be evaluated here. The widespread perception that such employment is usually a political payoff without requirement for productive effort doesn't help improve the level of service in either of these terms.

Repair and maintenance are often custom offerings that have high potential for cost avoidance and customer convenience. The auto or refrigerator that won't work represents direct expense and lost time to its owner. Timeliness of service can be a major factor in the value and quality of service to the customer. Repair and maintenance services must be flexible and responsive. They must work to priorities rather than on a strict first-come first-served basis. If the service is mobile, taking service directly to the repair site, some efficiency in application of time may be found in efficient sequencing of stops to reduce unnecessary travel. But, overall, efficiency is not primary in managing repair and maintenance services effectively. The needs of the individual customer must be considered first.

Because repair and maintenance are dominantly service oriented, approaches to operations management should emphasize efficient, flexible scheduling for minimum operating cost and maximum service response. The furnace repair technician in midwinter may work continuous double shifts to prevent his customers' pipes from freezing, then wait long periods between jobs in the summer. The emergency room physician may have no time for so much as a cup of coffee on Saturday night, but go hours without activity on Monday night. Service cannot be inventoried and kept on the shelf; it must be supplied at the time and place needed. Emergencies are part of the business. A source of low-priority, non-time-constrained tasks to fill in the gaps may be useful for assuring continuous productive application of the employee's time, but repair and maintenance, like emergency medical treatment, demand real-time response to customer need that puts unimportant work or interest aside for the duration.

Hairdressers and barbers must supply a high degree of personalization in their service offerings. Timeliness is much less an issue in this business, though grooming for special events may dictate occasional timing requirements. Fortunately, most such needs can be handled through advance appointments for the desired time. The greater part of this service is in meeting the customer's expectation for enhanced personal appearance. This is always a matter of individual taste. The beautician or barber chosen must determine how the customer ideally sees him or herself and work to achieve that image. The service provider who satisfies his or her own personal vision of good appearance in the customer without concern for the customer's perspective may seriously disappoint the client's expectations. Commodity grooming products like hair colorings or tonics are an important part of the business because they enhance the service, add to the profit line and are conveniently included in the service offering at no added effort on the service supplier's part. This is, perhaps, the best kind of blending of commodity and service offerings in that the commodity supports individualized service, adding revenue and profit at no appreciable increase in labor.

A similar emerging service is that of wardrobe consultation. The consultant assists clients in choosing the wardrobe appropriate to their professional roles, drawing on either custom-tailored or commodity offerings as appropriate to satisfy the need. This new service is closely related to wardrobe management in the theater or movies. Help is offered in achieving the desired image for the audience addressed in both instances.

The greater part of education in today's economy is a strict commodity offering. In the public arena, powerful political forces shape a bland, safe offering that offends no one of importance, removes most of the excitement from learning and largely rules out any individualization of service. Even special education for the handicapped or exceptionally bright is specifically programmed and budgeted according to bureaucratic plan. But education serves no purpose of value until it makes the desired impact on the individual student. Served up as a commodity offering to the public, it must either fail with significant frequency or offer a product that is pitched at the level of the lowest common denominator. Nor does education as commodity enjoy any of the efficiencies of cost normally associated with a commodity. The discomfort of students and teachers, cast in the wrong mold, denied service and the opportunity to offer service, creates friction and mischief in the system. Individual tutoring becomes, in many instances, a necessary support of the system to permit minimum success at high cost. In an earlier age when teachers had the freedom to experiment and explore with individual students, teachers often enjoyed heroic status with students and parents. In the current age, teachers must struggle to make a largely unworkable system work as best they can and frequently find themselves cast in the villain's role by angry students, parents or administrators. A strong teacher's union is a virtual necessity if teachers are to just hold their own in this kind of political free-for-all.

Education has become an example of a service that is wrongly miscast in the commodity operations mold, rendered incapable of supplying adequate, much less high-quality, service. Until and unless education is reorganized to permit delivery of customized service to each student/customer, it will be subject to continuous, often bitter, customer complaint. Higher education has the freedom and the potential for offering superior service if the teacher is personally capable of relating to individuals. Because of their focus on scholarly research, many college professors do not have time for relationships in their brief encounter with often transient students. To fill the gap, most universities provide extensive counseling, advising and tutoring services to their students—again, at high cost. The occasional sensitive professor who can diagnose and solve students' learning problems is a giant among his or her colleagues with students. Even here, though, the commodity emphasis on standard educational content, well represented in the style and scope of standard textbooks, undercuts much of the fundamental service mission of higher education.

Libraries, long an essential adjunct of education, do a somewhat better job of servicing clients. The commodity aspects of library work—storing, handling, record keeping, selecting and ordering new titles—are nicely separated into specialties that do not often impact the customer. If shelves are open and brightly organized, customers may serve themselves. Librarians are trained in their craft, thoroughly familiar with their inventory and the organizing system applied to it. Indexes and cross-indexes, references and cross-references present opportunity for each customer to pursue an individualized course of search and research. In the middle ages, the book itself was the service. Access to this service was limited to legitimate scholars. Now, books are the commodity, and provision of systematic, easy customer access to them is the service. It is significant, perhaps, that libraries have had a lengthy span of time to evolve into effective service providers.

Mail and package delivery services offer still a different perspective on service operations. The U.S. mail began primarily as a service, relatively unencumbered with bureaucracy. As a government agency that enjoys a significant monopoly on its service domain, the U.S. mail was destined to grow fat and slothful. Like any monopoly, a service that has no real competition will raise prices to the maximum, reducing service at the same time to a minimum. In the case of domestic mail, the cost of mailing a letter has escalated to a level where it is often more effective to use electronic communication—phone lines predominantly—as a more convenient and often lower cost alternative. With the emergence of real competition, mail delivery has turned to commodity operations methods to reduce or control costs and retain customers. The lure of a commodity solution to operating problems is not new in service industries. A service that cannot supply service, however, is in as much trouble as one that is under competitive siege.

In small towns, service can be found in the post office. Postal employees are well positioned to learn customers' names, home addresses and some of their interests. If they do so without appearing nosy or engaging in gossip about customers, they can begin to offer individualized service on a major scale. In larger central cities, mail service is likely to be a strict commodity offering—formal, impersonal, bureaucratically regulated by the book. Postal employees could readily enough use customers' names addressing them, smile and suggest related services that might improve delivery or save money, but that is still a rarity in big-city post offices. A service that will not offer even basic individualized services must inevitably appear uncaring to its customers. Overemphasis on efficiency in a commodity mode of operation is not effective management in a service industry. Some basic effort must go into creating a service.

Package delivery has followed a somewhat different line of development from mail delivery because of the special quality of competition offered mail service by UPS, Federal Express, Airborne Express and others. These operations are widely noted for their emphasis on efficiency in operations. They base their competitive strategy almost wholly on efficiency and cost control. UPS, self-proclaimed as "the tightest ship in the shipping business," employs commodity operations methods on a level with the most advanced factory production lines. The core of its service is fast, low-cost delivery of packages. Work performance standards are strict. But UPS customer contact is typically also pleasant, courteous and helpful. That has not prevented competitors like Federal Express and Airborne Express from cutting into UPS's market with more individualized service in the form of pick-up, package monitoring or speed of delivery. UPS has been hard-pressed to retain its superemphasis on commodity-style operations efficiency while responding to the accelerating expectation for service among its customers.

Lawyers, accountants, insurance agents and stockbrokers purport to offer personalized service, though often it is on a strictly formula basis. A large part of today's practice of law, accountancy, insurance sales and stock transactions could readily enough be programmed in menu form on computers and delivered by trained, knowledgeable paraprofessional specialists. The routine services offered in law are commodity offerings in every sense of the term. Customers demand only a sound product at a fair price. A commodity offering at inflated price is a contradiction in terms. The pretense of added value through individualized professional service is frequently only an excuse to drive up the fee. The potential for genuine service, though, awaits discovery. Law as a legitimate service can be a blend of counseling, business acumen, political involvement, real estate and tax knowledge and contributing to community leadership needs.

In similar fashion, a good accountant does not just keep books. In this age almost anyone with a personal computer can do that competently. He or she is an advisor on cash needs or sources, monitors for dishonesty or error of employees and helps keep clients from running afoul of tax and labor laws. A knowledgeable insurance agent will help clients get adequate coverage at the best price and will also point out important options in the way of inexpensive added coverage for special vulnerabilities of the individual client. The customer who does not know about flood, extended liability or business interruption insurance may be needlessly exposed to major and very real loss. Stockbrokers are dependent on their sales commissions for a living and, if not sufficiently service oriented, may focus excessively on generating account activity. Brokerages that offer no service or advice can and do easily discount their fees to customers. In the longer run, though, abandoning the service opportunity may be self-defeating to stockbrokerage firms. Clients who need information or education on investment risks or options can find it through a knowledge-able broker. If the broker knows the client's personal interests and re-sources well enough, he or she can alert the client to unusual opportunity and assist in hitting the critical timing windows. These can be valuable services, indeed.

Real service is available from these professions when the professional knows how and is willing to offer it. All, however, are subject to the error of a commodity and efficiency approach to management and pricing of their service. Until blended skillfully with genuine individualized service, the commodity side of any service offers a dead-end to professional and customer alike. The commodity dimension alone does not offer sufficient value to justify a professional fee rate. These four professions are plagued today with bad reputations because so many in their practice insist on the professional fee scale while offering nothing beyond basic commodity service. The prevalence of this abuse is so great that many clients have no expectation of anything better than low-value service at inflated prices. As paraprofessional and computer programmed alternatives emerge, service professions like these will be sorely challenged to find clients who want to pay for service that has no individualized character. There is going to be some big trouble in Profession City.

Certainly, clerical, printing and data services must be included in any survey of service industry characteristics. In the electronic age, services in this group that once were distinct have blended. The most popular data services deal with either custom printing of manuals and reports or creation of proprietary mailing lists. Typesetting no longer requires molten lead slugs; the copy comes directly off a computerized keyboard and is instantly electrophotographically copied or etched. The core of clerical services has become editorial in quality. The skilled typist who can correct spelling and grammar as copy is entered for storage or staging to print is today's one-person mass communication technician. Her or his tools are computer, printer, paper and telephone lines. The computer has gone from R&D invention to mass commodity in less than two generations. Printers range from under $200 upwards to multimillion-dollar commercial presses, all dependent on computer-processed words and graphics for the fodder they feed on. Out of this milieu has come a major new service industry. The one-person office at home serving the exact communications needs of local customers has become commonplace. Office services have become a frequent storefront occurrence in busy shopping plazas. Variety in this style of service proliferates almost daily to meet customer need. Ultimately, the customer, him- or herself, sets up shop in a spare bedroom to obtain the absolute maximization in custom communication service.

On the organized commercial level, mailing lists are created and maintained for sale by specialized segment to salespeople seeking to target direct mailings to potential customers. Lists are generated and regenerated using every conceivable device, constantly seeking to identify unique customer segments with ever more accuracy. Truly, it is in the burgeoning targeted communications industry, from cottage to corporate in size, that the spirit of the new service industries is to be found. Society is in the process of reforming to support the individualism this industry thrives on. Personally addressed and formulated mailings using the customer's name and referencing personal preferences daily revolutionize the meaning of mass merchandising. Records of choices and preferences by individual customers fill computer data banks, driving product/service design choices as well as sales approaches. It is fast becoming difficult to get lost in a crowd. There is a salesperson out there somewhere who wants to get to know you and service you better.

At the other end of the economic spectrum, commodity items like automobiles and refrigerators now must compete dominantly on the basis of their ease of use and reliability in operation. "User friendly" is a service concept. Value arises out of the blend of utility and pleasure derived from a purchase. Henry Ford could offer any color Model T to the public "as long as it was black." Every color of the rainbow can be found on today's roadways, befitting the vast variety of taste differences that prevail in the world. A refrigerator that does not defrost itself or make ice cubes overnight cannot find a market today. The serviceability of the product is its most important sales feature. The cheap commodity that quickly and crudely fills a heretofore unmet human need has become a rarity. The traditional operations tools and methods that served commodity production still dominate in service operations, even though they are not suited to a service economy. The means and methods of business operation that have been in place for as much as 200 years are suddenly inappropriate to the new service-oriented marketplace. We must continue to "render unto commodities that which best serves commodity operations." But a new age of operations is at hand in managing services. Service operations in a noncommodity mode require a wholly new management approach.

This brief survey of selected service industries illustrates many of the challenges and opportunities that face service operations in today's world. Where a commodity element is part of the service offering, it is critical to identify it clearly, manage it appropriately to achieve efficiency and control cost, then take every action to prevent it from dominating the offering to the exclusion of expected service. Always, the service element needs different treatment from the commodity side. The service side will require different skill and temperament from that required by the technical, commodity aspect of the offering. The methods and attitudes that differentiate a true service offering from a commodity product or service are the core subject of this book. They are extensively treated in the chapters that follow.

Chapter 3

Effective Service Delivery

"If it doesn't locate the customer, it's not service!"

Service is a troublesome concept. It is used in many peculiar or confusing ways in day-to-day speech. We speak of various branches of the military as service, describe the opening volley of a tennis exchange as service, call a ritual of religious observance service and refer to the wires that connect our home to electricity as service. The term comes to us from the latin *servus*, meaning slave, which seems minimally connected as a meaningful root term to these usages.

Service as a business offering, perhaps, embarrasses when thought of as an act of enslavement to the customer. Free men are too proud to accept servile status before their fellows. The notion of service is, as a result, revised or specialized in ways that avoid that harsh association with inferior status. We may apply the concept of service more easily to religious worship because the object of service is an abstract, omnipotent God. Racqueting the ball over the tennis net is either a friendly or aggressive act depending on the competitive climate of play. Machinery and similar inanimate equipment is easily relegated to status of servant. The strict discipline of military duty is enough like enslavement to merit description as service in its original sense, and is employed almost as a synonym for duty.

In private business relationships, though, getting down to the nitty-gritty of service as catering to the customer, slave-like, goes down hard with proud, free people. Some forms of service seem to reverse the power relationship, making the server the master. Medical doctors treat and prescribe to their patients, who are clearly subordinated to the expertise of the attending physician. Public servants may uncompromisingly enforce laws on their employers, the citizenry, making mockery of their status as servants. Teachers subjugate their students to their superior will and knowledge, making virtual order-takers of their learner customers.

Business is widely conducted on a take it or leave it basis with customers. "It's what we have in stock" rolls easily off the tongue of the salesperson. Commodity production is inherently standardized, suited to a limited, producer-defined set of customer needs. Availability of variety to fit individual customer preference depends on the vigor of competitive enterprise. Giant high-volume producers of commodity products have little concern for the individual customer. Efficiency and low cost are deemed service enough.

Those who provide genuine customer-centered service in today's economy are almost a special breed, often lavishly compensated for their willingness to serve. Waiters in the best restaurants expect extravagant tips on top of sizable bills. Realtors who chauffeur customers about town, offering advice, reinforcing the desire for the best property, softening the blow of the high price, all without assurance of any recompense, finally collect their liberal fee reward at the closing of the sale. Elected public officials, periodically subjected to the whim of the voting public, expect the perks of power and high status in their jobs, then award themselves large salaries or retirement benefits as compensation for their electoral insecurity. Customers complain about arrogant waiters and the high cost of dining out. Property sellers object to high property sales fees. Citizens complain about high taxes and limited services from government. These are all points of chronic friction in our social and economic system. They persist, unremedied, because of our attitude toward service. The certain belief persists, often unspoken, that giving true service demeans the server. We are often too proud to serve, and we frequently treat with contempt those who will serve.

A commodity economy relies on the argument of efficiency and cost control to dismiss real service as cost ineffective. Service in a commodity-dominated economy has, to some extent, been redefined as efficient, low-cost provision of the economic basics. Those economic doctrines and systems of production that have characterized the past 200 or so years of Western society were based on the imperative of mass output to overcome want and scarcity. That doctrine and those systems have largely run their course. Commodity abundance no longer justifies them. Only a fundamental rediscovery of service as the basis of value in commerce will satisfy today's customer expectations. For nearly two centuries, we have all been servants of the commodity production strategy, convinced of our dignity and freedom because we were servants of no other human being. Now we must rediscover the rewards and satisfactions of being both master and servant in a world where only service satisfies and succeeds.

FROM EFFICIENCY TO SERVICE

Before World War II, everyone within a twenty-five mile radius of Manhattan shopped in Macy's on Herald Square and went to the movies at RKO Radio City. Each in its own way mass merchandised on a scale formerly unheard of. The excitement of the great metropolis with towering buildings, underground transport caverns and incomparably innovative product/service offerings drew crowds to its center from great distances. Today, going into mid-Manhattan at night is on a par with visiting an active war zone. The excitement is still there, but only a particularly hardy breed of cliff-dwelling locals will be found who frequent the nighttime streets on foot. Once the most magnetic center of commerce for the world, the metropolitan business district is rapidly becoming an historical curiosity.

The life-style of the central metropolis has been its own worst enemy. The variety of choice offered, the freedom of movement, stimulation of crowding, the novelty of varied human type and, not least, the abundance of commodity-produced wealth all round have transformed it from the tight-knit, mutually supportive community it once was into an impersonal, faceless megalith of grasping, teeming humanity. The absence of service in the form of basic social courtesy and human outreach has destroyed the soul of the big city. It has evolved to a rat race for riches and self-satisfaction. When the product of mass output is raised in value above the customer, society reverts to competitive survival of the fittest. Lowest cost is king. Civilization suffers for it.

Commodity production and sales require centralization of resources and business activity. Large, efficient factories require extensive populations of laborers located close by. Efficiency of sales demands centralized inventory in a limited number of locations. In rural America, the traveling salesman once went door to door vending kitchen supplies, farm implements or Bibles. The efficiency of a universal postal system on rails and wheels, connecting gigantic centralized mail-order warehouses directly with the public, killed that style of personal service in merchandising. The great depression of the 1930s brought back door-to-door sales for a time, but efficiency drove it again into the stores. Bread and milk were once universally delivered to the buyers' doors to assure freshness, but mass commodity merchandising ultimately won out. Cost reduction demands that commodities be handled efficiently. Adding personal service to their delivery is deemed too expensive.

The nearest thing to customer convenience in commodity sales today still is the central and accessible store location. Supermarkets for almost anything are carefully located next to the exit ramps of superhighways and along major thoroughfares. Crowded, noisy, sometimes dangerous, these superstores compete vigorously on price, often only a few pennies different, while they define service in terms of range of commodity merchandise or speed of completion of the sale. The most successful retailers, Wal-Mart or Nordstrom, for instance, extend personal service and cover the cost through higher volume sales or lower advertising cost. Ultimately, all must return to service as the bedrock of sales success.

Physical location of plant and store have dominated customer service for the largest part of the twentieth century. Good, central locations, though, are becoming harder to find, more expensive to maintain. Taxes, security, liability, theft, high labor cost and a variety of associated, escalating costs threaten their viability. The attractive excitement of the casbah-styled megastore, be it a gigantic integrated shopping plaza or an old-fashioned metropolitan shopping district, gives way to a blend of fear and boredom.

Location for service is a different issue from location for low cost. Once the advantage of cost in commodity product and mass commodity sales location wanes, location is a wholly new problem, even though there still may be an element of cost as part of the commodity side of service that must be considered in physical location. The emerging and potentially greater dimension of location is psychological. As the casbah-styled megastore formerly fed the psychological need for excitement and diversion, expectation of genuine and intense personal service will drive the configuration of new business locations. The likely solutions will be in the form of more temporary megamarts styled on today's flea markets or country fairs, more mobile service at the customer's door and more sales over electronic media using much enhanced phone and TV linkups.

Service must be found at or near the customer. Decentralization is indispensable. Corner grocery stores, once a feature of every city, are returning in the form of "convenience" stores. Personal service from hairdressers or barbers has always been dispersed into local neighborhoods. Gasoline stations must be widely distributed about communities to serve customers where they live. Doctors, insurance agents and realtors all must locate increasingly nearer their customers and their territories. The ubiquitous automobile, formerly the magic carpet to the outside, centralized, efficient world, has become an expensive, dangerous, pollution-spewing nuisance that further detracts from health by encouraging indolently unhealthy, hazardous commutes. Service is more often located in the neighborhood where its customers live.

The problem with much of this redeployment of service offerings is often found in zoning ordinances that bar business in residential neighborhoods. Business as the sale of efficient commodities has taken on so tarnished an image that no one wants it for a neighbor. The usual solution, after much complaint from adjacent homeowners, is the minimall or small shopping plaza on open land near a major local intersection. Meanwhile, cottage industry of considerable scope and magnitude expands into residential neighborhoods as small service operations—telephone answering services, child care, clerical offerings and other electronic, low-customer-traffic activities—move silently into private homes, using basements, spare rooms or garages for convenience of service and reduction in overhead.

In their transitory form, these businesses are both a problem and an advantage. They avoid regulation and taxation because they are small and often invisible. This reduces cost, which encourages and supports start-up growth. It threatens to erode the tax base, though, since business-zoned real estate is taxed proportionately higher than residential property because of its efficient business utility. It is easier to raise business taxes than residential ones when business is concentrated because business can pass taxes through to customer as an invisible tax on purchases. The fixed, efficient, central location of business property also sometimes makes it more vulnerable to political exploitation. The coming deconcentration of business in all its various forms will create a major political and tax crisis.

Much service already comes on wheels. Home and yard maintenance, ambulances, some veterinary clinics, appliance repair and mobile libraries are a common sight in many residential neighborhoods. Business on wheels does not require an expensive, high-visibility business location. Vehicles are cheaper and shorter lived than property. They are depreciated, sold or replaced more easily. These service offerings, as a result, will be harder to regulate and tax. Taxes that visibly and directly increase cost paid by a limited base of closely served customers are subject to earlier, stronger protest from those same customers.

Thus, the changes that appear likely in the delivery of service are ones that have the potential for broad-ranging change in the political economy. Smaller, more self-contained communities where local service is the norm will be more self-regulated, more sensitive to local need. Taxes will be harder to impose on this service business base. Big government will also be less welcome to business owners and customers alike. Therein lies the blueprint of a major economic revolution.

LOCATING SERVICE TO FIT THE CUSTOMER

If it can't locate the customer, it's not service. The location of the customer is not strictly physical, though. In many if not most instances of service-giving, location is preponderantly psychological. Even physical location is likely to be chosen for its psychological "image" association or its easy exploitation of well-established customer habit. Successful service is always as much an entertainment as it is an economic utility. Finding the customer where he or she lives psychologically is the first priority of good service delivery.

Psychological associations and images that drive human behavior tend to be specific to the individual, or, at minimum, subject to categorization only at complex levels. Some physical locations appeal to one category of customer, turn off another and leave a large number with feelings of indifference. The rooftop restaurant in a big city hotel is a magnet for those who find exhilaration in the rooftop view, a terror for those with acrophobia, without attraction to those interested only in a quiet, moderately priced meal. Those who shop or commute by automobile seek out offerings with adequate parking, while those using public transportation will look for services convenient to their route of travel, particularly those at the points of departure and destination. Major airports, the intersections of the world, often look like supermarkets. Major highways offer intersections or access ramps where traffic must slow and stop. These are natural locations for service stations and restaurants. Any main route of vehicular travel has potential for customer attraction by businesses along the way.

The near universality of mail and phone service has turned mailboxes and personal telephones into business locations in their own right. Toll-free phone numbers, postage-paid return order forms preprinted with customer name and address, preapproved credit in the form of cards and accounts—all contribute to one's shopping ease without ever leaving one's home. Home, of course, is the most personal and intimate of locations at which to find and do business with a customer. Telemarketing expands rapidly to exploit the advantages of this ideal service location. Intimacy may not always be an advantage to sales, of course. Modern-day telemarketing methods that use phone contact at home near the dinner hour can be self-defeating when they intrude unwanted on personal or family time. The conceit of the high-pressure supersalesperson who wants efficiency in generating "contacts" to make more sales overrides good judgment in these instances, inappropriately imposing a commodity sales design on a contact located in the most personal of psychological circumstances.

Location can generate a magic or mystique all its own when it is attractive enough. It is no accident that Disney World is billed as the "magic kingdom." An aura of magic is exactly what promoters *must* create around this distant, isolated, crowded place. The local bar or restaurant strives to create an aura of romance or an ambience of relaxation to attract the sought clientele. Shopping malls strive for a carnival or holiday atmosphere to give customers the experience of a happy diversion on their shopping trips. Energizing excitement, warm romance, significant opportunity for accomplishment, enhanced personal status all serve to attract customers to distant service locations. The greater the attraction, the greater the perceived value of the location and, perhaps, the service. Location without special or personalized attraction must depend on habit or convenience to draw customers. Where specialized attraction, habit or convenience do not support location, price, service and quality are the only available substitutes. Price without service is a clear commodity offering strategy. Quality is a fundamental and pervasive dimension of service that will be dealt with at considerably greater length in subsequent chapters (see Chapters 10–13).

MAKING SERVICE ACCESSIBLE

Convenience of service may be a matter of layout, service provider skill, hours of availability or timeliness of service. Service must meet the competition and find the customer in his or her personal psychological space in these terms too.

Layout, in the most general of terms, must be conventional enough to feel comfortable to the customers, novel enough to entertain and guide them. Large hospitals often fail in service to customers because they are so illogically laid out. In the effort to expand or contract to maintain cost and service effectiveness, hospitals can easily become a crazy quilt of services that confuses and frightens its customers. The layout is more often fitted to the convenience of staff and employees, sometimes intentionally confusing as a security measure, generally without purpose or meaning to customers. The layout of some government offices is little better. Comprehensive instructions and maps are needed before customers can find their way around.

At the other end of the spectrum, the layout of a major airport, even the most complex, is simplified to the maximum for customer convenience. Departures on one level, baggage and arrivals on another, airlines grouped logically around clearly marked corridors and gates, extensive use of airline logos and colors to identify its gates and equipment—all greatly ease the otherwise complexity and confusion of air travel.

Supermarkets and department stores strive for a certain level of layout simplicity, but put layout concerns behind the need for novelty that avoids customer boredom with the store. Often, they sequence offerings in ways that create associations between products that generate added sales. Low-margin mass-commodity items are frequently located furthest from the entrance, requiring customers to pass high-margin specialties to reach them. As a result, it is often hard to find specific items in large stores. Layout is a psychological game played with the customer that refocuses attention on items that might otherwise be overlooked. From the customer's point of view, the more the manipulation of layout to maximize sales, the less the service. The most successful superstores, like Wal-Mart, minimize the game playing and maximize the layout to fit customer preference and need. Commodity operations habits of thinking continue to characterize many other retail stores. On the whole, they are a liability to those businesses that apply them. Customers appreciate service and resent manipulative psychological games substituted in its place.

SKILLS THAT SERVE AND HOLD THE CUSTOMER

Service supplier skill should be distinguished on at least two levels. The first is the technical product/service knowledge level. The service giver is expected to know the offering in depth and detail so that information about its utility and application can be provided on demand. He or she must also be technically competent to deliver the service expected, adapting as needed to varied or changing customer need. The second level of skill pertains to customer relationship. Here it is often as simple as whether the service-giver treats the customer as an object to be controlled and used, or as a unique, important individual to be served.

A certain level of product/service offering specialization is inevitable with respect to technical knowledge. The auto salesman must have a minimum working knowledge of an injection carburetor or the air conditioning system that is part of his product. The copier salesperson must understand some optics, some electronics and some of the qualities of paper. A nurse must understand some of the uses and side effects of drugs commonly administered to hospital patients.

Technical knowledge is usually a commodity item that can efficiently and cost-effectively be communicated to those who need to know. The quality of information comprehension can be measured and verified. Many businesses leave this education to chance, letting employees inform one another—sometimes erroneously—supplying fragmented information in a ad hoc manner and expecting workers to absorb it through job experience. This is a cost-ineffective design that need not be tolerated. Indeed, it is a basic dimension of service quality that must not be left to chance. Technical knowledge can be communicated in the classroom, on videotape, on audiotape, in printed word and illustration. It can be verified by test, by customer rating, or by mystery shoppers assigned the duty of questing for information. There is no excuse for failing to assure high quality in service supplier product knowledge.

It is in the domain of customer relationship that skill becomes difficult to train and impart. The early success of McDonald's hamburger stands was partly based on price, consistency of quality and cleanliness—all commodity operations successes—and partly based on the friendliness of counter personnel. McDonald's sales personnel were selected for their warm and winning smiles. Store managers were instructed to watch for habitual facial expression and screen *out* those applicants with bland, unexpressive countenances or, worse, combative, haughty ones. Habitual anger or sadness in expression were easy, automatic rejections. McDonald's looked for those people who naturally related positively and easily with other people. This was a significant, major service operations strategy that paid high dividends. Given the strict commodity base of McDonald's operating methods, recognizing the opportunity to frost the cake with a major service element like warmth and friendliness was a stroke of genius, a most profitable one at that.

Expansion of McDonald's and other fast-food franchises on a grand scale has diluted the quality of warmth and friendliness offered. Where once managers could skim the cream of the applicant market for those with a natural outgoing manner, a pressing need to expand the supply of counter-personnel labor has made that impractical. More often, counter people with poker-faced, impenetrable visages are found at once happy register stations, efficiently dispensing orders. Where personal warmth is not available, efficiency, perhaps, can be made to do.

Basic, open friendliness, it would appear, is a deeply set habit that cannot easily be counterfeited where it does not naturally already reside. Service with a smile is easy to propose, difficult to impose. Only a limited few people communicate easily and consciously through facial expression. The norm is unconscious habit, which often reveals inner confusion, boredom, fear or repulsion in one's facial expression. Chronic expressionlessness is a useful substitution and often replaces transparency of feeling tone as the habitual mode of facial expression. Smiling is a superior service manner as long as one is willing to deal with the outpouring of need for contact with another it can elicit. The waitress with the warmest smile gets the biggest tips and fends off the most passes. In an efficient, largely impersonal mass commodity economy, friendliness is sometimes in desperately short supply. Demands for and upon it may become intense at times.

Service industries face a dilemma where expression of warmth and friendliness is needed in customer contact—which is nearly everywhere, nearly all the time. There may not be enough of this precious quality to go around to all customers. Habits that have long supported the delivery of commodity efficiency easily interfere, usurp and supplant the warm smile. How can personal service be offered in these circumstances?

Up to a point, perhaps, close concern for the customer's specific needs can offset expressionless efficiency. Still, there is no more powerful defense against aggressive verbal assault than a confident smile. There is no better sugarcoating for a bluntly truthful retort than a smile. Smiles at the point of customer contact are the cheapest, most effective means available for solving the inevitable communication impasses that arise. A smile is the hallmark of service. Service without a smile is a contradiction in terms.

Employees can sometimes be trained to smile. Standard behavior modification methods can be brought to bear in service of training new habits. One's smile, though, is often a reflection of how one feels about oneself. It is an expression of self-confidence and self-worth. Self-image is not easily changed by mere exhortation. Even the most confident person may be shaken by unmerited criticism. It is hard to keep smiling when one is personally, verbally assaulted by an angry customer. The best training may collapse in the face of substantial personal threat. It is all well to talk about maintaining positive relations with the customer. When the customer has no interest in positive interaction with the service giver, it becomes a one-sided, difficult goal.

Service givers must be trained specifically how to handle the most difficult situations without losing their self-confidence or poise. They must be sold on the proposition that coolness under fire is a mark of personal class. Mere behavior modification or dependence on good facial habit is not enough and probably never has been. Positive interaction with customers is a major skill that must be developed and supported in service industries. Extensive practice, feedback, and evaluation in service giving skill is basic to creating a service atmosphere. It may be only the first step toward understanding and dealing with the customer as an individual, but it is the indispensable foundation of that dimension of service. If the service giver cannot relate positively with the customer neither can he or she psychologically locate the customer as a unique person. We will expand on this subject, discussing service provider training in Chapter 14.

TIMING SERVICE TO CUSTOMER NEED

Timeliness of the service is the remaining quality of service under the category of convenience. Unless waiting is offset by some alternative form of service, such as an entertainment, it is usually considered a mark of poor service. Restaurant patrons who wait in the bar may satisfactorily entertain themselves with drink and discussion. Some of the Disney World waiting queues wind at length through and around other entertainments like rock concerts or strolling Disney characters. When the boredom of waiting in line for attractions cuts into Disney World revenues, this arrangement will have to be expanded and enhanced to permit waiting to occur in a dominantly entertainment mode. Waiting that serves no other purpose quickly palls on the customer. Service must be timely.

This generally means that capacity for service through provision of sufficient personnel, assuring appropriate ranges of personnel skill among service providers, supplies of tools and equipment associated with the service and physical space must all be in sufficiently abundant supply to comfortably meet peak customer demand. Customers will walk away from poor service and seek either good service or alternative service. Insufficient capacity to serve generates an image of poor service, loses customers and revenues and generally makes the competition ecstatic.

Timeliness of service and capacity for service are inseparable. As we also clearly note, capacity for service is a key element of cost. Capacity and cost are core variables in successful delivery of high-quality service. They will be intensively examined in Chapter 4.

Capacity for Service: The Fundamental Strategic Challenge

"Capacity is the tightrope that service managers must walk."

The first rule of service is that limited capacity equals poor service. The second rule is that excess capacity equals high cost. Measurement of service quality is difficult because the customer is its ultimate gauge. Misconceived in the execution, quality measurement can seriously mislead. Quality issues will be treated in later chapters where their complexities can more fully be developed and evaluated. That will not prevent us from a careful and thorough examination of capacity and cost issues at this stage of argument. Indeed, quality as it applies to service offerings cannot make complete sense until the capacity-cost issues that constrain it are themselves adequately grasped.

Discussion of capacity must be anchored in an understanding of long-standing economic policy concerning quality that arises out of conventional commodity production practices. Mass production of commodity product assumes scarcity of the tools of production. Machines and factories are the principal investment base of production. They are designed for maximum simplicity and efficiency of operation. The people who staff the factory and operate the machinery are equipped with only the most basic skills supplied by a commodity-oriented, mass education system and augmented with minimum on-the-job training. The central economic object of commodity production is to keep the machines and factories humming. The product they turn out offers mass employment to a largely unskilled work force and pays the high mortgage and interest return demanded by those who finance purchase of factory and equipment capacity expecting quick, generous return on their investment. It is a tightly logical and self-contained system of exchange. The beans must be transferred with all due dispatch.

Within the conventional mass commodity production system, the highest priority is maximum utilization of physical production capacity. Costly, specialized production capacity cannot be wasted without near-term loss to employees and investors alike. The demand for high-capacity usage of production plant is so well set in the thinking of managers that it is employed by the Federal Reserve Board as a basic measure of economic health in industry. The Fed's Bulletin G-3402, issued monthly, reports capacity utilization in manufacturing and public utilities nationwide. Much of the time, overall productive capacity floats in the low 80s percentage range. As it rises toward the 90s, the economy moves into high gear, slowed only a little by the need for marginally cost-effective capacity to be brought on line to meet expanded demand. When capacity utilization falls toward the 70s, the economy begins to falter.

A large part of the meaning of these measures is found in the conventions applied to gathering the Fed's data. Production capacity that has been written off the books or simply abandoned is not included in the calculation. Provision to meet peak demand is typically covered by a cushion of marginal production capability such as outdated plant and equipment or multishift production. Where production is conventionally scheduled only five days a week during daytime hours, only that formally scheduled capacity is reported in the Fed's numbers. Even an operation scheduled over two shifts and working Saturdays runs slightly less than half the available working hours in a 168-hour week. The Fed's measures apply only to normal scheduled working hours of America's commodity production plant and facility. Only a limited segment of industries like petroleum and chemical processing or public utilities routinely schedule capacity as if every hour of the week were available for production. Those can be underutilized only through shutdown for lack of demand. If shut down for an extended period, they may disappear from the Fed's plant utilization statistics.

A century or more ago, the typical plant was routinely scheduled seventy or more hours per week, reflecting the then much higher value of plant investment in the total economic calculus. The relative worth of plant and equipment, once the major force in improving the quality of human life, has diminished along a slow down gradient over an extended span of time. Today's measures of plant capacity utilization factor in generous allowances for personal and leisure time of the work force. The longest hours are worked by the most highly skilled, often top managers and staff, whose time and talent are in relatively short supply. Their work often goes on well past plant shutdown. Their longest hours are likely to be when either the economy is poor and plant utilization is low, or when business is excellent and plant capacity is strained. Variation in capacity requirements makes commodity production management's job tough. Steady demand at optimum capacity makes it easy. The ideal for management of a commodity operation is stable production at the planned optimum. While that condition prevails, management's work life is a downhill coast.

The transition to a service economy thus begins with long-standing, deeply scored habits of thought concerning management of capacity. Working at less-than-full scheduled capacity is known with certainty to be cost-inefficient. Meeting peak capacity that exceeds planned maximum is equally cost-inefficient. Large inventories are maintained as buffers for variation in demand to support stable, minimally varying production at the planned optimum. Adjustment to variation in demand otherwise is a major, sometimes crisis, management decision. It is similar to the crew of a racing yacht that goes into maximum action whenever there is a change of course or wind, but that has time to rest and recover when on a steady course. Service, on the other hand, is a tightrope walk during which demand is continuously shifting, sometimes moment by moment. Capacity must be adjusted to fit varying demand without incurring excess cost as operations adjust. Rest is permitted only when all customers have been fully served.

The central change of thinking required to meet the needs of a service economy has to do with the plant and equipment that support service and the level of skill required of the service supplier. Plant and equipment must be available in sufficient excess capacity to permit fast, flexible switches from one work activity to another. Continuous, exclusive assignment of low-skilled labor to each machine or workstation becomes a gross waste of labor and, correspondingly, a source of excess cost. Equipment that is tied up in continuous use cannot be made available in a timely manner to meet customer need. Service suppliers who cannot move from workstation to workstation, varying activity to fit customer requirements, cannot supply the expected service at a competitive cost. Worker skill levels must expand and rise to meet the challenge of service. Both equipment and labor must be flexibly scheduled to fit the customer's timetable.

Service cannot be cost-effectively inventoried to await customer demand. It must normally be supplied *on demand*. This changes the entire ball game. Old habits of thought and expectation carried over from the commodity arena of production necessarily become a barrier if not a liability to sound service operations management. Capacity policies must be thoroughly reconceptualized. A new philosophy is needed.

Indeed, it is philosophy that is most in need of revision. Physical resources are no longer the primary barrier to productivity. They exist in such abundance that half or three-quarters of a week's physical capacity routinely sits unused in even the "fully utilized" commodity production operation. It is the shape, pace and rhythm of the work schedule where change will be most dramatic. Plant and equipment for service must be much less specialized than under commodity operating conventions. Depreciation and write-off of physical equipment in the service era will be on a slower, more extended schedule. Salvage and resale value of newly acquired equipment will consistently be higher. This will support increased excess capacity of plant and equipment and permit greater flexibility in its use. Financial pressure for intensive equipment use to quickly pay off specialized plant investment will be less acute. Some tools and equipment may be dedicated to the individual service supplier or even to the specific customer. The major changes will be in the way plant, equipment and workstations are scheduled to fit customer need and service supplier skill. These changes will produce the service operations management revolution.

THE BASIC SERVICE CAPACITY MODEL

New ways to think about capacity are required if service operations are to be managed effectively. The characteristic of service that is most common and troublesome is the waiting line. Service on demand virtually insures some kind of waiting line. The elaborate appointment book maintained in a doctor's office or beautician's shop doesn't look like a waiting line, but it is a queue of customers waiting for service all the same. It is an organized sequence of customers waiting for delivery of service. Some service can't or needn't be delayed. Doctors build in provision for emergencies that can't wait, and some beauticians accept walk-ins on a service-as-time-is-available basis. This is all part of the phenomenon of waiting lines. Some form of waiting line characterizes almost every kind of service.

Absence of a waiting line occurs only where the service can be held in inventory awaiting customer demand, which means that service capacity must substantially exceed customer demand. It may be necessary to maintain an inventory of available skills in sufficient excess capacity to assure delivery on demand. The trick to service operations management is to do this without excess waste of paid labor hours. This presents two major capacity concerns to the service operations manager. He or she must manage waiting lines without incurring excess cost and maintain an inventory of relevant human skill that can be flexibly applied to customer need as it arrives looking for service with minimum waste of labor time. The rest of this chapter will look at waiting lines.

THE UBIQUITOUS CUSTOMER QUEUE

Waiting lines are a widely studied, well-understood phenomenon. They occur regularly in banks, at service stations, at traffic lights, at supermarket check-out stations, in amusement parks, at restaurants and at any number of similar points of service demand. Waiting lines are described and analyzed mathematically through an operations research discipline called Queuing Theory. They can also be simulated on a computer. The mathematical model of waiting lines provided by queuing theory is a clean and clear point of beginning for this examination of capacity issues that can be examined first.

Queuing was developed by A. K. Erlang in 1905 to permit accurate and cost-effective capacity planning for assignment of human operators to telephone exchange switching boards. Using statistical averages of rate of demand and service time to connect calls, Erlang calculated the average customer waiting time at varying levels of operator availability. The object was to reduce customer waiting time for switchboard service to a tolerable minimum without needlessly increasing labor costs through overmanning the switchboard positions. Using accurate records of customer demand for service and sound standards for service time, Erlang was able to schedule operators hour by hour during the workday to assure a satisfactorily high level of service response to customers. Even today, the number of automated switching stations in a telephone system is carefully planned using Erlang's original model of waiting lines to assure that the system will adequately handle peak demand.

Planning of phone service capacity has been so effective using operations management aids like queuing theory that it is rare for anyone to associate waiting lines with phones and phone service. In the age before satellite and microwave communications transmission, when long-distance lines were all still hard-wired, peak demand on special holidays sometimes caused long waits for phone service. Today, waits occur only when the system fails. Mechanized, automated phone service capacity is more than sufficient to handle any peak levels of demand. The wait is more likely to be for a human operator to come on the line when we need information or have trouble, for repair or for installation of new service.

Exhibit 4-1
Single-Channel, Single-Station Waiting Line Service Model

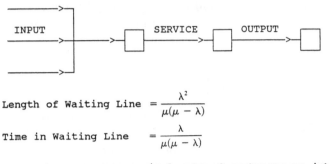

Length of Waiting Line $= \dfrac{\lambda^2}{\mu(\mu - \lambda)}$

Time in Waiting Line $= \dfrac{\lambda}{\mu(\mu - \lambda)}$

λ = average arrival rate of customers or jobs

μ = average rate at which customers or jobs are served

Real wages are much higher than they were in 1905, which means that service capacity policies that require the human touch must be less wasteful of worker time.

It is significant and instructive that the primary model for service capacity analysis was developed almost a century ago to support capacity planning in an emerging service industry. It is equally significant and instructive that the waiting-line model as applied to telephone service reduces and sometimes substantially eliminates the existence of waiting lines. An important measure of service quality is the speed and timeliness of service. The existence of a waiting line of any length can impair service quality. The longer the waiting line, the poorer the service. Indeed, the waiting-line model from Erlang's classic queuing theory is a useful and powerful model of the trade-off between the cost of excess service capacity and quality of service as measured by waiting time for its delivery. It deals with and illuminates a fundamental service operations decision point. Let's examine it more closely.

The most basic version of Erlang's model, in strictly technical terms, is the single-channel, single-server, negative exponential model for an infinite service population, illustrated in Exhibit 4–1. Almost any service setting can be simplified into a single-channel, single-server model without diminishing the basic accuracy of the model. The waiting line for tellers in a bank, for instance, can be reorganized from a line at each window into a single line that feeds from the head to the next available teller. The total number of tellers, like the total number of phone operators, determines the overall service capacity available.

"Negative exponential" is no more than a mathematical description of the variability of service time compared to the variability in arrival times. It assumes that these variabilities are about the same. An infinite service population means that there is no practical limit on the number of people who can show up at any time looking for service, and that, by chance alone, a *very* large number could arrive all at once. The available service population must be quite small before the difference between a finite and an infinite model begins to exert a practical influence on the model. Waiting lines for attractions at Disney World most certainly vary as a function of the size of the visiting crowd on a given day, but that, ultimately, is a function of fixed service rates and random variation in daily arrivals at the main gate. Disney World is a special case of random sequenced internal flow of jobs in a closed system.

All queuing models assume that service is on-demand and customers arrive on a randomized schedule. The queuing model, in general, is robust—that is, it is little influenced by minor departures from the underlying assumptions. Clearly, special cases that involve unusual variability in service times or very small customer populations might better be examined using the more specialized versions of the model that are available. To introduce queuing methodology as a decision-making guide for service capacity, though, we need look no further than the basic single-channel, negative exponential model, infinite customer population. Use of this model to examine service capacity policy is enhanced by the fact that the length of any waiting line in waiting *units* (people, cars or whatever) is dependent solely on the level of service capacity. Waiting *time* is a function of the units of time used in setting average arrival and service rates. The Erlang model is truly capacity sensitive at its very core.

Exhibit 4–2 illustrates graphically the relationship that characteristically prevails between level of service capacity and length of customer waiting lines. Inspection of the curve reveals that waiting lines reach an average level of about one customer waiting in line for service at around 70% capacity utilization, and thereafter rise rapidly, going into a near vertical ascent as the curve passes through the 90s range of percent capacity usage.

Several major service policy implications can be drawn from the model as presented here. For one, it is foolish, if not ridiculous, to expect to operate service at very high capacity. Theoretically, at least, operating at or above 100% capacity should generate infinitely long waiting lines. At minimum, every potential customer in the vicinity of the service will be waiting in line. At Disney World, 100% capacity usage would produce something akin to gridlock. It is a phenomenon that is otherwise dramatically demonstrated by the long waiting lines at Moscow stores sometimes

Exhibit 4-2
Length of a Waiting Line as a Function of Capacity Utilization at
Independent Workstations

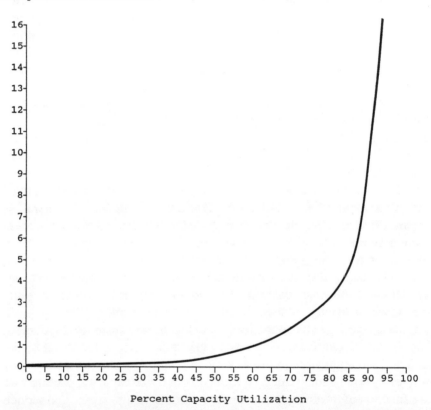

Percent Capacity Utilization

shown on TV news. Demand that exceeded available capacity for gasoline in 1974 and again in 1978 produced waiting lines at gas service stations that did not stop growing until the station ceased pumping gas for customers. When the capacity for service is exceeded by demand, waiting lines can grow to gargantuan proportions. The only rational management choice is to select some level of *excess* capacity at which the level of service sought matches operations policy.

Inspection of the curve reveals that a change of 10% in the level of capacity utilization has very different service implications in the higher ranges of the curve than in the lower ones. The difference between 80% and 90% capacity utilization is an increase from three to eight people (or service units) waiting in line, whereas the difference between 10% and 20% is a change from three-hundredths of a unit to five-hundredths of a unit. Presumably, the difference in cost of added capacity is the same over either of these ranges of movement. The apparent change in level of customer service differs enormously between them. A difference of three percentage points service capacity at the top of the curve can make a major difference in customers' perceived quality of service, whereas a difference of thirty points on the lower end may pass completely unnoticed by them. A firm's location on the capacity utilization curve has major implications for the quality of service.

Yet another implication of the capacity utilization curve is found in the trade-off of cost for service. A labor-intensive service industry may find that a relatively high level of capacity usage can reduce costs significantly, giving the firm a distinct price advantage over a low-capacity utilization competitor. Alternatively, in a cost-insensitive capacity usage situation, it is foolish to try to save money by increasing capacity. Where cost of capacity is neither trivial nor large, positioning on the capacity utilization curve may lead to creation of distinct business niches; one business may serve customers who don't mind waiting if cost is a bargain, another may serve those who are happy to pay a higher price for faster service.

Level of capacity utilization has important implications for low-priority "filler" work available when customers are not present demanding service. If filler work is available to cover 20% of service suppliers' working time, it makes no sense to try to raise capacity utilization above the 80% mark. However, any attempt to reduce the level below 80% will incur real costs in lost labor utilization. Cost is a direct function of the availability of deferrable, low-priority filler jobs. Occasional cost improvements may be obtained in either range through careful adjustment of capacity to reduce cost without decreasing service level. Every service industry must be sensitive to peak demand, which can stretch capacity beyond its limit, impairing its service reputation. Where peak demand is hard to forecast, the ability to flexibly expand capacity can be an important solution.

Capacity bottlenecks occur most rapidly and unexpectedly when chronic but unpredictable delays in provision of service occur at the highest levels of capacity utilization. Any avoidable delay that gets factored into average service time directly increases capacity utilization at a constant level of customer demand and thereby reduces quality of service. When high-capacity utilization is unavoidable, it can sometimes be less costly to improve efficiency of service scheduling than to increase capacity, which usually means speeding through customers headed for a known bottleneck. If, on the other hand, service utilization capacity is already set at a very low (high excess capacity) level, there may be little merit to examining the efficiency of service delivery to improve cost, and may even be some virtue to enhancing service by stretching it out when the waiting queue is otherwise empty.

The cost/service trade-off implications of the waiting-line model are fundamental to sound operations management decisions for any kind of service where capacity is limited or costly. When capacity is cheap, it is generally best to set the maximum at expected peak or with some safety margin beyond expected peak capacity. Service with insufficient capacity is invariably poor service. Most service industries will either set capacity utilization standards low enough, usually well below 50%, to provide near instant service, or will carefully set capacity in a moderate upper (60% to 85%) range where service is competitive and satisfactory against industry standards.

Real estate offices and auto dealers, for instance, typically staff at a level where a salesperson is *almost always* available to greet the next customer through the door. Service is the key to the sale. Capacity utilization here is usually somewhere around 10% or 20%, or even less. Compensation is matched to the capacity usage requirement and is on a straight commission for sales basis. This makes unapplied labor time (i.e., excess capacity) entirely an expense to the salesperson.

Airlines operate in the other end of the range. Break-even for the average flight has typically been in the vicinity of 65% passenger load. This meant that the typical last-minute traveler who has not made prior reservations would sometimes make the desired flight, but would seldom have to wait for more than one later flight to reach his or her destination. An increase in airline break-even to 80%—which represents a decrease in excess capacity from 35% to 20%—could mean that last-minute passengers would rarely make the first attempted flight and would normally stand by for three later flights before being boarded.

Lawyers, doctors and public accountants try to work at high levels of capacity—approaching 90% if at all possible. It is nearly impossible to reach a busy professional by phone; many tries may be required. Waiting time in the outer office can be tediously long, and deferral of already once-scheduled meetings or jobs is common. Those professionals new in practice may either be suspect because they are not busier, or attractive because they can offer immediate, fast service. Once established, they may require new customers to wait in a separate queue before they can be included as regulars.

These variations in style and quality of service are made fully compre-hensible by reference to Erlang's queuing model. Capacity utilization is fundamental to the shape and pace of the service offering. Competitive adaptations to market change always require careful consideration of capacity considerations and implications. Change in capacity should never be undertaken without first considering the implications to service of cost and waiting time for customers. Capacity utilization is one of the central and major variables of service operations strategy. Its implications must be understood if service operations are to be managed effectively.

Chapter 5

Building Inventories of Flexible Service Supplier Skill

"Cost-effective service requires flexible, multiskilled workers."

If there are many stubborn old habits of strategic thinking to be broken in redirecting capacity decisions toward increased excess capacity of plant equipment and tooling in support of service, there is potential for even higher drama in changing those customs that pertain to worker skill. The conventional strategy for managing skill in American industry is to keep it narrow, specialized and cheap. The first priority of keeping plant and machinery fully utilized is to assign one worker to one workstation on a permanent or semipermanent basis. Thereby, both worker and equipment capacity are kept near full application merely by keeping the machine loaded to maximum capacity. But if service-supportive plant and equipment must be utilized at significantly lower than normal, full capacity, as suggested above, labor hours are inevitably wasted by a strategy of using minimally skilled workers. And, whereas plant and equipment depreciation are merely book costs that can be reallocated through a change in pricing or depreciation schedules, paid labor hours are a *real* dollar cost. There is no way to escape this cost except by finding strategies that keep labor applied to *real* work.

A worker in a commodity output operation is similar to an actor who plays a series of single parts in one long-run play after another. Some parts run for years before change in the role occurs. Service suppliers, by contrast, are analogous to players in a repertory company who do a different role every performance. They may also manage properties, move sets and take tickets as needed. The variety of jobs that need to be done are widely mastered within the repertory group and roles are reallocated to cover the need at each performance. Service industries require the role flexibility of good repertory players.

The transition from a single- to a multirole work setting is a substantial, perhaps even a revolutionary, one. Casting for the long-run part is easy; the applicant actor need only be measured against a single part. Small parts in long-run plays can often be learned in an afternoon, making replacement of actors who move on to bigger things an easy matter. A handful of understudies for major roles covers the bigger contingencies arising out of illness and personal crisis. Every performance is a rehearsal for the next one. Once the momentum of the run is established, it runs with a minimum of added effort.

Converting into a repertory mode changes everything. Casting requires actors with long experience and great flexibility. Plays chosen for production will often be selected for their fit to the talents of the company. Everyone plays many small parts and some big ones. Illness of tonight's star is easier to cover by doing a different play than by carrying an understudy. Each performance is a unique creation in its own right, which may never quite be duplicated again. The adaptive, insightful skills of each player are called upon fully at every performance.

Service demands worker-suppliers who can quickly adapt to shifting market demand. This requires a new depth and breadth of worker skill, reliable means of identifying and verifying each person's repertory of skills and artful allocation of available worker capabilities across the jobs to be accomplished. Operations strategy in the management of service supplier skill is at an entirely new level of complexity from anything ever previously seen in commodity-styled operations. Planning and forecasting for future business requires that the probabilities of likely needed skills be estimated as accurately as possible. Scheduling incoming tasks requires that the inventory of available skill be scrutinized to assure availability in stock of the requisite skills and determine if other jobs may have a prior claim on it that will influence the schedule. Skill now becomes a major asset in the firm's stock in trade. Skill must be acquired, developed, maintained and validated. Lost skill must be replaced or else planning must account for its probability of loss through worker cross-training. Workers' repertories of skills are critical to an operation's competitive posture and success.

Managing a service operation's skills inventory begins with an exhaustive listing of all possible, conceivable and useful skills that may be supportive of business and customer need. Each skill must be specified and defined. Definitions should be framed both in terms of the human aptitudes and abilities required for its performance and the outcomes expected from its application. The fundamental skill of a direct service supplier is that of maintaining good relations with the customer. The principal aptitude required is an easy and open manner in communicating with all people, friends and strangers alike. Self-confidence is required where communication occurs under stressful conditions. The interpersonally competent service supplier must be able to listen well, identify confusion that needs clarification, answer questions clearly and accept responsibility for success in communicating. The outcome should be a clear understanding of the customer's specifications, accurate performance against specifications and customer satisfaction with the result.

As with many human skills, this one is actually a package of interrelated skills and attitudes that are flexibly applied in the customer contact setting to fit the emerging situation. In its simplest form it might be described in these terms:

- maintains eye contact and smiles at customers
- listens and clarifies facts
- keeps the customer happy

In the strictest terms, these are three distinct skills, each requiring aptitude and practice. For the sake of parsimony in inventory record keeping, they can be packaged as a single, customer contact skill. Technical skills, such as ability to pilot a C-5A transport aircraft, disassemble and clean a sink trap, give a permanent wave or prepare an income tax form are all, similarly, packages of basic skills combined to achieve a unified service purpose. The skill is demonstrated in the whole performance but is based on elements, some of which may be stronger or weaker than others. Assuring adequate quality in the package of skill will require specific identification and verification of the underlying elements. Ultimately, it is the elements that must be trained, assessed and verified in validating the possession of skill. The skills inventory, then, must be flexibly designed to operate on either or both of these levels.

It is the skills packages, though, that service operations must build on, schedule and manage effectively. Instead of job descriptions—the administrative staple of every commodity production operation—service requires carefully drawn skills descriptions, with definitions of the underlying elements fully specified. The entirety of a good service operation is organized around skills packages that serve the customer's needs. There are no longer any jobs or positions, there are now only tasks and skills. The service supplier is a repertory player.

Organization of service operations begins with identification and definition of the skills packages that are fundamental to the business. Each must be documented clearly and specifically so that the requisite skills can be trained, verified and validated as available in stock for delivery to the customer.

The next step in managing service skill is to assess the probability of customer demand and determine the market (pay) value of each skill. Customer demand may be measured from past history where historical records are available. Few businesses at present keep records of sales by skill package, which means that most existing records will have limited value for this purpose. The more practical approach will be to assemble a panel of experienced individuals and ask them to estimate the frequency of demand of each skill in a week's, month's or quarter's time. While they are at it, an estimate of the hourly worth of the skill might also be obtained.

A panel of this sort can be made up of personnel available in a plant, experts contacted by mail or phone, consultants hired for the purpose or just about any mix of these approaches that is workable. The larger and more variable the panel membership, the better the data gathered. Substantial agreement on probability of demand or level of pay suggests that the issue is stable and predictable. Major disagreement points to the need for closer management of the skill to pin down its demand and value. Skill descriptions should be independently rated by this or a separate, special panel for accuracy, comprehensibility and clarity. Skills can be rated in terms of percentage of working time in application, percent of jobs they would be applied to, ease or difficulty of recruitment and development of personnel holding the skill and any other relevant dimensions. Skills can also be ranked from most to least important to the business.

Identification of the skills requisite to effective delivery of the service is fundamental to effective management of service operations. It is always done informally in some fashion or other. A hospital medical department, a law firm, a university department or an appliance maintenance company will recruit or develop personnel to enhance the mix of the firm's available skills. The individual with multiple skills will almost always be a stronger candidate than one with only a single skill. The major exception will be that situation where the single skill is the dominant element of mainstream customer demand, or where it is rare and complex enough to merit a specialist on staff. Most such firms will be small and will center around an owner/founder who is distinguished by unusual breadth and scope of skills called for in the business. After everyone else is applied to their best

Exhibit 5-1
Skill Allocation Using a Simple Heuristic Principle

```
Heuristic employed:  Assign first those skills which are rarest.

Example:  Auto Repair Shop with six mechanics

    Skill Capacity:
          All can handle brakes, exhaust, batteries, starters
              and suspension systems.
          Four can handle engines, electrical systems.
          One of the four can handle transmissions.

    Scheduling rule:
          Transmission repairs are assigned first.
          Engine and electrical systems are assigned second.
          Brakes, exhaust, batteries, starters & suspension
              are assigned last.
```

skills, the central and most versatile member of the firm covers whatever is left over. A simple heuristic for allocation of available skill from among multiskilled workers is offered in Exhibit 5–1. It is an example that takes advantage of a common set of skills in auto repair in a small shop setting. Here multiskill is both necessary and manageable on a relatively non-complex level. The scheduling heuristic generally assigns the rarest skills first, proceeding in sequence to the skills most widely prevalent as the last set of assignments.

In larger service firms, specialization is more likely to be feasible and, because of its simplicity and conformance with commodity operations strategy thinking, will prevail. In the longer run, though, specialization is much the riskiest and costliest operating strategy. Specialists in service firms can too easily be either under- or overutilized. They will be defensive of their specialized turf, slow to pass on their skill to others and competitive with other specialists. It must be anticipated that demand for specialties will vary with cycles or changes in the service market. New specialties will appear, old ones will disappear. Specialists are harder to manage and are more easily outmoded by market shifts.

The more versatile and cost-efficient service operation will be the one that despecializes its work force to the greatest extent possible, requires multiskill qualification of every worker and allocates the available skills variably as a function of prevailing market demand or business mix. Response to the widest range of customer demand will be superior. Unapplied wages due to excess waiting worker time can be minimized. Cost and capacity are thereby best counterbalanced to fit the market.

WHAT IS THE RIGHT MIX OF SKILLS FOR THE BUSINESS?

Once a comprehensive inventory of the needed and relevant operating skills has been assembled and rated, the mix of skills and numbers of qualified people possessing each can be estimated. This is the equivalent of setting inventory levels against forecasts of demand. A new and different factor is introduced into the skills inventory, though, in the possession of multiple skills by each worker. We must assume that only one skill at a time can be applied. Indeed, where it is possible for one person to blend and apply simultaneously two or more skills effectively to a job, that capability should be specified in the inventory system as a distinct skill package in its own right. The allocation of skills over tasks subtracts from inventory *all* the skills in the repertory of the worker assigned to the task as was demonstrated in Exhibit 5–1. Depth of skill allows flexibility of assignment but can mislead the operations manager by suggesting that a bigger inventory of skill is available for assignment than actually is.

This presents three levels of decision making for the service operations manager. First, the number of workers needed to cover anticipated business demand must be forecast. This can usually be specified in terms of standard labor hours required to cover expected sales and approached as a problem in aggregate labor planning. Most businesses will attempt to cover all work with no more than 10% unapplied labor with provision for rapid expansion of capacity when required. Usually, a margin of error on the side of a small amount of unapplied labor time will be tolerated to assure service without undue delay. This decision will be reevaluated periodically—at least quarterly and perhaps weekly.

The second decision pertains to which skills to hire, develop, encourage and otherwise enter into inventory in anticipation of the business. If each worker possessed *all* skills required by the business, there would be no difficulty here; people could be randomly assigned to whatever work needed to be done. More likely, each worker will possess his or her own unique repertoire of skills and the operations manager's concern will be to allocate so as to best utilize those skills in shortest supply given present demand.

The same panel of experts that evaluated and rated skills can estimate the frequency with which each skill would be needed to meet customer demand. The proportion of jobs on which a given skill would apply or the percent of total labor time during which a given skill would be applied to jobs would be a useful start. This sets the proportions of workers who should possess each key skill as an individual foundation skill. Addition of skill to an individual worker's skills inventory repertoire in other skill

Exhibit 5-2

Linear Programming Allocation of Available Labor Hours in a Law Firm

Givens: 1560 hours of clerical time are available each quarter.
3120 hours of legal skill are available each quarter.
Divorce cases yield $10 per hour profit over expenses.
Accident cases yield $12 per hour profit over expenses.
The average divorce case requires 150 hours clerical and
    200 hours legal time in total.
The average accident case requires 100 hours clerical and
    250 hours legal time per week.

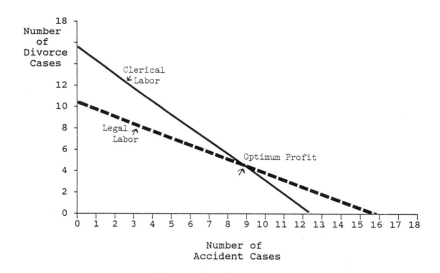

areas should then be kept in the same approximate proportions up to either the point where each skill is inventoried at two to three times its normal, expected demand or is possessed by all workers. In more stable service industries this decision can be subjected to a linear programming analysis. Exhibit 5–2 is a graphic example of how linear programming might be applied to allocation of multiple skills in a law firm.

The third level of decision making comes with actual allocation of available skill to the current task load. If skill is in limited supply and a linear programming or similar analysis is available, the feasible maxima of tasks can be directly determined. With sufficient depth of skill on hand in the inventory, though, there should seldom be any practical limitation. Now a more complex assignment heuristic may be required. This heuristic for assignment is straightforward; from a simulation or forecast of task and skill requirements, calculate the proportion of each skill category that will be needed to cover present tasks. Assign first from that category of skill on which proportionate demand will be greatest. Assign second from the category that is next greatest and so on until all jobs are covered. A supportive heuristic will be to check all remaining categories at each level of assignment to assure that sufficient skill allocation remains for application as needed. If allocation to another skill drains any yet unassigned skill category below level of need, assign the threatened category first. This is the heuristic equivalent of recalculating proportions skill category demand after each assignment, which, of course, is yet another and still more complex way to accomplish the same end. In many cases, a simple computer program can be constructed to effect the desired efficiency of allocation, perhaps directly from the computerized skills data base.

Skill capacity is the key to cost-effectiveness in service. The level of operations management effort and competence that has formerly gone into management of physical inventory must now be applied to management of the human inventory. The principal inventory in service is human time and skill. The methods and systems needed to manage human time and skill to assure capacity to meet market demand are very different from those required in a commodity setting. But the same level of effort is needed to manage skills in inventory as is needed in mass commodity operations.

ASSURING QUALITY OF THE SKILLS INVENTORY

Building an inventory of service skills requires adequate means of verifying skill possession. When comprehensive skill descriptions have been generated as the foundation for a skills inventory, though, the experience and aptitude on which skills are founded will be identified, and the elements that must be trained, developed, tested and validated are known. What remains is the specification of skill samples or tests that can be applied to each individual who claims mastery of a skill. The most appropriate device for validating skills is a verification committee composed of management and workers who are themselves already qualified. Candidates for skill verification can apply for committee validation. Almost any conventional form of work sample can be used. The results of supervised apprenticeship, a formal paper and pencil test, a sample of skill performance on the job or in a simulated work setting, references from customers or instructors, licensing from a private or public agency or a committee interview to test job knowledge are all appropriate methods.

Compared to the conventional commodity operations strategy approach where the hiring manager or supervisor merely satisfies him- or herself as to the candidate's qualifications and then uses a brief period of probation as validation of skill possession, service operations call for a more formal and thorough process. The skill verified may not be put to use immediately, and when applied, must be competently employed to the satisfaction of the customer. Skills that are not regularly used under the observation of supervisors or customers may require periodic revalidation. In the manner of a pilot who cannot maintain flying status without logging regular flying time, service suppliers must demonstrate ongoing command of their claimed skills on a regular and recurring basis. A log of skill application in some form will be required to verify skill exercise just as for the pilot. It is as if a conventional inventory system were to require periodic reinspection of items in inventory to assure that they are fresh and useful. A full-scaled skills inventory might be integrated not only with the scheduling system to allocate skills to work in process but also to maintain a full historical record of skills applied to actual work. Any skill not applied within the past ten days, for instance, might require reverification before assignment to a current task.

Reverification might be as comprehensive as full validation committee rereview, or as informal as a brief conversation between operations manager and service supplier before assignment. Brief special supervision by a supervisor or a skill-certified co-worker at the outset of task performance could satisfy the need. Supervisory or project management skill would, of course, require validation in its own right and would be allocated from the skills inventory just like any other skill.

PLUSES AND MINUSES OF A SKILLS INVENTORY APPROACH

The advantage of flexible skills allocation is found in the added flexibility to meet customer demand it offers. There is also the potential for increased variety and autonomy in the service supplier's work that comes with any form of job enrichment such as task rotation or job enlargement. These are proposed by many management theorists on grounds that they offer motivational impetus to workers from increased job autonomy and variety. Where a customer's project can be followed through from beginning to end by one person who possesses all the skills necessary to its completion, opportunity also exists to obtain greater accountability for quality and on-time performance, as well as the increased pride in performance that can go with full responsibility for the job.

The major disadvantages of a skills inventory system for allocating service supplier labor hours is to be found in the transfer losses that are inevitable as workers switch from task to task, in the higher training and skill replacement cost and in the higher pay that may be required. In a commodity operations setting these disadvantages are assumed to be sufficiently critical and costly to require their avoidance as intolerable inefficiencies in the operation.

Transfer loss is inevitable because each task is different, each skill requires a fresh mental set. Investment of time to adjust is necessary. The only sure way to avoid process loss completely is to insist on continuous repetition of the same task and skill. The next best thing is frequent shifts from one skill base to another, which, eventually, become quicker and more efficient with repetition and practice. Service suppliers can and must learn to shift quickly and comfortably from task to task, skill to skill. In the traditional commodity operations setting, flexibility is, indeed, costly because it is unpracticed. Production workers who are expected to be flexible in application of skill, as in the new institution of manufacturing work cells, gain skill in transferring from task to task quickly with minimal process loss. Indeed, it is perhaps at this point of policy shift, from specialized rigidity to multiskilled flexibility, that the crux of the new service economy is to be found. Commodity operations demands consistency in routine and expects repetition to be efficient. Service demands flexibility and requires practice in variety of applied skills to become increasingly effective. The underlying assumptions of each policy perspective are self-fulfilling because they fit their respective operating circumstances.

Multiskill has its own advantages. Training and replacement costs are potentially minimized in the flexibly allocated service operation by the availability of overlap in skill possession among workers. Where skill exists in sufficient depth, the worst that can happen when someone quits is that everyone else works longer hours or that the total incoming work load manageable in the system is reduced. Training will be continuous and ongoing in the service operation that allocates skills flexibly using a skills inventory. And, whereas turnover in a commodity operations setting is disruptive to smooth operations, enough surplus depth and scope of skill availability can be planned into the inventory to offset normal turnover. Adjustment to normal change is thereby routinely built into service operations strategy. There need be no unusual or extraordinary costs associated with the inevitable turnover of worker or customer populations.

Turnover may sometimes be troublesome in service operations where there are areas of necessary high specialization or exceptional skill variety, loss of which might mean loss of business. Even here, though, a variety of operating strategy options exist to offset the risk of loss. Exceptional, critically central skill can be backed up in some cases with consultants, part-time moonlighters, job shoppers or professional temporaries, retirees and other alternative skill sources. Where skill loss is intolerable and backup is excessively costly by other means, skill can be locked in with high wages or extension of ownership in the business. A little-noticed practice of major corporations is that of bringing the highest, most critical skills up to corporate staff level where they become generously paid teachers, evaluators and backups to practitioners of the skill in operations.

In service operations, pay systems and scales must necessarily be revised to account for the higher value of multiskilled workers and reflect the market value of specific skills as well. A change in compensation systems for the service industry represents a major shift in operating strategy, but it is an investment in strategy development that is long overdue anyway. Pay for routine, highly specialized, unskilled and semi-skilled work has escalated rapidly over the past fifty years. Workers in dull, inherently uninteresting jobs have demanded high pay as compensation for the discomfort of their work. Many have come to be paid *as if* they were highly skilled. The pay differential between skilled and unskilled work has, as a result, compressed significantly in many industries. The once significant advantage of low wage rates for low-skilled work has disappeared in most Western economies. Even in Japan, which used wage differential competitively to breach the U.S. market for autos and electronics in the 1950s and 1960s, unskilled workers now expect generous pay for their labors. Some offshore, Third World industries still possess a major wage advantage over Western industry, but that too will rapidly disappear with industrial success and rising expectations of workers.

It is timely to abandon the tired and worn-out approaches that have characterized pay systems in commodity and service industry alike. The opportunity exists to alter expensive and unworkable compensation practices in the transition to a fresh package of service operations strategy innovations. It is an opportunity that should not be missed.

PRICING SERVICE SKILLS

If at the time skills packages were originally identified and cataloged, estimates of hourly wage value for each skill were obtained along with ratings of skill importance, the foundation of a constructively revised compensation system is already partly in place. Wherever feasible, the estimates obtained from an expert panel should be cross-checked against actual prevailing wages for similar skilled work in other businesses or industries. Wages must be competitive with the labor market. The value of skill is established in a silent auction among employers who seek to attract the available talent. Rates of pay that are significantly above or below market—20% or more either way from the average—create signif-

Exhibit 5-3
Pay Range for Entry-Level Position

```
Average Labor Market Pay Rate:   $8.30 per hour

Policy:   Pay 5% above market for full performance.
          Bring in at 18% below full performance rate.
          Raise in 6% increments every six months.
          for effective performance.
          Full pay rate is adjusted only for:
          added skill increments and
          cost of living (inflationary) creep.

Full pay rate is:  1.05 * $8.30 = $8.72 per hour.
Entry pay rate is: 0.82 * $8.72 = $7.15 per hour.
Raises at six, twelve and eighteen months are: $0.52 per hour.
```

icant problems for worker and employer alike. Underpaid workers will find it easy to get alternative employment at an attractive increase in pay. Those within 10% or 20% of the average may have to move laterally in pay to the new and uncertain environment and will change only when clearly dissatisfied in their present circumstance. Workers paid above the average will have trouble changing without a cut in pay, and those 20% and more above in a stable labor market will typically find themselves trapped, especially if they don't like their jobs. Overpaid workers generally feel they can't afford to change but can still insist they are underpaid because they are so dissatisfied with their job circumstances.

Satisfied workers will rarely change employment when they are in the plus or minus 20% of average range of market pay. Pay slightly above the average will hold most critical talent and pay rates slightly below the mean may encourage turnover, which permits sifting through the market to find the best, who can then be rewarded more generously. It remains only for the employer to provide reasonably pleasant working conditions to hold a fairly steady work force. The major disruption to stability under these policies will be a surge in demand for skill in the labor market. When that occurs, wages must be quickly adjusted to meet the market if key personnel are to be retained.

The hourly wage estimates of experienced experts will almost always reflect their market experience with wages for the skill estimated. The advantage of a panel estimate resides in the range of estimates obtained that can be averaged. The estimate range may also suggest the appropriate full-rate point at which pay can be pegged. In some circumstances, it may be accepted practice to start new and entry-level people below the full-rate of the pay range and use periodic increases up to rate as an incentive to overcome their learning obstacles. The estimate of an expert panel plus available benchmark comparisons with pay for similar skill in other firms will establish the level of pay and entry-level increments appropriate for each skill. Exhibit 5–3 illustrates the way such a pay range might be calculated for an entry-level position that is pegged at a full-rate market average of $8.30.

In service operations, of course, it is expected and appropriate that each worker master several skills. It will be necessary, therefore, to take account of the repertory of skills each worker possesses in establishing his or her pay. Most skills that make up a worker's skill set will be close in pay, even to the point of overlapping rates and ranges significantly. The appropriate method of wage assignment will be to identify a major or foundation skill as the basis of pay. This may be either the most important skill to the business or the most valuable skill in the labor marketplace. Each skill added to the set after the foundation skill will then merit an added pay increment to reflect the worker's greater flexibility in work assignment and value to the business. Successive increments will usually diminish. The average total increase in wages brought about by added skills should average 20–25%—about the same increment that many incentive plans offer, which is high enough to supply incentive to add skill but moderate enough to leave the worker with some career mobility.

The first skill increment over the foundation skill, for instance, might be in the range of 8–12%, depending on its business importance and market value compared to the worker's foundation skill. The next could be 5–9%. The fourth or higher added skill would fall in a range of 3–6%. Departures from this schedule could be made for skills that introduced exceptional value or flexibility into the skills inventory.

Pay for skill increments as a system of compensation must fully supersede any preexisting system of pay for performance. Under this system, skill is the equivalent of performance. Beyond pay for skill, the only other adjustments in pay appropriate to this system are a periodic general increase to account for increases in the total firm's productivity and an increment to cover any creep introduced into wages by continuing inflation.

Compensation for added, extraordinary productivity is often best handled as a group incentive option and paid out as profit sharing into a tax-sheltered trust in lieu of a retirement plan. Inflation increases that once provided the illusion of performance-based pay increments are better handled periodically and uniformly for all workers on a nonscheduled and certainly anything *but* an annual basis.

Periodically, each skill must be evaluated against the labor market for any change in its value reflected in market pay rates. Where significant change—10% or more—has occurred, the firm's full-rate structure must

Exhibit 5-4
A Skill-Based Pay System for Service Industries

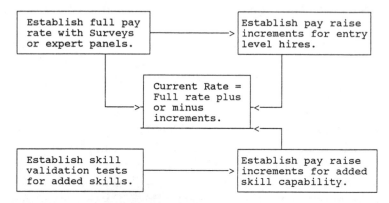

be adjusted and all workers in that foundation skill category adjusted accordingly. New entry-level employees are still paid below the market rate for their skill and are expected to earn their increases up to rate by consistency of performance. This is the traditional probationary break-in of the as yet inexperienced and untested worker. Otherwise, the firm need only establish its general policy of pay—usually either meeting the market average or setting pay 5–10% above the market average for each skill when labor stability is a competitive advantage—and stay with it consistently.

The strength of a pay system administered along these lines is in its objective simplicity and practical commonsense soundness. Basic, foundation skill pay can be routinely adjusted for inflation and changes in market value. The only "motivational" aspect outside probationary increments is the incentive to develop and validate added skills to one's repertory of skill capabilities. Otherwise, employees are expected to apply validated skills fully and satisfactorily as needed to meet work output and quality standards. Exhibit 5–4 illustrates how the system would work.

Capacity for service demands an entirely new philosophy of operations managers. Full-capacity usage of plant and equipment, formerly the unquestioned goal of every commodity operation, will not support high levels of customer service. Uniskilled workers cannot be efficiently applied to plant and equipment that is used at a suboptimized level of excess capacity that supports exceptional customer service. Excess plant and equipment capacity and multiskilled workers are indispensable to good service. Together, they make a world of difference in how service delivery will be organized and managed tomorrow.

Chapter 6

Basic Operating Policy: Service versus Commodity

"Commodity methods apply when price competition is the key to success!"

Skillfully rendered, service adds major value at minor cost. The uniqueness of the service offered makes cost comparison difficult and sometimes impossible. The value of true service is in the eye of the beholder. Cost squeezes like those typical of large-scaled commodity offerings are unlikely because the customer's investment to discover and develop an acceptable new source is likely to be high. In a true service situation, a substantial set-up or start-up cost must be incurred by both customer and supplier in arriving at specification of the unique dimensions of service to be supplied. In strategic terms this is sometimes referred to as the customer's "switching cost." The higher the switching cost, the larger the price differential required to seduce the customer away to a new supplier.

The skilled service supplier controls the cost of start-up by applying a clever system of client screening at the outset. This pins down the major dimensions of client need permitting the service giver to quickly and sensitively fine-tune the offering in the early stages of the new client relationship. The method of client screening applied may be subtle enough that even the client doesn't appreciate its power. Once a satisfactory relationship has been created, the investment required of a competitive supplier to surpass it will usually be prohibitive. The client's willingness to seek out a new supplier will require either major increases in cost or significant sacrifices in level of service. These barriers to change of supplier are likely to be awesome.

This is by no means a new formula. It is the prescription for success in the sale of almost anything to almost anybody since the beginning of organized commerce. The difference is that in our pursuit of vast wealth using complex tool systems to mass produce megaquantities of uniform product we have lost sight of the power of personalized service. It has seemed easier to drive price down through continued application of ever more efficient, sophisticated and capital-intensive methods of production. Ultimately the customer takes low cost and ready availability of the offering for granted, expecting it always to be a bargain. The cost of tooling up for production (supplier's start-up cost) becomes so great that only business behemoths can play the game. Prices stabilize at a level that allows an acceptable return on investment for the now-consolidated, capital-intensive industry, and competition shifts toward research and development of either better methods of production or an alternative product. For half a century or more, mass media advertising has supplanted salesmanship for introducing product innovation. Service has been largely subordinated to engineering technology as these strategies have run their course. The power of service to build a stable customer base that is less subject to cutthroat price competition has been consigned to a dusty back shelf and largely forgotten. Large-scale customer defection from stodgy commodities may quickly bring about its rediscovery.

As service regains its rightful place in the economy, it must displace mass production and mass advertising as the prevailing foundations of the system. Those powerful tools of commodity abundance are most certainly here to stay, but their long dominance of business operations will quietly recede. The operations strategies that support service offerings are already gaining prominence. They will be the subject of succeeding chapters. First, though, we must evaluate the contribution of commodities and their operating methodologies to a service economy. The commodity part of a service operation will continue to be subject to price competition if for no other reason than improving profit margins of the supplier. That part of the cost calculus which pertains to commodity elements of service must still be managed competently as a problem in commodity operations management.

MANAGING THE COMMODITY OPERATIONS SIDE

Commodity operations are, above all, cost-efficient. Scientific management, pioneered by Frederick Winslow Taylor a century or more ago, continues to be the foundation of cost-efficiency in mass production operations. In delivery of services, it is necessary to recognize those instances where efficiency contributes to cost containment without diminished service. Only if called out and recognized for their special utility can cost-management opportunities be exploited. Delivery of quality service and management of costs, if allowed to mix, tend to the domination of one or the other. They must be blended with care. The other imperative for recognition arises in the need to separate commodity and service work cultures in order to coordinate them effectively and avoid needless conflict between their radically disparate value systems.

Commodities are often the building blocks of service. To be a true commodity in support of service, a product or service in its own right must be readily available at minimum cost in minimum lead time. This usually means that there is a competitive market where multiple suppliers vie for the business on a price basis. Between firms, these circumstances will usually be easily recognizable. Within a firm where the offering is subject to integration and coordination under a single management head, cost analysis will be required. Lead time to provide the required level of service will necessitate stockpiling of those elements of the offering that can be inventoried cost-effectively because they would introduce unacceptable delay if produced and delivered to order. Commodity elements must be managed so that they efficiently and cost-effectively blend as part of various ultimate service offerings. If too specialized, a commodity is subject to obsolescence or may deteriorate waiting in storage. The commodity element must move quickly and predictably into the work flow. This requires reasonably accurate forecasting of customer demand and cost-efficient inventory control.

All the classic operations methodologies used for cost control of mass produced output apply—specialization of low-skilled labor, accurate sales forecasting, work flow management keyed to critical lead times and close management of inventories are crucial to efficient management of commodity elements. It is, further, little relevant that the elements may be tangible or intangible, hard product or soft service. The advantage of low skill, for instance, is in the ease of its availability, the low cost of training in putting it to work and the simplicity of laying it off. Skill that takes years to create and is in frequent demand must be inventoried because the lead time to develop it is unacceptable in the marketplace. Lead times of all kinds must be anticipated and managed as part of commodity operations, including commodity services.

Commodity operations must anticipate demand for both competitive and cost reasons. The first or nearest supplier with the commodity in stock will probably make the sale. Short production runs are likely to be uneconomic, high-cost and noncompetitive. Sales must be forecast with precision and care. High-cost production equipment or facility will require intensive use. Machines or processes may run round the clock to keep up with forecast demand. Workers, usually unskilled or semiskilled, will work a fixed schedule at a specialized, tightly defined job.

The work culture of service as contrasted with that of commodity production will differ markedly. Service is altogether "market driven," gaining its power in responsiveness to unique and emerging customer needs. It requires close attention to the market and its environment with consistent concern for the special, the novel and the individual. Service is not constrainable to a fixed time schedule—it must be delivered whenever and wherever the need exists. Service providers—firemen or retail sales people, for instance—are on call, some instantly. Lead time is reduced to response time. While waiting, these service providers train and prepare for future service need. Service flows with the tide of demand, serving need where it emerges, using first one skill then another of the provider. The quality of service output is immediately apparent to the customer and is the first concern to the provider.

These are cultures that are built upon the different values, attitudes and life-styles of the people who populate them. The culture that underlies a strong service orientation will be explored further as this discussion develops. Here we will examine more fully the qualities of the commodity production culture and the operating methods it requires.

EFFECTIVELY MANAGING THE COMMODITY CULTURE

The culture of conventional commodity production is best known in the current age for its pathologies. The facelessness of the work force, labor unrest, management that is often out of touch with the operation, low standards of quality, sometimes even sabotage of the product are all common themes in the popular literature of production. These are the negatives of commodity culture, often created by inability to select workers who fit the culture, sometimes the result of careless or unskilled management. Intensive use of the commodity operations model, as with the military in wartime, requires induction and employment of too many people unsuited by temperament to that culture. It also requires that marginal leadership skill be called into service. The resulting product can be considerably less than optimal.

The problems of commodity operations arise principally out of the imperative of tight organizational discipline to support cost and output quantity goals. There are excellent positive models of what it takes for a commodity offering to succeed. A championship football or rowing team requires the very highest levels of player commitment, teamwork and discipline. Everyone must be focused first on the goals of the team; self-interest comes last. A successful military operation depends on this kind of disciplined spirit. The U.S. Marine Corps, for instance, makes a specialty of this quality of discipline.

It works for business organizations too. Outstanding examples of cost-conscious commodity production can be found in companies like Lincoln Electric and Nucor Steel. Japanese manufacturers succeed grandly in this department as well. The discipline and teamwork of a well-trained battle unit characterize these operations. Personal satisfaction seems to come principally from being a member of an standout team. The athletic star who loses his commitment to teamwork in self-centeredness typifies the once effective commodity production employee who loses interest in team success. Unless they happen to be the top boss who typifies team discipline, organizational stars in commodity operations are usually organizational liabilities.

The culture of commodity production requires a special personality and temperament. The great success of the Japanese appears to rest as much as anything on a culture broadly trained and inured to close teamwork, which chronically subordinates individuality to the good of the greater whole. Given the aggressive independence of Americans, it is a wonder that mass production succeeded as grandly as it has over the past century. Without the continuous influx of European immigrants, long habituated to subordinacy, it is probable that the great American industrial complex might long ago have run aground on the shoals of worker defiance. A wage far above that justified by the modest levels of worker skill needed has been required to keep it going even so. The rigorous discipline of commodity operations is ill-suited to the independent temper of many Americans.

The lessons from companies like Lincoln Electric and Nucor Steel suggest that, much like the U.S. Marine Corps., success of teamwork depends in part on selecting and acculturating only those workers whose temperament can be fitted to the culture. The other critical element of teamwork seems to be top leaders who exemplify in their actions the discipline demanded by commodity operations. Leaders must set the pace for workers in commitment, teamwork and self-discipline in service of the goals of the greater whole. Bosses who sit behind closed doors swapping stories or jokes, who disappear from the workplace into countless meetings that yield little or no product, who insist first on their personal perks and complain stridently about poor work attitudes in the plant themselves set the tone for worker alienation and cynicism. They have abandoned their teams while in pursuit of their own perks.

Commodity operating culture is easily undermined. Mixing commodity operations with service culture operations is likely to be volatile. The essential and unavoidable interface between these operations can be a major problem. The service temperament expects to be catered to by the commodity culture. The commodity temperament chafes at the lack of respect for rules and procedures expressed by service providers. The communications interface can succeed where an unusually sensitive service representative grasps the differences found in the culture. The extreme emphasis on individuality that characterizes good service is antithesis to the selflessness demanded for superior self-discipline and teamwork. The rare team player who appreciates subtle differences in style or temper of colleagues may communicate effectively with the service culture. But the selfless teamwork that characterizes good commodity operations is the enemy of adaptive, unprogrammed action central to good service.

Thus, particular care must be placed not only on picking the right temperament for the culture but also on the even rarer and more complex temperament of the liaison representatives between disparate cultures. In service industries the more common solutions are to permit service goals to dominate the commodity elements of service to the detriment of cost control, or to allow the commodity dimension of organization to overwhelm its service purposes to the detriment of service quality. It is, perhaps, this push toward one polarity or the other without concern for the needed blend that defeats service industry effectiveness more than any other factor.

The operations philosophies of commodity and service operations are similarly polarized. Blending service with commodity operating strategy offers a parallel challenge to that of managing these disparate cultures. The operating methods that must be consistently applied within a commodity operations culture are well-established and described in the literature of management and production engineering. Short jobs or production runs must be avoided. The are likely to be uneconomic, high-cost and noncompetitive. Positions should be filled by unskilled, cheaply trained, easily replaced workers from the mass labor market. Product sales and material usage must be forecast with all due exactness. Inventories and work flow will be tightly controlled against forecasts to minimize cost. These are basics of conventional commodity operations. To the extent that they are appropriate, these methods should be applied to contain cost in commodity-oriented service industries.

In service settings that don't fit the commodity mold, expensive, specialized equipment or facilities that require intensive use will be a liability. Flexible, multiuse equipment or processes are now more often required. Running production round the clock to keep up with customer demand is probably a sign of inadequate planning and capacity. Specialized workers who work at the same task day in and day out are no longer cost-effective or productive. Broad cross-training to permit adaptive reassignment is more common. Quantity goals supported by quality inspection are replaced with blended quality-quantity goals where the worker is directly assigned responsibility for results in both domains. Lengthy production runs in lockstep work flow are replaced by a flexible variety of output, keyed to individual customer need. Adapting toward a project orientation becomes a way of working life.

Adaptiveness to emerging market need demands a very different operating approach from that of the commodity operation. Facing the need to adapt, cost-efficiency is likely to be obtained by gathering the right mix of equipment and skills together and skillfully allocating them to varied project types of situations. I have dubbed this the *project shop*. Projects may be either of a product or service nature. The service project shop is rapidly becoming a prevalent style of operations in service industries. Operations management tools for the service project shop are introduced in the chapters that follow. A service project shop requires that costs be controlled in every way *except* through enforcement of high-volume scheduling. But that is a departure that changes almost everything. The basic theory and principles that guide project shop management are spelled out more fully in my *Management Strategies for Today's Project Shop Economy* (Bassett, 1991).

OPERATING METHODS: THE TRANSITION FROM A COMMODITY TO A PROJECT ORIENTATION

High-volume cost-effective production typical of conventional commodities depends heavily on carefully engineered work flow that divides up the tasks leading to the end product into precisely engineered segments. Each task in the flow is a one-station waiting line for the next workstation. A poorly designed work flow is characterized by numerous bottlenecks with accumulated work-in-process waiting in front of the bottleneck station. Solving bottlenecks requires either a cut in production feeding the bottleneck or addition of capacity at the bottleneck. The payoff for a skillfully designed work flow system is continuous flow through the system without delay for bottlenecks, which maximizes utilization of machine and labor resources committed to the system. Cost is contained by assuring that workers and machines are continually busy when the full line is in operation. If the line itself represents high cost capital investment, continuous or semicontinuous operation can be scheduled to maximize return on the investment.

In a project shop where long production runs give way to short, customized spurts of output, the cost of reengineering lock-step flow with every new job is likely to be prohibitive. Even where the sequence of work flow is standardized, task times will vary widely, sometimes unpredictably, and bottlenecks can emerge at any point in the flow without warning. Applying traditional production engineering methods to the management of this flow is impractical. Even the attempt to make flow of work lockstep in this setting is self-defeating. Machine and labor time will be wasted in large amounts unless an alternative approach is used. Engineered work flow fails in these circumstances.

The most direct solution is to increase the capacity of machines and workstations to a level where substantial excess capacity exists in the operation. Queuing theory, discussed in Chapter 4, offers guidance in establishing the approximate standard of excess capacity needed to avoid excessive waiting lines on available workstations. Indeed, it is in the effort to keep machinery and plant capacity loaded that the problems of project shop work flow begin. As Exhibit 4–2 illustrated, at very high-capacity utilization, waiting lines lengthen rapidly. As capacity usage falls, waiting lines wither and almost disappear. At 67% capacity utilization the average waiting length is one job. This compares to an average waiting line of eighteen jobs at 95% capacity usage. At capacity usages in the 20–30% range it is rare to find a workstation in use when a job moves into it.

Thus, if equipment or machinery can be held in readiness against need, something approximating queueless work flow can be achieved in the project shop, even when work flow is randomly sequenced. Attempting to maximize or even just raise capacity utilization of equipment will snarl work flow and defeat service objectives. Capacity must be constrained to a moderate or even substantially suboptimized level. Equipment and workstation capacity must be liberally "wasted" in the effective service industry project shop.

Two major changes in operating methods are required to support intentional suboptimization of equipment and machinery capacity. First, prices may need to be raised to recoup the return on investment required to justify the capital investment. Analysis of the actual percent increases required reveals that the price advance needed to justify underutilization is often modest and may be easily supported by the added value of customer service available from it. Decelerated depreciation of flexible, multipurpose equipment is an economically sound alternative which supports suboptimized capacity.

The second change required is in the skill level of workers assigned to tasks. It is no longer possible to keep a narrow skilled worker on the same workstation continually. The waste of paid worker time *would* be economically prohibitive. Workers must become more broadly skilled in the use of multiuse machines. The best skilled workers may carry a job through from beginning to end, employing brief waiting line delays encountered to review specifications and for quality checks. This will require a revision in methods of training and compensation for project shop workers.

A probable essential in support of project shop, short-run queueless work flow is a work flow simulator into which every job is entered on arrival at the shop so that its impact on internal capacity usage and overall work flow can be estimated in advance. Bottlenecks in the project shop will emerge temporarily, then disappear. The opportunity exists in a simulator to identify potential temporary bottlenecks and experiment with revised scheduling sequences to assure their fullest utilization. The simulator can also be employed to allocate available labor hours so as to avoid wasted labor in the schedule. In advance of any major change in job mix, the simulator can be employed to evaluate capacity constraints so that person-power can be properly allocated, added or new equipment can be obtained to offset anticipated bottlenecks or the new business can be rejected as incompatible or unprofitable.

Almost all operating methods used for management of operations in support of service are familiar ones in the operations realm. It is mostly in the purpose of their use that the more dramatic shifts in operations emphasis will occur. Complex and costly set-ups, for instance, are likely to be scheduled to support straight through, queueless work flow in support of service and quality goals. Some set-ups may even be held in place until final acceptance of short-run or one-of-a-kind items. Set-up on low-capacity utilization equipment can be scheduled as work in its own right without concern for lost production time. Lead time for set-up is scheduled exactly as lead time for a continuous flow MRP-based (materials requirements planning) system would be in this new approach to work flow management. These will be major departures from past practice wherein set-ups were amortized over the length of the production run and offset against inventory holding costs.

FORECASTING AND WORK FLOW POLICIES

The purpose of good forecasting, like the purpose of all commodity operations methods applied to service industry, is to control or reduce cost. Good forecasting, more often, identifies costs or cost-saving opportunities that might otherwise be overlooked. It permits anticipatory cost control. It must be competently practiced in all the qualitative and quantitative ways possible in service industries, and will be particularly important in managing commodity operations aspects of service. Forecasting a service project operations situation requires greater emphasis on manpower scheduling and flexibility. Those issues will be treated in more detail in Chapter 9.

In traditional commodity operations, forecasting is also used as a guide to capacity expansion or reduction decisions; to identify critical lead-time constraints on labor, materials or capital investment; to establish manning levels in all positions; and to establish production levels. Forecasting is an early warning and planning tool. It is typically based on past experience and tables of probability. Thus, forecasting is subject to error, sometimes on a grand scale. In conventional commodity production, forecasting sets goals for future output that determines the press and pace of work flow. MRP work flow management systems are driven by forecasts that establish end objectives for output, then trace the work flow backward through all elements of work and their lead times to determine what the critical constraints are on meeting the goal. A computerized MRP system might be thought of as a simulator of sequenced, engineered work flow. But because it is typically used to establish production standards and goals, MRP is subject to numerous distortions and subterfuges by those who input the base data. Lead times, for instance, are typically inflated to guarantee sure success in meeting them. If there is fear of revision upward in the plan, surplus capacity may be built invisibly into the plan to assure successful response to the revisions. MRP can easily become the ultimate bureaucratic routine in the commodity production operation.

Where used strictly as a simulator of work flow, MRP can perhaps make a more consistent and cost-effective contribution to operations management. The usual error in business planning is failure to look at all major contingencies inherent in the forecast. Many plans, patently, are clearly best-case and serve more as examples of "cheer leader" enthusiasm than as models of planning. Probable and worst-case scenarios are too often ignored. This is an error that flows from loss of sufficient discipline in commodity operations work flow. The literature of service management may need some new management-style guideposts that warn of error in planning. We might propose a theory "R" (for realism), which requires everyone to expect the worst and have contingency plans in place for its occurrence. Severe penalties are assessed against those who fail to anticipate eventualities that should have been obvious to them. Then there is management theory "H" (for hopeful), which anticipates the best and blames hostile external factors when disappointed. Theory R demands realistic contingency plans for layoffs, diversion of resources, cancellation of purchase orders and general belt tightening. This is ugly stuff that could upset employees, and, perhaps, customers too.

Theory H is more popular because it is presumed to create an upbeat working environment that motivates workers to meet optimistic goals. It offers assurance to customers that their purchase decisions will be sound and timely. Everyone can rest comfortably in their easy chairs, repeating past action whether it is appropriate or not, letting the situation rock along to its presumed destined end point without messy or inconvenient adaptation. Theory R, by contrast, demands that everyone stay alert and on their toes.

Sound service operations strategy demands realism, sometimes even cynicism. Forecasts and plans that do not look at the downside will often set traps in the path of operations managers. The downside of commodity operations in support of a service industry is variation in customer demand that approaches chaos. Service project shop operations managers must anticipate variety and the need for extreme flexibility. Sound commodity operations *rule out* variety in work flow and flexibility of response as excessively costly. They are rejected as cost-ineffective practices. In the service project shop environment everything must be revised to permit cost control without the benefit of long-term production runs that allow routine application of conventional operating methods and depend on lockstep work flow.

Blending commodity with service culture and operations represents an entirely new dimension of operations management skill in service industries. A full appreciation of the differences is required along with awareness of the need to buffer these two disparate sides of the organization through sound organizational structure. Wholly new kinds of operating interfaces are required. The best output of each dimension will be needed in many or most service operations. That is today's challenge for operations management of service industries.

Chapter 7

Planning/Forecasting to Meet Service Demand

"It's all as simple as following the path of a butterfly."

Anyone who tries to predict the future must tolerate a substantial margin of error. Efforts to foresee what lies beyond the immediate time horizon can yield anything from an approximate good guess to fanciful prophecy. The most comprehensive model of forecasting we are daily exposed to is that of the weather. In many ways, we are as well informed of the potential for tomorrow's weather just by knowing the season of the year as we are from elaborate computer models. In precomputer times, the experienced weather watcher could anticipate near-term changes in the immediate geographic vicinity by observing atmospheric pressure, wind direction, cloud patterns and temperature changes. Meteorologists still use these cues to assess the potential in current weather. The computer is indispensable for generating the elaborate visual graphics used on TV to depict weather systems, but as far as prediction is concerned, computers are still dependent on and often less accurate than experienced judgment. The programs they are based on, indeed, are entirely derived from the judgments of experienced weather forecasting experts.

Forecasting business activity is little different. If one knows the season of the year, current interest rate, today's sales level compared to last week's or last year's, along with current rates of births, marriages and housing starts, a businessperson can usually plan realistically for what's immediately ahead. Scheduling is largely a matter of keeping enough flexibility in the plan to permit corrections as needed.

Where it operates on a large enough scale to find safety in averages, or when service is managed as a commodity offering, forecasting service demand in this conventional mode is entirely appropriate. Disney World, McDonald's, the phone or electric companies and commercial airlines can predict with considerable accuracy levels of demand by season of the year, day of the week, even hour of the day. Even so, they will be caught every so often in errors of forecasting that result in significant over- or undercapacity because of unforeseen changes in political and economic factors. There is very little that can be done to avoid it. Chance is ever present in matters of foresight.

Conventional commodity production uses finished goods inventory as a buffer against unpredictability of demand. Sometimes demand is so great that inventory is wholly depleted. Other times, inventory sits on the shelf gathering dust till it becomes obsolete. Error in forecasting here is translated directly into some amount of inventory holding or back-order cost. The customer finds the desired product waiting in stock with an increment added to the price for inventory costs or otherwise awaits its availability. The better the forecasting, the fewer the stock-outs and the lower the price.

Conventional commodities and real service offerings equally will effectively meet customer demand and price competition as a function of the accuracy of the sales forecast. Too expansive a forecast generates excess inventory, which adds to cost and price. Too cautious a forecast that avoids inventory cost but leaves shelves empty or service unavailable will send customers looking for an alternative source of supply. Sales, and perhaps market share, may be lost. Strategically, every reasonable effort should be put on increasing the quality of business forecasts. Poor forecasts increase cost and threaten competitive position.

Every business or industry has its own pattern when it comes to sales predictability—or unpredictability. If sufficient excess capacity is maintained to permit adjustment to variable levels of demand, sales may bounce about, day by day or week by week, varying with the caprice of random buying patterns, but will ultimately average out over a month's or quarter's time. A commodity product must be inventoried at a level that absorbs the random ups and downs of consumer whimsy. A service must respond with sufficient flexibility to rise and recede with the tide of demand and meet peak demand. Flexibility of service response begins with ample excess capacity in physical capacity or supporting inventory stocks. Cost control of these elements of service is a matter of identifying significant cost breaks that minimize added value to the service offering but eliminate lengthy or costly waits in service delivery. More discussion about cost breaks follows in Chapter 8.

Cost control of the labor in support of service requires:

1. close control of any excess capacity in labor hours kept available to assure quick customer response,
2. some form of on-call labor resource that can be added or deleted to meet unexpected demand,
3. flexibility of individual worker skill repertory that permits reallocation of available paid labor time, and
4. individual worker flexibility in rate of output or hours of work that can be invoked to meet expanded demand.

The options are complex, but not unusual or uncommon. Excess capacity of available labor hours is used up in study and planning by real estate and auto salespersons. Police or fire departments have provision for call-in of off-duty personnel for a major emergency. Where the emergency is extended and severe, police or fire personnel may work extended hours and extra shifts. When business is unexpectedly light, restaurants and retail stores send personnel home early. Supermarket stock clerks work at the cash registers when checkout lines become too lengthy. Experienced waitresses increase their pace and efficiency of service as crowds of customers arrive.

In one form or another, capacity expands and contracts within an established (forecast!) range to cover variations in service demand. Some form of background forecast that establishes the minimum and maximum range of likely demand is always necessary as the framework in which to manage variation. The forecast may arise out of experienced judgment, long-standing policy or carefully analyzed historical records. However it is accomplished, it is inevitably a forecast prediction of one kind or another. It is appropriate, thus, that we examine the types of forecast strategy that are available and commonly applied in service industries.

A good forecast is essentially a balancing act. On one side, the forecast should ignore the random bounciness of past sales history. On the other, it must be sensitive to real changes in the wind that may require adjustment of capacity, revision of work schedules, expansion of skill requirements and all the variables that go into meeting customer demand in real time on its own ground. Many forecasts begin with available historical sales data. A historical time series of sales data embraces a natural blend of randomness and meaningful pattern. These are referred to in forecasting jargon as error and trend. Meaningfulness in the pattern may also include elements of seasonality or the influence of an economic cycle. Because of the complexity of forecasting patterns, it is often difficult to discriminate between error and trend. The art of forecasting requires that meaningless variability in sales over a short span of time be ignored, but that real, emerging change be astutely recognized. A forecaster is continually asking him- or herself: Is today's change in level of business a mere fluke of chance or is it a signal of future market directions?

A useful analogy for understanding error and signal is found in theory of communications systems. Every channel of communication has both noise and signal constantly flowing through it. The trick in making the channel serve the purpose of communication effectively is in distinguishing between the two. The widespread prevalence of remote phones, for instance, offers experience with channels where the signal is weak or the noise is high. It is sometimes necessary to ask for repetition of a message or to listen with extra care to make out what is coming in on the remote phone channel. Mistakes in communication are still common because it is impossible to clear up every source of noise without blurring or masking the real signal.

That is exactly the dilemma of the business forecaster. Crude incoming signals that the market offers may be indistinguishable from randomness and thereby are lost in the clutter. Alternatively, noise that sounds vaguely like a message may be mistaken for signal and acted upon inappropriately. Communications systems damp noise or enhance signal in a variety of ways, most of them electronic. The mechanisms for damping noise or enhancing signal in forecasting are somewhat cruder and simpler. To damp out excessive noise, the forecaster averages two or more data points, thereby smoothing the forecast line in some degree. To enhance signal, greater emphasis is put on the most recent data points, sometimes by accepting them raw as indicators of market change, sometimes by weighting them more strongly into some type of average.

THE TECHNOLOGY OF FORECASTING SERVICES

Forecasting services is no less difficult than forecasting conventional commodity production, but it is more critical in terms of the cost of error. MRP-styled commodity work flow requires only a summary sales forecast figure for a month, quarter or year. Planning proceeds backward from the gross goal supplied by the forecast, filling the intervening capacity in the manner judged most practical. Usually this will result in a stable, relatively level stream of output. Variations in demand over the period may be met with surplus inventory or through backordering. The convenience of a steady work-force level, the day-by-day predictability of output, the comfort of a familiar routine—all serve to make the levelized output strategy a popular one in support of conventional commodity output. Small adjustments to changes in demand are easily buffered with inventory. Intermediate adjustments are met through overtime or short-term layoffs. Only the big mistakes of forecasting will demand major adjustment in the commodity production operation.

Most conventional commodity forecasts, thus, are rather informal, even crude in their formulation. A production controller or a sales manager projects past sales forward with some simple mathematical system (increase last quarter's sales by 3%, for instance), the forecast is modified or approved by higher management and a production plan is drawn based on the agreed-to number. In a very-high-volume conventional commodity production operation, nothing more is necessary or practical. The whole process can be carried out on the back of an envelope.

Forecasting is more sensitive in service industries. True service must be delivered when and where it is needed. Poor prediction of either the when or the where can cost revenue and customer goodwill. Police or medical emergency personnel must respond to the emergency call, proceeding in a timely manner to the location of the call. Repair and maintenance technicians must be sent quickly to the site of a downed power or telephone pole. Package delivery service must locate the sender and receiver quickly and efficiently. Forecasting of demand for services such as restaurants, airlines, schools or barber shops may require accurate prediction of variation in demand for capacity, sometimes on a day-by-day basis. Considerably more accurate approaches to forecasting are needed for these purposes. Excess unused capacity will be costly. Insufficient capacity is lost revenue and customer goodwill. Expecting each day, week or month to merely be a trend-modified clone of the previous one will not do here.

Some service offerings are subject to sudden, frequent changes in industry capacity due to competitive factors. Where barriers to entry into or exit from the industry are low, competitors may come and go almost overnight. A new restaurant or beauty shop in the neighborhood can immediately reduce revenues of existing ones. A bleak business picture can turn bright overnight if a major competitor closes up shop first. Ted Turner's superstation barely survived its infancy to become a cable network star because an Atlanta competitor station unexpectedly went out of business.

Forecasting in service sometimes requires an elaborate system of intelligence gathering. If the opening of a new video rental store in the neighborhood is not anticipated and met with equivalent sales promotion to defend share, serious loss of revenue may ensue for an existing one. The qualitative side of forecasting in service may require contin-

Exhibit 7-1
A Severely Erratic Pattern of Sales

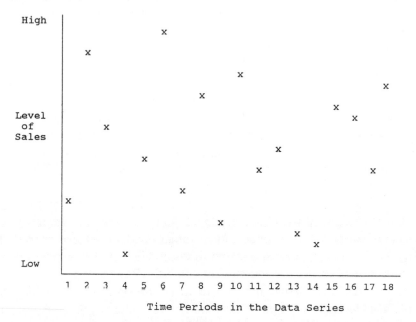

uous monitoring of building permits or licenses issued in the area, seeking out talkative friends in the employ of competitors, periodic direct observation of (i.e., spying on) competitors' businesses, regular review of local and industry advertising, including the want ads, and careful cultivation of knowledgeable experts and consultants in the field. A service industry with a sales force will gather intelligence through its own field representatives. Successful service providers must acquire the skills and habits of an investigator and business analyst as a foundation for sound sales forecasts.

Forecasting for service operations must often proceed on multiple levels of analysis. Qualitative intelligence that provides insight into probable competitive changes is essential to preparing for major threat or opportunity. The forecast itself may begin with calculation of last period's activity in terms of customers, units and/or dollars of sales. A shift toward fewer customers providing more revenue may look like a sales increase when it represents, in reality, only increased vulnerability to reduced sales if a larger customer is lost. The customer base must often be analyzed customer by customer, especially for major customers, to identify opportunities or vulnerabilities that should be factored into the forecast.

Exhibit 7-2
A Seasonal Pattern of Sales

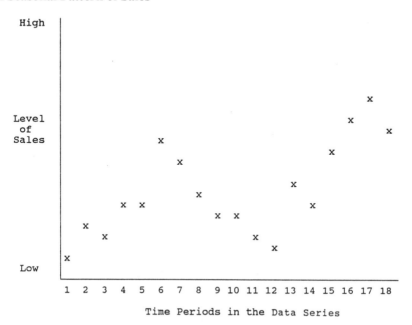

Units of sales may be important. Attempts to forecast are often confused by the influence of chronic inflation. Dollars of revenue can increase as unit sales decrease and the customer base erodes. Good past records are needed, not only for tax and other legal purposes, but for sound forecasting as well.

The available history of sales, however brief or lengthy, is the beginning point for the quantitative analysis that a forecast is based on. The simplest, most easily understood form of analysis is a line or bar graph. It is good practice to get into the habit of plotting sales by total dollars, units or customers on a daily, weekly, monthly or quarterly basis. The time period chosen for graphic display will depend on the variability of business. When changes from period to period are gradual, allowing connection of the graph points with a gently flowing, curved line, the period employed is probably stable enough to be used as a forecast base. If levels of sales fluctuate wildly, shooting up one period, dipping deeply another, another approach is required. Usually this will call for use of longer periods as the basis for a forecast. Exhibit 7–1 offers an example of wide fluctuation in sales. On occasion, variation in sales may indicate that seasonal variation must be examined as shown in Exhibit 7–2. Service is frequently variable

Exhibit 7-3
Hourly Arrivals of Bank Customers

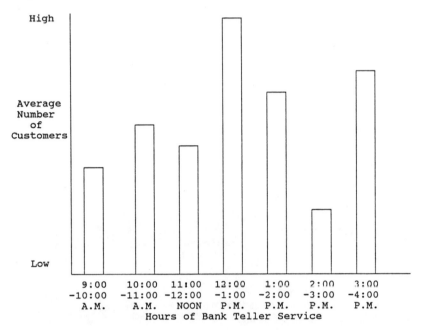

on a day-of-the-week or season-of-the-year basis. The service of advertising can be variable by day of the week and hour of the day as a function of newspaper readership or television viewing patterns. Exhibit 7–3 illustrates this pattern of sales variation. Some services, like air or bus transport, restaurants or amusement parks, may forecast certain seasons or holidays specifically based on expected variation from the current quarterly or annual sales. The quarter's sales, for instance, may be increased or decreased by prevailing economic conditions onto which sales are uniquely superimposed according to characteristic holiday or seasonal patterns. Exhibit 7–4 illustrates this sales pattern. Here, appropriate seasonal or holiday records must be used as the basis for estimating the extent of departure from the current baseline of sales.

Small amounts of erratic variation in sales that appear to have no weekly or seasonal significance can be smoothed with a moving average. Any number of immediately prior time periods—from two up—can be averaged. The average calculated may either be plotted as the midpoint of the averaging period for purposes of creating a graphic curve of past sales, or projected to the next future sales period as an estimate of coming sales activity. Exhibit 7–5 illustrates the moving average curve plotted against

Exhibit 7-4
A Seasonal Pattern of Sales Reflecting Holidays

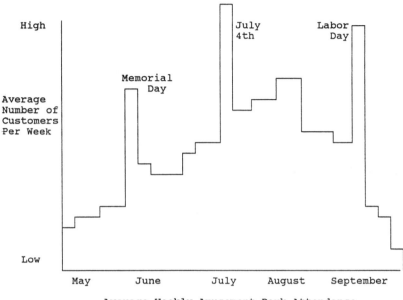

Average Weekly Amusement Park Attendance

the midpoint of the five data points, while Exhibit 7–6 shows how the same moving average appears when projected forward to the next following sales period as a forecast. A simple mathematical evaluation of forecast projection versus actual sales known as Mean Absolute Deviation (MAD) can be calculated as an index of the accuracy of moving average forecast for different averaging periods. A discussion of MAD can be found in any standard operations management text (see, for instance, Chase and Aquilano, 1989).

A relatively smooth curve that offers a reasonable guide to upcoming sales activity when projected forward is the product of a sound moving average approach to forecasting. A moving average either offers usable results or it doesn't. The proof of utility is in the results of use. Where sales activity is chaotic to the extent of offering no apparent pattern at all, it may be necessary to use a best straight-line fit to available data as a means of estimating whether sales are level, up-trending or declining. The technical name for this forecasting method is regression analysis. It is a time series analysis much like a moving average, which simplifies the data into a single straight line and measures the angle of its slope: upward, downward

Exhibit 7-5
A Centered Five-Week Moving Average for an Amusement Park

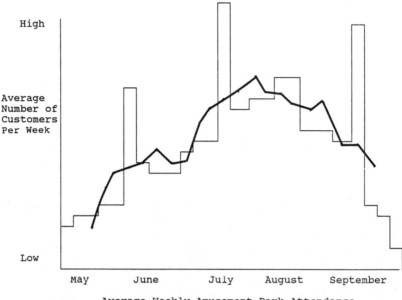

Average Weekly Amusement Park Attendance

or level. Exhibit 7–7 illustrates a regression line forecast as applied to the extreme variation offered in Exhibit 7–1.

Regression or straight-line forecasting centers on a single average for the total time series of data analyzed. Mathematically, that average is set at the exact midpoint of the time series that fixes the center point of the regression line. The line is then rotated (mathematically or visually, depending on your devices) until it centers across the data points at minimum distance from their collective dispersion, to find the best straight-line fit across the totality of data points. The regression forecast carries the moving average concept to its logical extreme, using a single average to anchor the line slope, then accommodating all of the data points in the series as closely as possible to the line.

Occasionally, a business may be subject to large cyclical or seasonal fluctuations that render near-term forecasting useful but extremely difficult. It may be useful here to calculate a base trend using linear regression, then superimpose expected seasonal patterns of sales on top of the straight-line trend. This is usually accomplished by adjusting any given period's data (day, week, month, etc.) by a seasonal index of expected sales variation.

Exhibit 7-6
A Projected Attendance Forecast Based on a Centered Five-Week Moving Average for an Amusement Park

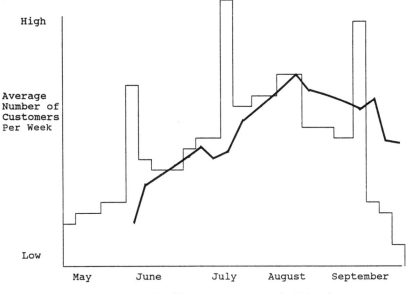

Average Weekly Amusement Park Attendance

Averaging smoothes out the error in a data trend series. The longer the data series included in the moving average, the greater the error damping accomplished. The shorter the series, the greater the influence of the most recent sales result. When the most recent sales period is used alone as the forecast of the coming expected result, the realm of error and noise damping is fully left behind. We are now dealing with raw signal.

The most extreme form of averaging is the calculated linear regression on all available time series data. At this extreme, there is a point at which forecasting is reduced to a game of throwing darts at all possible eventualities on a target. A business that is dependent on a few large customers may be subject to unpredictable surges and falls in demand that come utterly without warning. A market driven by fashion may bloom and fade overnight. The only workable strategy here is to build enough flexibility into the planning and work flow systems to permit rapid response to major variation. Good forecasting comes down to recognizing the impossibility of close prediction. Today's sales often are the best indicator of tomorrow's business.

Exhibit 7-7

A Calculated Regression Line Applied to a Severely Erratic Pattern of Sales

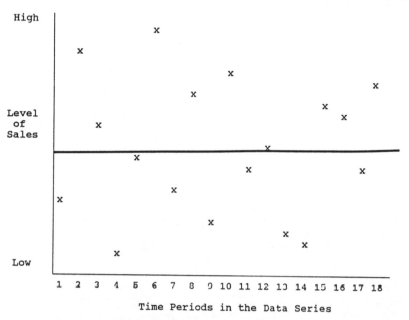

When no amount of averaging helps, the alternative is to give emphasis almost entirely to the current level of sales as a best available portent of the immediate future. This is sometimes referred to as a "naive" forecast. Naive or not, it certainly demands an element of experienced judgment to bet heavily on today's sales as the dominant indicator of future sales activity. Other factors in the social and economic context may have to be added to the consideration to make the bet a sound one. For instance, greatly increased sales at raised prices add credibility to the notion of real change in demand. Conversely, greatly reduced sales at lowered prices may readily suggest that the bottom is about to drop out. Either steady sales or a fall in sales with the entry of a new competitor probably should be seen as a sign of things to come. A change in sales that parallels a change in interest rate or a major promotional effort ought to be taken seriously. The economic and political context within which business is done often has a bearing on the meaning of sales data that should be factored into the forecast.

Under the right conditions, raw current sales results *should* be read as trend. But the safer approach to forecasting still is always to build a blend of error damping and signal enhancing into the forecast. One of the more

Exhibit 7-8
The Exponentially Smoothed Forecast Model

```
Requisites to the Model:
    Some forecast based on an average.
        For instance:
            A regression projection to the forecast period.
            A moving average over several recent periods,
                projected to the forecast period.
    Actual sales result for the most recent full sales period.

    An experienced judgment as to typical period by period
        variability in sales.  For instance:
            Sales figures are subject to high variability
            or
            Recent sales are sensitive to near-term change.

    Weight the average of the forecast and recent actual sales
        to reflect period by period variability:
            Weights must sum to 1.0.
            Weight forecast highest if variability is high.
            Weight sales actual highest if near term is
                sensitive to change.

    Once calculated, the exponentially smoothed forecast
        figure becomes the sales forecast for the next
        period's forecast calculation.

Example:
    A neighborhood beauty parlor -
    Five-period moving average for a beauty parlor is calculated
        at $4750 sales weekly average.
    Most recent week's sales is $6100
    Weekly sales are highly variable:
        weight moving average .9
        weight recent actual sales .1
    (.9 x $4750) + (.1 x $6100) = $4885 sales forecast for the
        following week.

    A rapidly growing videotape rental store -
    A three-week moving average for video rentals and sales is
        calculated at $7350 weekly average.
    Most recent week's sales is $7950.
    Recent sales are sensitive to actual growth
        weight moving average .2
        weight recent actual sales .8
    (.2 x $7350)  + (.8 x $7950) = $7830 sales forecast for the
        following week.
```

preferred forecasting devices is the exponentially smoothed forecast that computes a weighted average using as one element some kind of averaged projection—usually a current forecast that has an element of averaging already built into it—in combination with a weighted raw current sales data as the other element. The weights applied respectively to the forecast and the current sales numbers can be adjusted either to give more weight to the damping effect of averaging or to increase the influence of current sales results. Exhibit 7–8 illustrates how this is done. Where there is a substantial discrepancy between the forecast number and current sales results, it may also be wise to build in sufficient flexibility of response to cover a range of demand possibilities in the coming sales period.

The mechanics of forecasting are, indeed, often very crude ones. Like crude tools in many other situations, though, they can yield impressive results in the hands of an experienced, skilled operations manager. A large element of experienced judgment enters into every forecast. The mechanics of the exponentially smoothed forecast, seemingly elegant and powerful, pale in importance beside the significance of the judgment that determines the weights to be applied. The most elegant computer model imaginable is useless if it doesn't fit the business or the industry. Every business must try and err in its search for the most appropriate forecast model. The emerging science of nonlinear systems—chaos, as it is sometimes called—suggests the underlying dynamics of the forecasting process; everything is predictable in the gross average, but something as trivial as the flight path of a butterfly in Bejing today may influence the weather in Cincinnati tomorrow.

Forecasting is always a chancy proposition. Error is inevitable. Our foresight into the future is inherently dim. As with anticipating the weather, we use the best experience, data and knowledge available to dispel our otherwise substantial ignorance of what to expect. Seasonality and randomness are accommodated pragmatically as needed. One must appreciate the greater accuracy of near-term forecasts and hold reasonable doubt about long-term predictions. The experienced manager blends close observation of salient detail with experienced judgment and quantitative analysis to form the clearest, most confidence-inspiring picture of the future as can be drawn. Then he or she follows the business plan and adapts to the surprises.

LEARN TO BEND GRACEFULLY TO THE WIND

There is no real alternative to forecast planning as a means to prepare for the future. If nothing better is obtainable from the crude tools we have, a sensible estimate of the range of variation from most to least can be teased out of available historical data and experienced judgment. The weakness of many business plans and their related forecasts lies in the failure to look seriously at alternative outcomes. The typical government budget is based on the best-case outcome for both sides of the ledger; revenues will be as high as it is possible for them to be, expenses will be as low as it is possible for them to be. When anything goes awry, and it certainly will, there is an instant shortfall. If every taxing body were required by law to plan on the basis of the worst-case experience for both revenue and expense based on the past dozen or so years, government spending would become considerably more rational. Many business managers have yet to learn the same lesson; worst-case contains traps that must be uncovered and anticipated.

Business plans also are often overoptimistic. The challenge to grow or to meet stiff competition evokes a competitive enthusiasm that sees only the positive side of the situation. Business strategies are too often rigidly formulated around a narrow set of optimistic goals. When things begin to get off track, chaos ensues. Forecasting and planning deserve our best commitment and energy once set in place as policy, but should look at all the possibilities, good and bad, in the formulation stage. Worst-case, best-case and most-likely-case forecasts are all equally essential to achievement of a realistic assessment of business opportunity and threat. The plan that is implemented in policy, in like fashion, must account for fall-back positions and contingencies. The manpower plan for a small law firm offered in Chapter 9 (see Exhibit 9–1) illustrates how this might be accomplished for basic labor hour requirements against best-, worst- and most-likely-case business forecasts.

A good forecast should specify the range of flexibility required to meet likely minima and maxima of customer demand. The business plan that flows from it must be flexible enough to meet the challenges of the entire range of possible outcomes. Capacities of all kinds, including supporting materials, skilled labor or plant and equipment must be effectively managed to permit cost-effective adaptation over the fullest range of possible sales results.

Chapter 8

Lead Time, Cost Breaks and Inventory Control in Service Operations

"A revolution in service operations methods begins right here."

Delay is the great enemy of high-quality service. Anything that introduces substantial customer waiting time diminishes service. Everything that eliminates delay without increasing cost proportionally enhances the competitive position of a service business. Delay most commonly results from complex processes with long lead times, which require significant set-up or changeover to adapt to market redirection, which necessitate investment to learn new skills, which must assess the special needs of a new customer or discover the emerging new requirements of an old customer, and in a host of related places. The basic rules that apply to minimization of delay in delivery of service are these:

- General-purpose parts and materials that can be stockpiled at very low or no cost must be inventoried in abundance well ahead of need.

- Long-lead-time parts or materials must be costed against the customer's valuation of superior service. If a price differential to cover inventory can be built in and still stay competitive, maintain an ample inventory. Immediate service always wins over small cost saving that requires backordering.

- Evaluate long-lead-time processes with a cost-flow analysis to identify delay that can be offset inexpensively with inventory, versus lead time that cannot be tolerated by the customer. Stockpile at favorable cost/service break points using sound inventory practice.

- Organize long-lead-time processes that are found to be unavoidable and evaluate with cost-flow analysis so that available material, skill and labor are best applied to achieve fast completion upon demand.

The objective that underlies application of these principles is to cut lead time whenever and wherever it is cost-effective to do so. Analysis begins with identification of task completion or lead times for every element of the total job. Lead times are routinely estimated when preparing work or production flow analyses in support of operations control. Materials requirements planning (MRP) systems cannot function without specification of lead times for every item and stage of work flow. Planning with any process from the most formal PERT (Program Evaluation and Review Technique) analysis to an experienced informal guess as to a delivery date requires specification of lead times.

The conventional context of MRP work flow analysis encourages conservative estimation of lead times. That is, a substantial margin for error is added to lead-time estimates to assure that production goals will be consistently met. Time is of the essence in service. Lead times with excessive built-in slack mean poor service. The more appropriate model for service lead times is found in the JIT (Just in Time) approach to work flow management. In the JIT environment, lead times are critically scrutinized to shrink out any built-in safety margins. Tight, realistic lead times based on equally tight, realistic labor standards are demanded by JIT. The better model for analysis and identification of cost/service breaks is JIT.

Long habit in a commodity-oriented economy, though, will often yield lead times with substantial slack built into them. JIT is new and unconventional in most work settings. When all lead times have been specified, it will be prudent and necessary to critically examine each for realism. Eliminating lead-time slack is the absolute lowest cost way to improve service. The soundest assumption is that every worker and every vendor wants to make their work lives easier by giving themselves plenty of time to do the assigned job. Service quality demands that every worker and every vendor give every job their absolute best in the way of quick, high-quality delivery. Permitting loose, high-slack estimates of lead time to prevail defeats service quality at the source. Nor is it enough to evaluate lead times once and forget them. The attack on lead-time slack never ends in the campaign to tighten lead-time standards. Continuous rereview of standards for lead time is basic to effective service operations management.

When sufficient confidence in the quality of lead-time estimates has been achieved, the next step in cost/service break analysis can be undertaken. It is now time to calculate the cost of stockpiling material or WIP (work in process) at each step in the work flow to discover and eliminate unnecessary waiting time. This analysis always begins at the start points of the work flow. For many operations, there will be multiple start points. Long lead time for supplies used in support of service should be treated as independent flow branches in the cost/service analysis. Critical long lead times will typically require stockpiling in advance of need to avoid intolerable lead times in delivery of service.

An example of a moderately long lead-time item that is critical in a service setting is that of whole blood used in hospital operating and emergency rooms. The quantities of blood required for a severely injured accident patient in the middle of the night would easily outrun the availability of donors available. Blood, of course, is priceless. The expense of taking blood from donors can still be high in the costs of nurses, technicians and equipment. In addition, the cost of holding it in inventory is very high due to its perishability and the requirement of close administrative control over stocks. On balance, though, it is an acceptable cost given the alternative of the unnecessary loss of a life merely for its absence. Maintaining whole blood in inventory is a sound, even indispensable cost/service break point for assurance of sound medical treatment.

The cost of carrying long-lead-time supplies in inventory is wholly a function of inventory carrying costs. These costs can include theft, deterioration, obsolescence, stock room space, inventory handling overhead, insurance on stock and the opportunity cost value (interest equivalent) of tying up working capital in physical stock. Carrying cost must be carefully calculated for every type of inventory stock to determine what the real savings from JIT inventory will be. Trivial costs will almost always justify inventorying of necessary supplies. Even some large costs, though, can be more than offset by the service value of availability on demand.

A typical holding cost incurred in service of JIT inventory policies is found in waste or spoilage of food prepared in advance of customer demand. The chef in a gourmet restaurant may find it cost-effective to buy more fresh food than required so that customers need never be disappointed in their menu preferences, even though some food supplies may be wasted. He or she may also prepare, well in advance of demand, certain sauce bases that require extended cooking or long refrigeration, knowing that some may be thrown out at the end of the day. McDonald's, the hamburger master, has specific standards on the amount of food, prepared in advance of sales to assure fast service, that should be thrown out because it sat too long in the service (inventory) bins. These all represent carefully thought through cost/service breaks, which accept inventory holding cost as the necessary price of high-quality customer service.

Exhibit 8-1

Cost Break Analysis for a Custom Limousine Offering On-Demand Service

```
Cost Break Trade-offs:

Fill gas tank at end of run rather than at start of run:
     Average impact on cash flow       $0.02
     Delay if not filled               20 minutes

Wash vehicle after run rather than at start of run:
     Frequency with which vehicle
          must be washed again at
          start of run                 50%
     Delay if wash needed at start
          of run                       20 minutes

Flat tire while carrying passengers:
     Cost of full sized, mounted
          spare tire in vehicle        $100.00
     Delay if carried                  15 minutes
     Delay if not carried              20-90 minutes

Provide clear directions to driver
          for the trip:
     Delay for clear trip directions   20 minutes
     New driver orientation in the
          territory - amortized
          over first 20 trips          $5.00
```

Exhibit 8–1 illustrates a simple service setting where cost/service breaks can be calculated and evaluated. This is a custom limousine service that provides service on demand. Most calls require response within thirty minutes, some allow up to two hours. Average time to reach the customer's place of departure is ten minutes. From this set of cost-break analyses it is apparent that as much as an hour delay is incurred when it is necessary to provide the driver with clear directions and then gas and wash the vehicle before starting for the customer. The degree to which service is diminished is compared with the cost of avoiding delay in this analysis.

The easiest decision is always to gas vehicles at the end of the trip. The small increment in inventory holding (gas in the tank) it requires is trivial compared to the service increment added. It is a worthwhile price to pay for quicker response time. Familiarization of new drivers with the territory looks like a good policy. A vehicle wash that costs $3.00 is more difficult to establish a policy for, inasmuch as the delay may occur anyway. The prospect of a flat tire, while remote, offers the potential for an intolerable delay if customer timing is tight, but the offsetting cost to carry a full-sized spare is high. For vehicles on long trips, the spare may be necessary. Shorter trips in the immediate area may permit quick vehicle substitution in place of carrying the spare. Cost/service break analysis here may require inclusion of considerations regarding vehicle assignment to differential jobs.

Cost/service breaks that occur near the beginning of the work flow process are easy to analyze, since costs are readily identified at or very near the point of the break. Longer chains of flow in service may accumulate costs over multiple operations, which must also be accounted for in the cost/service break analysis. The end result, though, is the same. The total cost of inventory holding required to prepare in advance for rapid delivery of service by avoiding the delays of otherwise long service lead times must be calculated. The holding cost in terms of waste and inventory holding expense is measured against the loss of service quality brought about by avoidable delay. If holding cost can be added to price as the price of high-quality service, and if customers are satisfied with the resulting price/service package, the cost/service break is a viable one.

In a complex service setting there may be opportunity for multiple cost/service breaks. Any single cost may appear merited for the benefit of added service time. When summed together, though, costs may be higher than tolerable. When more than one good cost/service break point can be identified where lead-time delays can be directly traded off for a measured cost increment in stockpiling, a prioritizing system is appropriate and probably necessary. Two variables are in play here, time and cost. It is useful to categorize all cost/service breaks in terms of significance of lead-time savings and the total cost increment added per unit of service to effect lead-time reduction. The list of available cost/service break opportunities can be categorized on a per unit basis, first by lead time saved, then, independently, by cost increment incurred through the savings. The most attractive alternatives will be those where a major time saving can be obtained at low cost. The least attractive are those that save little lead time at relatively high cost for holding inventory. Those cases in the two remaining intermediate categories can be individually examined for importance of contribution. This can be an opportunity to reevaluate lead times selectively to determine which can be reduced further without stockpiling, as well as to scrutinize holding costs to see where they might be reduced.

Sometimes a weighting system can be applied usefully to cost/service break analyses. The simplest and crudest weight would be to divide lead-time delay by inventory holding cost per unit held. This yields a comparative index of service delay reduction as a function of inventory cost. The larger the index the greater the attractiveness of the savings in service delay on a purely time/cost basis. This index does not take into account very large delays that could severely reduce service quality. Cost may be less important than the major increment of service quality available in avoiding the delay. The choice at this cost/service break point may be obvious and imperative, in which case it is directly implemented. If not, an additional weight can be added to the analysis that increases the delay element by some percentage factor, 125%, 150% or even doubling it to 200% of its raw value.

Once indexes have been calculated, they can be rank ordered from highest to lowest. Then, one at a time, delay should be subtracted from current required total service time and cost should be added to the current pricing structure of the service. It will be useful to identify points of discontinuity in the rank order—those points at which either delay drops or price rises sharply. A panel of customers or knowledgeable judges should then rate the trade-off of cost and service along the scale of feasible delay reduction presented by the available break points. The objective of rating is to locate the most attractive cost-service trade-off point in the available array of possibilities.

The methodology used with these ratings is first to compare the two most extreme possibilities, most delay and lowest price, with least delay and highest price. This establishes the primacy of cost or service. The preferred polarity is then held and compared with successively closer options from the opposite end of the rank order. When comparisons reach equality, the comparison moves one position toward the middle from each point of equivalence and begins again. The comparison process is repeated in this fashion until the exact midpoint of preference is located. Where possible, this comparison process should be carried out with a substantial number of customers and their preferences plotted on a graph. If the distribution is normal, choose the midpoint. If it is bimodal or flat, it may be worthwhile to consider offering a differentiated range of prices and service (delay) levels that reflect differential delay and cost trade-offs, segmented to different classes of customers.

Experienced operations managers will note that the cost calculus offered here uses an inventory holding cost that does not take into account one element of cost commonly included in inventory cost analyses. This is the cost of acquisition of stock or set-up of processes. Acquisition/set-up cost, if substantial, can be offset only when sufficient inventory is held in large enough quantities to require periodic acquisitions or set-ups to hold inventory cost down. Where inventory is not currently held, and acquisition/set-up cost is large, the presence of significant acquisition/set-up cost alone may be sufficient argument for changing policy and holding inventory. Thus, the only influence that a high acquisition/set-up cost can have on the cost/service break analysis is to raise the point at which cost of holding inventory when it reduces delay is already acceptable. An adjunct to the cost/service break point analysis may be to examine stock acquisition/set-up costs to locate any points where the cost of holding inventory would be largely offset by the reduced acquisition/set-up cost available from quantity orders or runs. If usage quantities are small and acquisition or set-up is clearly inexpensive, this element of cost can probably be safely ignored. If quantities are small and acquisition/set-up is costly, it becomes necessary to add acquisition/set-up cost to the unit price for purposes of calculating carrying cost.

INVENTORY FOR SERVICE

Two separate and distinct kinds of inventory must be managed in service industries. The more conventional inventory has to do with control of those inventory costs that accompany commodity elements of the service offering. As we have seen above, opportunity cost of the inventory investment, storage and administrative control, as well as damage or obsolescence of goods in stock all have potential to add undesired cost to the expense line of service when inventory is carried.

The unique dimension of inventory in service pertains to available stocks of human skill, talent and time. Some of the same costs apply here. There is investment in training or learning, deterioration from lack of practice, obsolescence due to change in machinery, methods or customer need and the requirement of sound administrative systems to validate and locate possessed skill when business need calls for it. The availability of specialized service is dependent on the stock of required human skill, talent and time ready for application on demand. Approached from a different direction, the inventory of skill, talent and time available to customers represents a firm's capacity for service. This inventory is fundamental to timely, competitive delivery of the desired service.

Growth in knowledge and skill is a standard element of service. Doctors, teachers, accountants, lawyers and other professionals are regularly required to upgrade and augment their professional skills, in some cases as a condition of licensing. For all types of service, professional and nonprofessional, the most cost-effective way of maintaining a broad-based inventory of varied skill is through extensive cross-training. The overly specialized, narrowly skilled worker sits on the sideline, wasting wages and available skill when there is no customer demand for his or her skill. The extensively cross-trained worker moves from one task to another as the mix of skill required to meet service demand changes. Inventories of specialized skill are costly and wasteful in service. Where the aggregate-level labor requirement can be accurately forecast, sufficient workers with depth of skill capability can be put in place to permit allocation across service demand without excessive waste of paid employee time. Where probable maximums of skill demand can be estimated, the mix of available skill may be established with precision through linear programming or related optimizing algorithms. Multiskilled workers, advised and compensated to acquire those skills that are most valuable to the firm, can be allocated across existing demand as demand shifts with maximum responsiveness to customer need and minimum paid lost time.

The challenge in providing service is to meet customer demand at or close to the point in time of the need. As noted in earlier discussions, surplus service capacity is typically unavoidable and even indispensable to providing high-quality service. Workstation and equipment capacity must be available at a level substantially below full capacity if service is to be delivered at a high level of quality. The cost of capital investment can be recouped through adjustment in pricing or decelerated depreciation. The cost of labor skill inventory can only be managed through cross-training and broadened worker knowledge. An ample range of algorithmic, optimizing and heuristic-based management science method, partly cataloged in Chapters 5 and 6, exists for application to the estimation of the desired skill mix. The major need is a fair system for compensating added skill. The value of multiple and secondary skill in the worker's wage can be determined through market analysis. The pay system can be revised to add pay increments for added skills. Allocation of available skill to current mix of service demand can be accomplished in real time with the assistance of computers. Computer-based skill banks, a creation of the 1960s, now reappearing in the form of resume data bases, can supply the necessary data base for skill allocation. Simulation using even a very simple allocation heuristic, as Exhibit 5–1 illustrated, can match skill with customer need to permit near immediate service response with cost-effective labor.

BASIC INVENTORY MANAGEMENT TECHNOLOGY

There will always be call and opportunity to employ inventory management and control methodology to the commodity dimensions of service. Inventory of physical goods offers opportunity for cost reduction in several important ways. For some kinds of inventory, the costs of *not* having stock on hand is so high that it is critical never to run out. Maintenance of one or two levels of emergency stock in separate, tightly controlled storage permits instant response when available open stock is depleted. Putting the key to the emergency stock room in the hands of someone accountable for *never running out* assures that a reorder will be placed simultaneous to access of emergency stock. Holding enough emergency stock on hand to cover the most severe worst-case lead time assures that recovery can always be complete and timely.

Some materials are so inexpensive and so important to the business that it is uneconomic to expend administrative time or effort on control of stock. A barrel of standard bolts, a bucket of common electronic resistors, a case of common gauze bandages or a box of telephone answer pads can simply be left in an accessible place. Instant resupply from a controlled backup stock will keep the stock flowing into use and simultaneously initiate reorder. The error of most early and even some present-day MRP systems arises out of assuming the need for exact control over every item of inventory, however trivial or inexpensive. The administrative cost imposed on operations by such compulsive attention to record keeping in trivial matters is prohibitive. MRP is generally the wrong model for managing service work flow. It is unlikely that MRP can be broadly applied to service operations needs, because it encourages not only lead-time padding but also permits nitpicking and exact record keeping to intrude on service inventory at the wrong time and place. The negative consequences to quality of service from running out of a cheap but critical piece of supporting stock are potentially severe in the form of customer disappointment or dissatisfaction. There is no excuse for letting that kind of stock shortage occur in a service setting, just as there is no need for systems and administrative overkill in avoiding that kind of stock-out.

Prioritization of inventory items is indispensable to effective management of service inventory. A simple, powerful prioritizing heuristic is available in the form of Pareto's principle, sometimes known as the 80/20 rule. Vilfredo Pareto, a nineteenth-century Italian demographer, ascertained that 80% of the wealth of Venice was at that time controlled by 20% of the population of that city. The 80/20 heuristic, never quite exact numerically but frequently close enough to fit, can be found in nearly every domain: 20% of customers account for 80% of sales; 20% of worker skills account for 80% of service demand; 20% of customers account for 80% of complaints;. 20% of workers account for 80% of days lost to absence; *20% of inventory items account for 80% of cost*. Let's repeat that last item: 20% of inventory items account for 80% of cost. Then let's revise and recycle it: 20% of inventory accounts for 80% of delay due to long lead time to reorder; 20% of inventory results in 80% of poor-quality service due to stock outages. The ubiquitous, dominant 20% discovered by Pareto accounts for much of our success and failure in operations management.

The quickest route to effective inventory control is to prioritize stock in terms of cost, lead time, frequency or criticality of defects and against any other standard that serves to reduce cost or improve service. Find that 20% of stock items or situations that are most troublesome. Manage them strictly. Apply high-cost administrative time and talent where it will pay off. The most effective system for managing work flow is to put 80% of time, effort and cost into controlling the highest priority 20% of inventory. The corollary to this rule is that as much as half of the remaining stock may merit 5% or less of management's time and attention to inventory control. The urge to stay on top of every detail is the greatest enemy of effective operations management, not only in service industries, but in conventional commodity operations as well. Quality is easily but erroneously associated with obsessively close attention to detail. Cost control in service may require that some details be allowed to take care of themselves because their impact on perceived quality is trivial or nil. Operations managers must classify those details astutely and deal with them appropriately.

Analysis of inventory cost decisions is useful in determining which details deserve to be managed and which can be left to happenstance. The principal and inevitable costs of inventory center around the price of holding and preserving it in readiness for sale. This is holding cost, which we have earlier identified and defined to include any of a variety of costs, beginning with the opportunity cost of value tied up in inventory that might otherwise be invested to yield a cash return. There may also be warehouse space, warehouse personnel, insurance against natural destruction, obsolescence through market shift or competitively outdated design and shrinkage from damage or theft to be added to holding cost. Some combination of these potential costs *always* attends the existence of inventory. Indeed, the inevitability of these costs might suggest that the surest path to inventory cost control would be to carry no inventory at all.

In theory, at least, that is the object of the JIT process flow. Only inventory is produced that can be immediately put to use in a salable item. In many if not most circumstances, JIT is a less-than-practical ideal. The American business press has recently taken note of the very high costs incurred by Japanese businesses attempting to realize the JIT ideal. A proliferation of very small deliveries by subcontractors has placed so great a demand on Japan's delivery capacity that roads have become overcrowded with trucks and the labor market for truck drivers has been stretched to its limits ("Just in Time Is Becoming Just a Pain," *Business Week*, June 17, 1991).

There is usually a cost incurred upon the occasion of inventory resupply. At minimum, the time and effort must be invested to place an order for resupply. This may seem trivial and it may or it may not be so. Overhead expense attendant to the company's purchasing department can be a major cost factor, sometimes to the extent that only very large orders are economic at all. Where there is a fixed cost for delivery, as with JIT in Japan, it is prudent to compare the added cost load on a small delivery with the inventory holding cost expected with a larger load. Close analysis may reveal that an intermediate-sized load, neither JIT-sized nor maximum, is the cheapest in terms of expense for trucking onto premises. If the cost of set-up (preparation to produce) is high, a cost trade-off similar to JIT trucking may be found. The expense of set-up should be contrasted against inventory holding cost to find the lowest point of combined cost. This can be accomplished through cost optimizing of summed holding and acquisition costs.

There are also possible instances in which labor cost may be lower with larger production runs. The efficiency of repeated practice of the work routine or worker specialization can influence cost when workers are narrowly specialized. Large swings or long gaps in the production schedule may result in higher costs from hiring and layoffs, especially when workers are not cross-trained in multiple skills. Inventory holding costs may partially or largely offset some of these labor change costs. The theory that cost control is best achieved by carrying zero inventory becomes practical only when there are no added ordering, set-up or labor costs incurred with small quantities of output. This is not a common occurrence.

The simplest model through which to examine these cost trade-offs is F. W. Harris' classic economic lot-sizing calculus. Simply called EOQ (for economic order quantity), this model directly contrasts all possible inventory holding costs with all possible resupply costs. Since the frequency of resupply is a direct and inverse function of average inventory lot size, the two are linked isometrically. As one increases, the other must decrease. Applying calculus, it can be demonstrated that the sum of the two is minimized (or optimized) when the opposing costs are equal irrespective of the actual cost of either. Exhibit 8–2 illustrates these relationships.

Using the logic of the EOQ model, a number of critical operations principles can be deduced. First, the only practical way to drive inventory lot sizes to the ideal of one is to drive resupply costs virtually to zero. When the Japanese find a practical way to order and deliver a JIT lot size of one at almost no cost, JIT will be practical at all times. Nor is flexibility of output likely to become fully cost economic until the cost of changeover is minimized to near zero. Mixing lots and types of output in a continuous

Exhibit 8-2

Trade-off between Acquisition and Holding Costs: The Classical EOQ Model

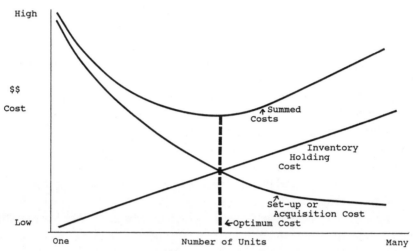

When Cost of Set-up or acquisition = cost of holding inventory, then

The sum of costs is equal, minimum and optimum.

$$\text{Optimum Lot Size*} = \frac{2 * \text{Annual Usage} * \text{Set-Up Cost}}{\text{Per Unit Holding Cost}}$$

*Mathematically derived from the above model

service or product flow requires instant switchover to be cost-effective. Otherwise it may be necessary to reduce costs by accumulating lots or customer types of the same kind to run continuously on a single set-up. We may take note from application of EOQ that when resupply/set-up is driven to zero, a lot size of one inventory becomes feasible and inventory is wholly eliminated, thereby setting the sum of costs in the EOQ model at zero. Reduction of resupply and set-up costs is critical to inventory cost control.

Second, when resupply or set-up is a major expense in the overall cost calculus, it may make no difference at all how much the inventory cost is. A one-of-a-kind job that is as much set-up preparation as it is time to run the job can require so high an investment of set-up that inventory cost is relegated to insignificance. Indeed, where set-up is several times larger than production costs, it can be cost-effective either to maintain the set-up in place until final job acceptance is obtained, or to produce an "unneeded" second or third run as insurance against problems on the first. The wasted extras may represent a cost that is far eclipsed by the possible cost of a

Exhibit 8-3

The Potential Excess Cost of Re-Set-Up (An Example from Film-Making, Filming a Stunt Scene)

```
Cost to set-up and tear-down the set          $60,000
Rental of specialized equipment, $2000 per day
Time required to complete filming, 5 days
     Cost of specialized equipment, one filming   10,000
Odds of a good take on first attempt, 80%
Quality of film take known 2 days after
     completion of filming
Good take on second try 99% certain


A 20% chance of the second set-up is worth:   $12,000
Cost of 2 extra days of rental is:              4,000

Maintaining the set-up is valued at:            8,000

A 1% chance of the third set-up is worth:         600
Cost of 2 extra days of rental is:              4,000

Failing to tear the set down costs:             3,400
```

repeated set-up. Indeed, the probability of unexpected rejection of the first-piece output can be used to calculate the expected value of re-set-up against the actual cost of the safety-margin extra pieces. Exhibit 8–3 illustrates how this might occur in a film-making situation.

With many service offerings, it is cost-effective to keep special set-ups in place until the customer is totally satisfied with the result. Attempting to find efficiencies through more intensive use of tools or equipment, or saving pennies by ordering one-of-a-kind of inexpensive but critical support stock so nothing is wasted, are fools' errands where cost reduction is the goal.

Third, the EOQ model can be used to deduce that, when both inventory holding costs and resupply costs are major elements of cost that cannot be avoided, those producers with dominant market share will always possess a clear cost advantage. They will enjoy proportionately smaller inventories and lesser frequency of resupply against total revenue compared to their competitors. Exhibit 8–4 shows how and why this is the case. The EOQ model provides a rare illustration of a hard-cash economy of scale. Where this condition prevails, it must not be ignored. Furthermore, it is seldom prudent to attempt to compete when one's market share is weak and large inventories are required for service effectiveness unless inventory can be tightly controlled.

SETTING INVENTORY POLICY

These are fundamental principles that apply to any business, service or product, project or commodity. The EOQ model is an immensely useful

Exhibit 8-4

An Illustration of Economy of Inventory Scale as Established by the EOQ Model of Lot Size Cost Optimization (see Exhibit 4-2)

```
Acquisition (reorder) cost and per unit holding cost are equivalent
between companies A and B for widget items.

          Acquisition cost = $100 per order
               (Paperwork, inspection, etc.)
          Annual inventory holding cost = $10 per unit
               (Opportunity cost, shrinkage, warehousing)
          Widgets cost $50 each


Company A uses 100,000 widgets per year

          Optimum lot size is 1414 widgets per order
          Sum of annual acquisition and holding cost
               is $14,142 (minimum cost per EOQ model)
          This optimum inventory holding cost is .28% of
               total inventory cost

Company B uses 200,000 widgets per year

          Optimum lot size is 2000 widgets per order
          Sum of annual acquisition and holding cost
               is $20,000 (minimum cost per EOQ model)
          This optimum inventory holding cost is .20% of
               total inventory cost

Company A's inventory cost per widget produced is 41.5% higher
          than Company B's
```

device for evaluating inventory policy in such situations. It must, of course, never be presumed that a cost-optimized lot-size calculated EOQ establishes the correct or proper order quantity for all situations. Further calculation of actual cost savings obtained will often reveal that they are trivial (the flip side of the 80/20 priority). Many other factors such as convenience, continuity of supply, shifts in cost or price structure, opportunity to combine orders and shipments and a host of related operations cost variables may count for more in the final analysis. EOQ is better applied as an analytical model than as a routine decision-making formula. In the management of service inventories, particularly, that should be its role.

Managing service-support physical inventory may be a minor or a major part of the service business. Inventory for restaurants or hotels, for instance, can be a central and significant element of the total service offering. Materials logistics for supplying the worldwide distribution network of a McDonald's or Pizza Hut can be awesome. The best of classical inventory operations management methods will be applied with a high level of professional skill.

Logistics in support of any offshore military operation—Operation Desert Storm, for instance—are equally critical and may be at least as important as tactical planning for actual military operations. Inventory management as a significant management science was developed in and practiced at its highest level in World War II. Allocation of war materials and supplies in that multitheater conflict involved scheduling materials flow in convoys of ships subject to the uncertainties of submarine attack, establishing production goals and lead times for the domestic military production complex and assuring that needed supplies and equipment got to the battlefront on time. It called on the highest level of logistical skill and knowledge. Operations researchers—specialists in applied mathematics—caused the materials of warfare to flow quickly and efficiently to the locus of use. At the end of World War II, one team of war-seasoned operations researchers headed by Robert McNamara, later U.S. Secretary of Defense, marketed its considerable collective skill and experience to the Ford Motor Company. Thus, operations management as a foundation management discipline came to maturity in World War II. The industrial disciplines of MRP and industrial process control were already fully developed and waiting when computers arrived to make them practical in any factory.

Inventory control, at its core, is little more than minimizing inventory holding costs while assuring that parts, materials and supplies necessary to effective production and customer service are consistently available when and where they are needed. Effective management of inventory holding costs and lead times is fundamental to good inventory control. Economic order quantity, parts explosions in the manner of product trees or bills of material, accurate specification of lead times and realistic priority setting are all powerful tools for managing commodity and service inventory. They must not be ignored or overlooked.

In commodity operating situations, EOQ contrasts inventory holding cost against acquisition/set-up costs to achieve the lowest sum of the two. In an alternative form, inventory holding cost is traded off against the costs of varying employment levels as an element of aggregate capacity planning. Steady, level employment in commodity operations is typically achieved by buffering market demand with finished goods inventory. The costs of hiring, training and layoff are avoided when level employment is maintained in an operation but inventory costs are incurred. Where inventory costs are excessive, market demand is met by increasing or decreasing employment in the plant.

Where market demand must be met in real time, as service typically requires, the choice is constrained to varying levels of labor. The discussion in Chapter 5 of skills and skills inventories was directly addressed to this requirement of service. The principal remaining cost control model that has direct relevance to noncommodity service is the cost/service break model discussed at the outset of this chapter. Parts explosions, product trees and bills of materials can be assimilated and applied in revised form by the cost/service break analysis model. Specification of all the materials and supplies that must be available to support service is absolutely sound practice. Establishment of lead times that go with them is indispensable. It is specific use of materials and supplies control systems and of lead times that changes in the service setting. Inventory management for service, while it builds on existing concepts and models, requires a major modification of standard commodity inventory management policies. Cost models must be custom fitted to service needs.

Accurate specification of lead times or, more precisely, toughly realistic lead-time estimation, has been adequately dealt with in the cost/service break model. Methods for prioritizing inventory items have also been discussed at length as part of the development of this model. What remains to be said about service inventory is fairly straightforward: Once the critical contribution of every element of inventory to customer service has been assessed as part of the cost/service break analysis, inventory within any remaining class should be categorized as either trivial or significant in cost. Trivial items should be managed with a minimum of fuss and controls. Compulsive record keeping is a needless cost here. Ordering and usage should be delegated as close as possible to the point of use. Inventory control can be a simple matter of occasional random audits of item use. Eyeballing the level of purchase will often be control enough.

Significant cost items should be controlled unit by unit with clear assignment of accountability for maintenance of a cost- and service-effective inventory level. Truly costly or service-critical items can be reviewed regularly by a higher level of management. Standard audit procedure will be adequate for control of most.

Service cost must certainly be controlled and reduced wherever possible. If cost control is not the responsibility of the service operations manager, it's probably no one's responsibility. Cost management is the very soul of good commodity operations management. But cost management in the service industry must *always* be tested against the impact of cost savings on the quality of service. Commodities tend to be cost-sensitive in the extreme. Cost trade-offs against service lead time in service, by contrast, can mislead. Service is more often cost-sensitive only at the level of gross cost differentials. Customers will pay a premium for quality service. Cutting the service heart out of the offering by driving cost to the minimum risks losing the customer.

At the other extreme, failure to manage cost intelligently can cut the profit margin immediately, and may risk loss of customers to lower cost but equal quality of service in the longer run. The decisions of an operations manager in support of service have longer range implications and potentially more serious impact on the broader business strategy than they do when made in support of commodity output. The quality of operations decisions has a more direct impact on the quality of service. Cost must be controlled, but single-minded pursuit of cost reductions cannot be tolerated here. Every inventory decision must be tested for its effect on service.

Indeed, every cost decision probably has a direct impact on service and many present-day quality problems in commodity manufacture are the result of ill-conceived, narrowly analyzed cost reduction decisions. Cost *always* has a quality consequence of some magnitude. Some costs clearly increase quality noticeably, others diminish it markedly. Narrow, single-minded operations managers who look only at the cost implications of every decision risk undercutting the quality of many standard commodity products. Adoption of a service philosophy in the management of commodities would greatly benefit those operations. Certainly the short-sightedness of tunnel-visioned cost cutting is a major liability in service industries. Ignorance of the importance of the cost/service trade-off in service operations will defeat the service purposes of a firm. A sound cost/quality balance must be sought and maintained in the successful service operation. Nothing less is acceptable.

Chapter 9

Work Load Modeling: Setting Priorities and Locating Bottlenecks

"A little bit of graphic preplanning yields large dividends."

Competition among service providers must eventually be won by the supplier who offers best price, highest quality, and most timely service delivery. These are all operations issues. Managing operations effectively is the difference between success and failure in service industries. Approaches to cost management were examined in earlier chapters. Those operating dimensions that determine service quality will be extensively analyzed in later ones. In this chapter, we will look at some techniques that are useful for improving work flow, reducing delay and generally getting the most utility out of available equipment and labor capacity. These techniques fit under the headings of work load modeling, priority setting and location of bottlenecks.

WORK LOAD MODELS AND PRIORITY SETTING

Modeling work load in a service operation picks up where forecasting leaves off. In some ways, work load models can be used to supplement forecasts. A good forecast of demand by service skill category, for instance, should include best-, worst- and most-likely-case scenarios. A model of available service capacity can then be employed to test for capacity overload and slack. Points of overload are potential bottlenecks where service quality may be stressed to the breaking point. Heavy slack may point to the need for more skill cross-training or more flexible working

Exhibit 9-1
Labor Allocation in a Law Firm

FORECASTS FOR COMING QUARTER (1 Lawyer = 500 hours of labor)

	LABOR HOURS REQUIRED Forecasting Condition			CAPACITY CONSTRAINTS	
	Best Case	Likely Case	Worst Case	Maximum Demand in People	Number of Qualified Personnel
Trial Work	1800	1500	1200	3.6	4
Legal Research	4500	4000	3500	9.0	32
Corporate Law	8000	7000	6500	16.0	15
Real Estate Law	1700	1500	1300	3.4	6
Criminal Law	3500	3000	2500	7.0	12
TOTAL HOURS	19500	17000	15000		
Equivalent Lawyers needed	39	34	30		

hours. Modeling the impact of potential high and low demand on the service organization's work centers permits intelligent planning for business contingencies.

Exhibit 9–1 illustrates how forecasting for various mixes of business in a small law firm might be modeled against available capacity. Five major categories of legal specialization are used here as the basis of the forecast and as rough indicators of differential legal skill. The forecast offered covers one fiscal quarter (three months or thirteen weeks) of calendar time and assumes a starting level of thirty-two legal professionals working for the firm. Variation in level of business activity from best to worst case is in the range of + 12% to – 15%. Assuming a normal forty-hour work week and 100% billout of hours, approximately 500 hours of billable working time (using round numbers) are available from each lawyer in a thirteen-week quarter. Hours of billable time are forecast and cumulated for the quarter by the five categories of skill/activity, then divided by 500 to obtain an approximate count of legal talent required to cover the anticipated business. Something between thirty and thirty-nine lawyers will be required to cover the forecast, depending on variation from the most to least likely level of anticipated business. For a business where the standards are more precise, the calculations might reflect added precision. Here and in many similar cases, round number approximations will serve the need adequately. Anything more suggests a degree of precision in forecasting and planning that is illusory.

Testing a forecast requires construction and use of a viable model to estimate how future circumstances are likely to stress available capacity. Modeling permits us to go beyond mere gross numbers of people required to cover the expected business demand. We may now identify the qualifications of current staff by skill/activity area—one person may be qualified in one, two or more skill areas—to determine what the effect of a best-case quarter will have on available skill capacity. The first question asked is: If the firm is lucky enough to get all the business that is possible in this period of time, can it handle the load?

Assuming that all personnel are qualified to perform basic legal research, any of the total firm strength of thirty-two can be assigned to this category. This is the maximal flexibility skill area. Entry-level law clerks who are yet unspecialized can be assigned here to cover the base requirement (i.e., worst-case demand, for instance), and anyone otherwise unapplied can pick up the remainder. The most highly skilled (and capacity constrained) categories are trial work and corporate law. In these areas, we find that the best-case business forecast slightly more than covers trial law, while corporate law is shy one full person. Overtime might be used to cover the excess for now, but as business expands further, it may be necessary to hire or develop qualified talent in both these areas. Real estate and criminal practice are both adequately covered by available talent as long as other areas of need do not suck up the excess in available talent in either of these areas.

With an assumed current thirty-two person legal staff, best-case forecast conditions will increase the work load by about 20% if no new additions are made to the firm. This represents one extra full day of work per firm member per week. Worst-case, on the other hand, will result in about a 6% underutilization of available talent. For both most-likely and worst-case forecasts, available talent will cover expected demand for service suitably.

The modeling process goes beyond mere revenue goals for the business. It compares capacity with anticipated demand to identify gaps or excesses that can either impair service quality or raise cost. These are the critical operations management issues for every service industry. Modeling in some form or other is fundamental to their analysis and resolution.

Beyond forecasting, a comprehensive model of the business' capacity for operations is a useful way to test the impact of incoming business demand on the available skill and work center resources. As each new customer demand is placed on the system, it is entered into the model to determine what effect the added service demand has on available capacity. Exhibit 9–2 shows, for instance, how available capacity in a small appliance repair business might be affected by the mix of incoming repair

Exhibit 9-2
Appliance Repair Service Capacity Table

Type of Appliance	Number of Qualified Repair Technicians	Technician Number			
		1	2	3	4
Refrigerators	2	x			x
Washers	1		x		
Dryers	1		x		
Dishwashers	1			x	
Electric Ranges	2	x			x
Electric Ovens	2	x			x
Microwaves	1			x	
Air Conditioners	1	x			

orders. Eight different categories of appliance repair are covered by this business. Maximum daily capacity for service can be determined by making reference to Exhibit 9–2. It is assumed here that the average repair time is one and one-half hours, with an average travel time to the job of one-half hour. Each job entering the order queue has an average potential of two hours of committed work and travel time. Most appliances are specialized to a single repair technician. Refrigerators, electric ranges and electric ovens, though, are each covered by the talents of two technicians. Each technician has at least two appliance repair skills. This permits some limited flexibility in the assignment of incoming jobs to specialists based on schedule availability.

Exhibit 9–3 illustrates the result of this skill mix on a near full day of work order loading. On the day illustrated in this example, the work load is near maximum: 87.5% (thirty-two normal available hours versus twenty-eight scheduled hours). Exhibit 9–3 shows that two technicians are fully loaded and scheduled to work a normal eight-hour day. Any further work orders in these two areas must either be covered with overtime or deferred to the day following. A surge in orders on the day following could create more overtime or diminish customer service seriously. The question becomes one of whether to incur the added cost of overtime to serve additional customers today or risk impairing service standards by deferring jobs and overloading the schedule tomorrow. Again, the operations trade-off is between cost and quality of service. Modeling makes the options clear and assists in making the best possible decision.

As the foregoing illustrations suggest, there is no requirement that modeling be difficult or elaborate. In some businesses, it might be handled

Exhibit 9-3
Appliance Repair Service Typical Day's Labor Assignments

Each call requires an average of 1.5 hours repair and 0.5 hours travel time for a total of 2.00 hours per job assigned.

Appliance Line	Maximum available hours of capacity	Assigned Jobs	Hours of Work for Repair Technician # 1	2	3	4
Refrigerators	2	2	2			2
Washers	1	3		6		
Dryers	1	1		2		
Dishwashers	1	3			6	
Electric Ranges	2	2	2			2
Electric Ovens	2	2	2			2
Microwaves	1	2			2	
Air Conditioners	1	0				
Total Hours Assigned for the work day			6	8	8	6

through a physical model. An advertising firm, for instance, might use a pictorial layout of the firm with each work area sized to represent proportional capacity. As work comes into the firm, the surface of each area involved in a job is physically covered to reflect the work capacity committed to that job. As each job is finished, the cover representing that job is removed. A visual, real-time picture of work loading is thereby offered, which points to delays and bottlenecks that may then be managed by subcontracting or reallocating available labor skill.

Indeed, the appointment schedules that characterize operations management control in offices of every kind, including those of physicians or lawyers, and personal services like beauticians or counselors, are, in reality, models of available capacity that can be used to allocate capacity as fairly and fully as possible across current customer demand. The salesman's appointment book is a capacity (time) allocation modeling tool. Models on a simple level are already widely and effectively used to manage service operations in many industries.

More complex capacity analyses may require a computer model, which need not be overly complex in itself. Indeed, the simplest and best model is likely to be one that is implemented on a personal computer using standard electronic spreadsheet software such as Lotus, Symphony, Quatro or Excel. Even capacity that must be simultaneously modeled for both workstations and labor time can be effectively and efficiently handled with no more than these basic tools. Exhibits 9–4 through 9–7 illustrate how a walk-in medical center might use a spreadsheet layout to schedule jobs and labor to best meet patient needs.

The example presented here is based on typical case demand in one walk-in medical facility. The ten cases offered represent the kinds of treatment sought from such a service:

Patient # 1: A routine preemployment physical exam

Patient # 2: A routine preemployment physical exam

Patient # 3: A minor fracture in the bone of one hand

Patient # 4: Routine prenatal physical exam

Patient # 5: Evaluation of report of minor chest pain

Patient # 6: Physical exam of a postcardiac patient

Patient # 7: A routine insurance physical exam

Patient # 8: A routine insurance physical exam

Patient # 9: Routine prenatal physical exam

Patient # 10: Severe laceration of foot, possible fracture

Exhibit 9–4 is the image of the inputs to a spreadsheet program that has been set up to capture data on patient flow. Entering patients have either a preestablished routine, as for a preemployment or insurance physical examination, or are screened by an available physician or qualified triage nurse who determines the stages of treatment required and estimates the time of treatment. This is a morning schedule that reflects an 8:00 AM opening surge of overnight medical problems. As such, the schedule must be completed as efficiently as possible so that patients arriving in the later morning or early afternoon will not be delayed by excessively backlogged work.

The available physician and technician personnel are almost fully utilized by this morning's schedule. Three physicians are on hand to handle physical examinations and minor surgery. Each is qualified for any of these tasks and all are interchangeable as far as meeting patient needs is concerned. Three medical technicians are also on staff, each qualified to handle any aspect of X ray, blood work, EKG or ultrasound tests as required. This is a very busy clinic. It is necessary to schedule work effectively to avoid wasted time and assure the highest level of patient service.

Routine physicals arrive with authorization forms that describe the exact extent of the examination to be performed. There are no life-threatening emergencies in this schedule, but if there were such emergencies, they

Exhibit 9-4

The No-Appointment Medical Center Work Flow Modeling System (estimated treatment time in hours; sequence of treatment shown with times)

PATIENT #	X-RAY UNIT SEQ.	TIME	BLOOD WORK SEQ.	TIME	ROUTINE PHYSICAL SEQ.	TIME	DIAG. PHYSICAL SEQ.	TIME	MINOR SURGERY SEQ.	TIME	EKG TEST SEQ.	TIME	ULTRA-SOUND SEQ.	TIME	TOTAL PATIENT TIME
1	2	.5	1	.3	4	.5					3	1			2.3
2	2	.7	1	.3	3	.5									1.5
3	1	.5					2	.5	3	1.5					2.5
4							2	1					1	2	3
5							2	1.5			1	1			2.5
6	1	.5	2	.3			4	1	5	2	3	.5			4.3
7	1	.5			2	.5									1
8	1	.5			2	.5									1
9			1	.3			3	.5					2	2	2.8
10	1	.5							2	1					1.5
TOTAL WORK CENTER TIME REQUIREMENT		3.7		1.2		2		4.5		4.5		2.5		4	22.4

ASSUMPTIONS:
    ALL PHYSICIANS AND TECHNICIANS ARE CROSS-TRAINED IN ALL SKILLS
    TECHNICIAN EQUIPMENT IS CAPACITY CONSTRAINED TO ONE PATIENT AT A TIME

would be given first priority at each stage of treatment, regardless of the effect on scheduling efficiency. The present schedule offers opportunity, in the absence of crisis treatment, to identify the points of heaviest demand and then sequence tasks so as to arrive quickly at those points and keep them busy. When this morning's patient load is estimated and entered into the spreadsheet model, we may begin to look for bottlenecks and set priorities for work flow.

First, it may be useful to assure that the load is manageable within the people resources on hand. By adding the time demands for physical exams and surgery, we may determine that eleven hours of physicians' time will be required. That should be sufficient *if* there are no undue delays getting major jobs through to the physicians quickly. It can be noted that patients, in every case, require some tests before they can proceed to see the attending physician. Some initial delay is inevitable and can be managed by offsetting the schedules of technicians and physicians by an appropriate increment of time. Care must be taken in choosing which patients to move through the early stages of lab and diagnostic testing to assure that physicians are quickly and fully loaded with tasks so that their time is not needlessly lost. This must also be accomplished without waste of a technician's time, since total technician time requirement for the morning patient load totals a heavy 11.4 hours for three people. The flexibility of physicians and medical technicians to cover all the task assignments in their respective areas is indispensable to efficient work flow. Without that flexibility, large blocks of time would surely be wasted in this schedule.

The first principle of work flow efficiency in a random flow project shop such as this is to schedule backward from any downstream bottlenecks (capacity constraints) to move work into and fill available critical capacity as quickly as possible. We may look at the diagnostic physical and minor surgery columns to find large jobs that can be moved through to fill this capacity with minimum delay. The biggest pieces of anticipated work here are related to patients #3, #4, #5, #6 and #10. Of the nine hours estimated in these two areas of service, eight and a half hours are accounted for by these four patients. The remaining two heavy-capacity use areas are X ray and ultrasound. It will be important to keep these two work areas loaded as fully as possible to prevent delays in work beyond them. Patient #4 requires ultrasound before moving into a diagnostic physical, which suggests immediate scheduling into that area. An EKG must be accomplished on patients #5 and #6 before they will move on to attention from physicians. Patients #3, #6 and #10 need X rays before moving on to a diagnostic physical exam or surgery or both. These are point-of-entry assignments that will support later capacity loading requirements while getting the initial bottleneck areas off to a fast start as well. Other work can be pulled in as needed to fill capacity in X ray and ultrasound task areas. Nonbottleneck areas of blood work and routine physical exams can be covered as patients and personnel become available in the schedule.

Exhibit 9–5 illustrates the result of scheduling to keep critical capacity areas loaded. As would be expected from the priorities established above, patients #4, #5 and #6 are put immediately into preliminary workup with three technicians who are instantly assigned to high-priority cases. Because patient #6 requires over four hours of total time in the morning schedule, it is critical to keep him moving. It is the time requirement as much as the medical condition (postcardiac) in his case that dictates the priority. The technician working X rays, therefore, delays follow-on work with other patients to complete a brief blood test on patient #6, which prepares him to move expeditiously on to the scheduled EKG. An alternative schedule would keep the technician doing X rays committed in this station while the EKG technician picked up the blood work on patient #6 upon finishing patient #5. This would introduce only minor changes into the overall schedule.

Patients #10 and #3 are quickly processed through X ray and moved on to other treatment as dictated by their priorities. From here on in, it is almost entirely a matter of who is waiting for the next stage of any given treatment. Once the early priorities are set so that they fill critical downstream capacity quickly and fully, the schedule is kept full easily. The only slack in this schedule is two twenty-minute gaps, one between patient #10 and patient #6 in surgery, the other between patients #4 and #9 in ultrasound. Technicians are otherwise continually busy from 8:00 AM to completion of all tasks, and physicians, once work is pushed through to them, stay busy until 1:00 PM. The afternoon patient load can be handled without any significant loss of capacity to work that has been carried over from the morning.

Exhibit 9–5 illustrates the correct approach. But this approach to scheduling must be contrasted with the more natural *and* the consistently recommended approach based on existing operations management practices. The approach recommended in virtually every current operations text is to move the shortest jobs through the system *first* because that rule of scheduling consistently reduces average time to completion when jobs generate at a common starting point. The shortest jobs through this system would be related to patients #2, #7, #8 and #10. Only one of these priorities overlaps the capacity loading priority system employed above.

Exhibit 9–6 illustrates the flow of work with a shortest job time priority assignment applied. Again, technicians are kept busy. Only one-half hour

Exhibit 9-5
Scheduling Patients in a Walk-In Medical Clinic—Scheduling to Fill Constrained Capacity

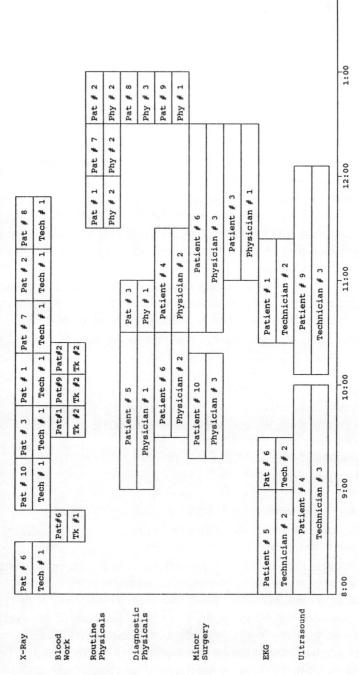

Exhibit 9-6
Scheduling Patients in a Walk-In Medical Clinic—Scheduling to Finish Shortest Jobs First

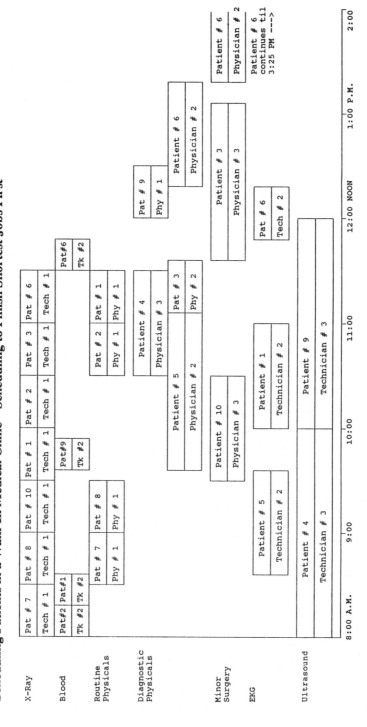

of technician time is wasted in this schedule when the EKG/blood work technician must wait for patient #6 to come from X ray. Because they are usually at the front of the patient flow process, it is easy to keep them busy with any prioritizing system. The physicians' work schedules, by contrast, are characterized by excessive starts and stops. One physician begins work a half-hour after the clinic's opening with a pair of physical examinations back-to-back. The balance of his morning schedule contains three large gaps of wasted time, each a half-hour long. Both remaining physicians have large gaps in their schedules and begin seeing patients twenty minutes later on the average than they would with the capacity loading priorities. One works beyond 1:00 PM, the other until after 3:00 PM. Considerable physician capacity is lost in the afternoon schedule with the shortest job time approach to prioritizing patients. This is solely a product of the scheduling rule applied. Were this an end-of-the-day schedule, physicians would be held over well past the end of their clinic day with unfinished work.

Remarkably, though, the schedules as measured by average job completion time clearly favor the shortest job time rule of priority. Exhibit 9–7 contrasts the completion times for all ten patients under each of the priority rules demonstrated above. The average completion time per patient with the bottleneck capacity loading priority schedule is 4.08 hours, while the average for the shortest job schedule is 3.49 hours, more than a half hour better. The result observed arises out of rushing several short jobs through the system quickly while leaving the longest patient until the end of the schedule. It is a quirk of mathematics that produces a superior outcome for the shortest job time priority schedule, not an increase in real efficiency. A bottleneck capacity loading approach squeezes slack out of the schedule, making best use of the available time and talent in this clinic.

Clearly, schedules can and must vary as a function of patterns that characterize the specific service industry. It is always easy to fill capacity at the beginning of the work flow. If the only capacity constraint is located at the start of the flow, shortest job time can be used to move jobs through quickly into other workstations and to avoid making customers sit around longer than necessary. People with small service time requirements do appear to expect faster completion of service than those with larger service time needs. Supermarket express lines encourage shopping for small grocery orders. The prospect of a long waiting line might otherwise send small purchase customers elsewhere. There is, at least, a psycho-logic to shortest job time priority schedules. The downside of requiring routine physical exam patients to wait while physician capacity is loaded for efficiency is in the appearance of slow service to these potential future

Exhibit 9-7
Comparison of Completion Times Under Alternative Schedules

Patient	Schedule to Complete In Shortest Average Time		Schedule to Fill Constrained Resources	
	Finished at	Elapsed Time	Finished at	Elapsed Time:
#1	11:30	3.5	12:00	4.0
#2	11:00	3.0	1:00	5.0
#3	1:05	5.1	12:30	4.5
#4	11:30	3.5	11:30	3.5
#5	11:05	3.1	10:30	2.5
#6	3:24	7.4	12:30	4.5
#7	9:00	1.0	12:30	4.5
#8	9:30	1.5	1:00	5.0
#9	12:30	4.5	1:00	5.0
#10	10:30	2.5	10:25	2.3
Sum of Elapsed Time		35.1 hrs.		40.8 hrs.
Average Patient Time in Process		3.5 hrs.		4.1 hrs.

customers who could breeze through the system under a shortest processing time priority. Provision of TV for watching or reading material may take some of the edge off the waiting time. Forewarning that the schedule is heavy and a return visit later in the morning when service would be quicker would probably help. If the model is accurate enough in normal use, physical exam patients might be scheduled for return later in the morning on an appointment basis. Without a model to predict work flow, though, it would be impossible to estimate the waiting time accurately and make such an appointment sensibly. The alternative is to waste valuable physician talent unnecessarily by failing to fill downstream physician capacity quickly and fully. Whenever there is a capacity constraint downstream from the point of entry for service, it will usually pay to move work through on a higher priority when it is scheduled later for the area of capacity constraint. Indeed, if Exhibit 9–5 were a typical morning pattern that repeated itself consistently, it would make sense for one physician to come in at 8:00 AM to assist in screening to establish the schedule and handle any early emergencies, then offset the remaining physicians on a 9:00 AM arrival schedule.

Use of an electronic spreadsheet to assess capacity demand on multiple service stations is a simple and powerful device for purposes of operations analysis and management of service work flow. A pictorial representation in the form of a graph or a scheduling board that lays tasks out on a time flow line can assist in shrinking out any excess slack in the flow system. At a minimum, postmortem analysis of several typical work days, weeks or months on a spreadsheet and timeline flow basis will test the utility of a capacity constrained prioritizing approach to task scheduling. It is a simple, powerful analytical device that can help measurably to improve scheduling efficiency, especially as it pertains to utilization of human talent. In those circumstances where scheduling is highly complex, it may be worthwhile to approach work flow on a project network analysis level. In those circumstances where service capacity is necessarily constrained but competition is stiff, it may be necessary to program a graphics display of work flow in real time so that jobs can be entered as they arrive, their impact on capacity at any point in the flow can be instantly assessed, and current flow reprioritized as needed to close up slack and maintain efficient flow of work. Indeed, this is the next generation of computer simulation technology needed to support complex service operations management need.

Scheduling efficiencies in random flow service situations are the most difficult of all efficiencies to achieve. Appointment systems are useful only when the customer can and will wait for service without seeking it out elsewhere. Immediate service always has an edge over delayed service. Walk-in service capacity will win over appointments as long as waiting lines are not excessive and service flow is expeditious. The advantage of efficient use of valuable talent must be cost equivalent as between service on-demand and service by appointment for that edge to become a competitive advantage. Only close attention to work flow with an eye to maximizing the use of capacity constrained (bottleneck) resources will make it possible.

FLEXIBLE CAPACITY AND BOTTLENECKS

In Chapter 4 it was argued that the best route to assurance of superior service is to build in surplus plant and equipment capacity. In the examples just discussed, most capacity constraints are a function of the need to utilize skilled labor efficiently. Indeed, that is where most bottlenecks will necessarily occur in a service economy. Rarely, equipment will also be a major capacity constraint. In a small medical facility, for instance, it might not be cost-effective to duplicate high-cost X-ray or NMR equipment.

Larger facilities might take advantage of their economies of scale to duplicate some kinds of expensive diagnostic equipment, but even here there will be basic cost constraints and efficient scheduling of bottleneck capacity may be more cost-effective. Sound operations management methods will then be the difference between high- and low-cost service.

It is of equal importance, though, to build maximum flexibility into the system in the form of versatile equipment and multiskilled service providers. Too much specialization of either is a potential source of increased cost. Specialization is an old, deeply scored habit of operations management in the commodity operations arena. It is a habit that is easily carried over to the service sector, where it can only add cost and create inefficiencies. Effective management of service operations requires that specialties be tolerated only where unavoidable, and that even unavoidable specialties be challenged as threats to cost. In many circumstances, for instance, it is unthinkable for a physician to perform technicians' work. That is a "waste" of skilled time and talent, even when the physician's time is being wasted anyhow. If efficiency and service are the objective, though, it must become "thinkable." The restaurant owner who refuses to bus tables when customers are lined up out the door can only reduce his own profit by wasting opportunity for effective application of his time. Moving to cover bottlenecked work is natural and inevitable in a service environment. But expecting workers to shift downward in the status scale to accomplish needed work is likely to bring disappointment. Moving down on the status ladder would be seen as a diminishment of one's value and status rather than as a contribution to organization effectiveness. It is often easier to cross-train technicians in skills that are on a comparable level of status. If moving down is hard, moving up without sanction is likely to be dangerous. The technician who practices medicine or the busboy who takes orders from waiting customers is likely to be censured by the legitimate status holders. But it is poor operations management to tolerate such attitudes. It is a source of waste to fail to cross-train and upgrade talent wherever it is possible to do so. It is arrogant to refuse to do low-status work that has become a bottleneck to customer service. Flexibility in all directions is fundamental to service operation efficiency. Every opportunity to enhance flexibility must be seized.

Upgrading into higher priced, unutilized capacity is standard in the hotel and airline industries. Late arrivals at the hotel reservation desk who cannot be accommodated in the class of room reserved can easily be upgraded into higher priced quarters that are empty without increase in reservation price. Tourist-class airline passengers who are too late to get seats can be upgraded to first class. Reservations of any kind that are oversold can be compensated with free service at another time if there is no flexibility to current capacity. These are common devices for dealing with capacity inflexibility. Luxury service or accommodations are priced to break even well below full capacity, so excess capacity in luxury domains is employed to cover excess demand for the "popularly" priced offering.

Opportunities for flexibility exist in many places when they are actively sought out by the service operations manager. They must usually be identified in advance of the need, though, when the pressure of time to meet customer need does not impede search for them. That is often the difficult part. When capacity is stressed to its limits it is obvious that help is needed from some source, but the time is not available for a comprehensive search to locate the right source. The quick fix is more likely. If it is good, it will be remembered and reused. If not, the search for better may be postponed until the next crisis. Old habits of operations management assume that departures from standard procedure are always temporary inconveniences. The new perspective on service operations management must treat them as important assets in the arsenal of service flexibility. Continual search for new and more powerful sources of adaptive flexibility that solve temporary capacity constraints is the very soul of good service operations management. Deeply grooved routine is the enemy of service operations efficiency.

Every decision that pertains to equipment and labor capacity should be made with one eye on the fundamental need for increased flexibility in service capacity. High-cost, leading edge technology that is narrowly specialized but more efficient than cheaper, general-purpose equipment is still a high-risk opportunity that should not be approved without a very large margin for error in costing. On the other hand, equipment that increases flexibility at equivalent cost is likely to become an asset to capacity constraint problems. When the time and opportunity are available, it is imperative that experiments in capacity flexibility be designed and carried out by service operations management with all forms of equipment.

Similar experiments with labor flexibility are essential to planning for capacity crunches. Slack time in the schedule can always be productively applied to upgrade training of workers. Multiskilled service providers who can be reallocated as demand changes offer superior customer service *and* enjoy greatly enhanced job security. Opportunities to learn, practice and demonstrate command of alternative skills must be aggressively exploited. Pay structure for alternatively skilled workers must then be restructured to recognize multiple skills.

Self-service offers potential for increased capacity. Automatic teller machines (ATMs) are employed by many banks to permit twenty-four-hour access to banking services. They also offer overflow capacity service during normal working hours when capacity is stressed. On-line networking with personal computers permits near real-time information on stock market exchanges. Computer input to sales and buy orders is technically feasible. Permitting customers to directly place, sell and buy orders on their own personal computers is a device that overcomes the broker's phone line bottleneck that occurs in heavy trading times. To the extent that such self-service devices please customers, they may occasionally represent an improvement in service, despite the absence of personal contact.

Any service business that can arrange it should always have backup personnel available on-call. Fire and police services already operate routinely on this basis. Supervisors in some industries fill the capacity gaps. Banks, hospitals, communications services and maintenance routinely expect their supervisory staff to cover excess demand. In those rare situations where higher management takes the opportunity to work side by side with line operations personnel, willingness of management at all levels to get their hands on the real work is increased. Awareness of opportunity for other flexibilities is often also enhanced. In those organizations where top management never leaves its ivory tower to engage the real work of the organization, narrow, inflexible skill must prevail throughout. In an on-call service situation everyone must be flexible. Even in those organizations where work flow is relatively predictable, an organization that is pervaded by skill and task assignment flexibility will be the competitively stronger one. Reallocation of time and talent is a primary resource for improved service operations cost efficiency and service quality.

Service organizations like Rotary, Kiwanis and Lions all know the power of flexibility and willingness to serve in any role. None permit leaders to serve longer than a specified term, usually a year as president, for instance. All have past presidents, presidents-elect and presidents-aspirant as sources of leadership in times of need. Illness or business exigency need never impair the organization's mission effectiveness. There is always alternative talent and backup experience ready to apply. Ample mechanisms exist to assign legitimate status and authority in the organization, but no one is indispensable. Everyone is available to meet the challenges of the moment.

Traditional business organizations with their relatively rigid hierarchies and status distinctions diminish role flexibility among their members. The more inflexible the business becomes, the less adaptable and the less competitive it is. Under stress these role and status distinctions become major liabilities. In the military, status distinctions between officers and enlisted personnel serve to maintain stability in peacetime. In battle where death can become the ultimate leveler of status, they are only old habits that assure clarity and continuity of communication under fire. Skill is what counts at every level, and anyone who can't fill alternative jobs is a liability.

The lessons of service flexibility are widely available but just as widely ignored within the context of standard operations method and policy. Specialization in many service industries and roles increases rather than decreases cost. Status barriers between organization levels don't improve performance, they waste manpower and talent. Flexibility and variety, rather than being the enemy of cost-effectiveness as they are in the commodity production environment, are its foundations in service. Flexibility is indispensable.

MONITORING FOR BOTTLENECKS

Capacity constraints—alias "bottlenecks"—can occur by chance anywhere in an unscheduled system, even one where capacity utilization is, by design, low. The best solution to capacity constraints is still the maintenance of a generous level of overcapacity in the system. But sudden surges in demand either overall or in some limited corner of the system, caused by factors such as equipment breakdowns or absent personnel, can overload capacity and demand an operations management fix. Where additional capacity cannot be brought on line, the recommended fix is to expedite jobs that can fill the overloaded workstation or labor capability quickly and fully to assure that the available capacity at that point *is not wasted*. If the bottleneck is not noticed, though, that will not occur. A high priority on every service operations manager's list of duties, then, is to maintain a continuous watch for emerging bottlenecks. It is accurate, indeed, to maintain that the core accountability of any competent service operations manager is to manage bottlenecks effectively.

Effective management of bottlenecks will usually require that all incoming tasks be preallocated across available capacity to monitor demand on a workstation-by-workstation, worker-by-worker basis. Managing service operations thus requires that the task time requirements of arriving work be competently estimated and added to a current work loading estimate. It is precisely this kind of monitoring that permits potential capacity constraints to be forecast so that work can be appropriately expedited into them. Where possible, large jobs that are on their way to or through the system and that will probably produce a bottleneck should generate immediate priority for movement through the system. Other jobs in the system that could be put through the impending bottleneck to utilize available capacity before it becomes loaded must also be expedited so that they will not needlessly end up delayed by filled capacity at the bottleneck.

In a hospital emergency room, for instance, it is highly desirable to have notice from the police or ambulance crews of a major disaster—a multi-injury vehicle accident, or a large fire in a crowded location—so that capacity can be expanded and patients en route to that capacity can be expedited through in advance of incoming crisis patients. Any incoming patients who will tie up a larger-than-usual number of medical staff signal the need to use that staff capacity *now* for any patients in the system. It may seem counterintuitive to load up capacity that is about to be over-loaded, but merely letting that capacity sit idle in wait is a grievous waste when there is work in-house that could be expedited to that station in advance of the surge.

Any forecast that suggests heavy demand for service probably signals the need to begin giving priority to work scheduled into the area of heaviest expected demand. The flight that is departing for a bottleneck air terminal should be moved out first. The train that must use a track corridor restricted by track repairs must be given priority over the one that does not need that corridor. The legal matter that requires intensive team negotiation should be given priority for research and investigation. The insurance policy that requires an unusual amount of actuarial investigation should get priority through the clerical stages of processing and any other work in-house requiring actuarial review should be expedited to that area *now*. The working principle of sound service operations management is expediting to load the potential capacity constraint. Once capacity is overloaded, there is little to be done except work it off quickly. Any jobs that must flow through one bottleneck to another are obvious and natural priorities for attention at the earlier bottleneck. Those remaining nonconstrained capac-ities in the system will largely take care of themselves on an as-needed basis. It is the bottlenecks that raise cost and diminish customer service. They demand first priority in attention.

Bottlenecks are always identifiable when waiting work piles up in front of the workstation. Long queues of waiting work, like long lines of slow-moving traffic, mark the obvious bottlenecks. Once the waiting work has piled up in front of the workstation, though, it is too late to take remedial action in the form of scheduling. The best that can be done is to increase capacity at the bottleneck and/or expedite work through the bottleneck to the next bottleneck—assuming you can identify the next one.

The trick in sound service operations management is to anticipate bottle-necks *before* they announce themselves with pile-ups of waiting work. That can be accomplished *only* by modeling the work load in real time to forecast the impending increased demand. That requires some form of graphic, tabular or computerized system like those illustrated earlier in this chapter. Only when overloaded capacity is identified is it possible to expedite the right jobs through the system to fill the limited capacity early and fully. Any other approach is a crap shoot. Managing service work flow in a complex flow environment means modeling flow against incoming work. That is an indispensable element of cost efficiency and customer service in service operations.

Chapter 10

Discovering Service Quality

"Service quality is found in its design, not its magnitude."

Quality is an inherently vague notion. The dictionary definition of quality makes reference to character or kind and then escalates to include the degree of excellence or superiority of the entity described. The Latin root is *qualis*, "of what kind." Quality is a concept that begins with categories of the possible patterns that may typically be encountered, then proceeds to rank those patterns on some scale of preference or desirability. The clearest and simplest definition, perhaps, is to locate quality as the antithesis of quantity; quantity may sometimes be *a* contributing dimension of quality, but quality is *never* something that has solely to do with size, amount or magnitude. Preferring something that is big or small merely because of its size has nothing to do with quality. Quality is found in design, patterning, features, attributes, traits and characteristics of the product or service. This is not to say that low cost is not an important dimension of quality. Indeed, we shall subsequently see that low cost is often closely associated with high quality.

Service quality is many different and varied things. Discovery of quality requires knowledge of the tools, skills, service setting, worker roles and organization structure out of which service is originated and delivered to the customer. The configuration of the service generation process must first be described accurately and in detail. This is a sufficiently formidable task in its own right. Later on, once an acceptable taxonomy of service types has been developed, we may move to the question of excellence or superiority of service quality. A useful system for classifying service and service quality is the indispensable starting point.

CATEGORIES OF SERVICE

The complexity of service offerings is reflected in the variety of categories necessary for adequate description and in the lack of continuity between category dimensions. Alternatively or simultaneously, service can be based on service provider specialization of some kind, on satisfaction of common but essential human need or on entertainment through diversion or recreation. There is, indeed, so much complex variety inherent in these dimensions that it is essential to organize them in some visual, graphic form to begin to grasp their workings. Exhibit 10–1 presents a tabular array of representative service industries against the dimensions of service common to each. Although the industries and professions included in the list are broad-ranging and diverse, they do not necessarily represent an exhaustive list of service possibilities. The list is supplied only as a representation of the range of possibilities in service-intensive business offerings that should reasonably be included in an examination such as this one.

SPECIALTY AS FOUNDATION OF SERVICE

The most pervasive service dimension in this list is that of a specialty applied on the customer's demand. The subcategories of specialty in Exhibit 10–1 include service supplier ownership, use or maintenance of specialized tools or equipment, the service production and/or delivery system configuration, specialized know-how of service suppliers pertaining to the field of service, individual service provider skill in the delivery of service and service provider licensing to reflect verification of threshold qualifications and other specialized access to resources not easily or otherwise available to the public.

Many kinds of tools or equipment are too costly to be owned and maintained by individuals. Alternatively, they may demand a high level of training, skill and even licensing to operate them on behalf of the customer. Very few consumers are capable of flying their own airliner or commanding their own cruise ship. Hospitals and physicians routinely use sophisticated, high-technology tools, sometimes costing millions of dollars. Ownership of equipment on behalf of the public, mastery of tool usage know-how and skill and application of professional judgment as to how, when and on whom they are to be used reside in the hands of the institutions and

Exhibit 10-1
Sources of Service Quality for Representative Service Industries

Industry Category	SPECIALTIES					SATISFY ESSENTIAL NEED			ENTERTAINMENT	
	Tools & Equipmt	System Design	Know-How	Skills	License Access	Low Cost	Mixed Cost	Luxury Cost	Passive Viewing	Discover Learn
Insurance			x		x		x			
Banks			x		x		x			
Hospitals	x	x	x	x	x		x			
Professionals:										
Physicians	x		x	x	x		x			
Pharmacists	x		x	x	x		x			
Dentists	x		x	x	x		x			
Lawyers			x	x	x		x			
Architects	x		x	x	x		x			
Civil Engineers	x		x	x	x		x			
Business Service:										
Advertising			x	x	x		x			
Stockbrokerage		x	x		x		x			
Recruiting			x	x	x		x			
Training			x	x						x
Corporate Staff			x	x						
Counselors:										
Weight Loss		x	x	x						x
Marriage			x	x						x
Addiction		x	x	x	x					x
Career Planning		x	x	x						x
Pastoral			x	x						x
Psychiatric		x	x	x	x					x
Communications:										
Telephone	x	x	x			x				
Postal Service	x	x	x			x				
Information/MIS	x	x	x				x			

Exhibit 10-1 (continued)

Industry Category	SPECIALTIES					SATISFY ESSENTIAL NEED			ENTERTAINMENT	
	Tools & Equipmt	System Design	Know-How	Skills	License Access	Low Cost	Mixed Cost	Luxury Cost	Passive Viewing	Discover Learn
Education										
Schools/Univ.		X	X	X	X		X			X
Libraries	X	X	X	X	X	X				X
Restaurants										
Fast Food	X	X	X			X				
Family/Diners	X		X	X			X			
Tray Service	X		X	X				X		
Service										
Churches		X	X				X			
Lodges/ Fraternities		X	X				X			
Social Clubs		X	X				X			
Service Clubs		X	X			X				
Maintenance										
Automobile	X		X				X			
Appliance	X		X				X			
Household										
Plumbing	X		X				X			
Electrical	X	X	X				X			
General	X		X				X			
Landscaping	X		X				X			

132

	1	2	3	4	5	6	7	8	9	10
Entertainment:										
Television	x	x		x			x		x	x
Movies	x	x		x			x		x	x
Theater	x			x			x			x
Amusement Park	x		x			x				
Cruise Ship	x		x	x				x	x	
Public Transport:										
Railroads	x	x	x							
Airlines	x	x	x	x		x	x			
Buses	x	x	x			x				
Taxis/Limos	x		x				x			
Personal Service:										
Health Clubs	x		x				x			
Recreation	x		x	x			x			
Beauticians	x		x	x	x		x			
Barbers	x				x					
Tailors/ Seamstresses	x		x	x			x			
Realtors	x		x	x			x			
Hotels/Motels	x		x				x			
Public Service										
Police/Security	x	x	x	x	x	x				
Fire Fighters	x	x	x	x	x	x				
Refuse Removal	x	x				x				

professionals who use them. Physicians who are trained in their use, for instance, have full power to decide who will be the recipient of the machine-based services of magnetic resonance imaging systems. Quality of service can be influenced by the availability of exceptionally powerful tools and persons trained to use them as well as in the skilled judgment of the operator.

Many other professionals similarly use specialized tools, know-how, skill and resource access to serve their clients. Architects employ their boards (or computerized CAD systems) and mock-up materials to model projects in two or three dimensions to help clients visualize the end result. They offer materials know-how and structural engineering skill that can be applied for the best blend of aesthetic and sound structural results. They, like civil engineers, are usually licensed as assurance of the soundness of their structural planning for the safety of clients and the public. Advertising agencies specialize in mass communications know-how and apply skill in the aesthetic layout of copy. They have unique access to advertising media by virtue of resource usage know-how and ongoing personal relationships with media representatives. They enjoy substantially greater influence because of their continuing business relationship with media and can often dictate advantageous ad placement that would be unavailable to their customers. Quality is influenced by the skill with which tools, know-how and access to resources are combined in service of the customer's unique requirements.

Business services of various sorts including recruiting and placement firms and training and specialized industry consulting firms offer experienced judgment to their customers. Even the corporate middle management staffers of moderate-sized to large corporations may enjoy a level of specialized know-how that sets them apart as professionals. Occasionally, these service givers may also possess particular skills, as in the recruiter's interviewing and assessment ability, the trainer's teaching ability or the staff consultant's skill at operations and industry analysis. While these are typically viewed as professional services, they seldom require licensing as a prerequisite to engaging in their practice. For these services quality is partly measured by the results obtained for the client by the service provider.

Landscapers, realtors, barbers and beauticians are licensed to assure mastery of basic know-how and skill in their service to the public. They may also use some specialized equipment tools, but their tools are seldom technically sophisticated or costly. Some of their materials may be proprietary or otherwise difficult for the general public to obtain for personal use, but a large part of their competition comes from amateur and do-it-yourself solutions to the need. Tailors and seamstresses, in like manner, are skilled in the use of their basic tools and knowledgeable of materials availability and suitability to customer purpose. Quality of service is in the overall blend of tools, know-how and skill to achieve the customer's objective.

Counseling services sometimes are subject to licensing, sometimes not. Pastoral counseling is protected under constitutional guarantees of religious freedom, but some kind of formal recognition of ministerial status— ordination, for instance—is usually necessary to establish the legal protections and privileges such as tax exempt status or performance of marriages that go with the role. Psychiatric counselors are almost always licensed, largely because they choose to be. Licensing serves as a guarantee to clients of certain trained know-how and adherence to a standard code of ethical conduct. Weight loss counselors, marriage counselors, alcohol or drug addiction counselors, career counselors and similar counseling services are less often licensed. These services are frequently performed by paraprofessionals or even volunteers who serve by applying some sort of systematic, formula approach to solving the client's problems.

Counselors typically presume to apply know-how and skill in the identification of personal problem causes or solutions. Some counselors, though, serve well enough if they can assist the client in a voyage of self-knowledge and discovery. In many instances the central service they deliver is provision of sympathetic, uncritical friendship. Quality of service thus may be measured at different levels of counseling skill. The highest is located in successful counselor discovery of a solution to the client's problem. Client self-insight is another level of quality of counseling service, and emotional support from the counselor is at yet another level on a descending scale. Measurement of quality of the service will be a function of the level of expectation for outcome held by client or counselor or both. The clever counselor goes for the easiest quality win in a sympathetic relationship with the client, and then claims credit for increased client self-insight or for solved problems. Counseling is an easy service category in which to claim success. Quality of counseling service is often ambiguous and illusive. At its foundation, the quality of counseling is likely to be found in the conscientiousness of the counselor in applying his or her skill.

Communications services like phone, postal service and computer information systems are typically based on some level of specialized equipment or system that introduces efficiency into the delivery of the service. Phone service frequently relies on very high technology for microwave or satellite transmission of signals. The U.S. Postal Service is a highly organized, elaborate systems-oriented bureaucracy that guarantees reliable handling and delivery of the mail. MIS systems such as credit reporting or mass mail lists could not exist without cost-effective computer support that permits low-cost crunching of the great masses of data involved. A basic level of experienced know-how is also typically required to operate these systems effectively, but the quality of system design is fundamental to service quality in each of these service areas. The quality of the system design in combination with the know-how of the system service giver almost wholly determines the value of the service.

Entertainment and transportation are variants on communication services. They are equally dependent on specialized tools and on highly organized systems for effective delivery of service to the customer. Television and movies, for instance, would be impractical without the complex of electronic equipment required to capture the story image, and they are dependent on complex networks of transmission and distribution to reach the public. Movie houses still supply early distribution of new movies to the public, then television distributes many of the same releases over the airways and on cable. Finally, videotape technology permits physical distribution through local video shops in the form of sales and rentals of the cassette-taped performances.

Quality here is partially the result of the skill with which the story image is created, partly of accessibility to the public through the appropriate distribution system. Beyond the electronic technology and distribution systems technology that supports television and movie entertainment, there is considerable skill on the part of actors, writers, directors, camera people and various other support technicians who contribute to the artistic creation of a TV or movie production. Advances in technology improve the quality of the physical image transmitted or distributed, but the basic quality arises out of the systems and the skills that go into creating the story image.

Amusement parks and legitimate theater specialize in the creation of illusion in a context of physical reality. The equipment applied to the task can be simple or elaborate. As a rule, the more technologically complex the entertainment system, the more realistic the illusion created. Theater depends on lighting, props and sound to present the illusion of real events being enacted before the audience's eyes. The amusement park uses the same devices plus active physical involvement of the customer in the entertainment. The theater rises or falls on the skill of actors, director, stage hands, writers and associated technicians who create the event. The amusement park succeeds or fails as a function of the excitement of the physical experience offered.

Cruise ships are a unique form of entertainment, combining, as they often do, travel to exotic places, gambling, musical theater, on-board hotel and restaurant services, as well as social mixing of passengers. The unusual event of living shipboard on the open sea is thrown in for added measure. In their special way, cruise ships are an exceedingly complex service system in which there are an unusually large number of opportunities for both good and poor service. Passengers can focus on the good or the bad as they choose, or arrive at some sort of averaging of service quality as an overall index of quality.

Public transport of every kind involves equipment at its core. Taxis alone are based on the conventional commodity automobile. Most other public transport relies on specialized equipment. Buses, rail locomotives and cars, commercial aircraft, oceangoing ships or limousines equipped with TV and wet bar are clearly specialized to their service purposes. Most often the design of transport equipment centers around cost-efficiency, though some forms may be configured for luxury. Operation of transport equipment requires some basic know-how in operations and passenger handling. Airlines routinely supply food and beverage on board to combat boredom and airsickness, an incidental service that often confuses the quality of transport service issue for some travelers. It is, more substantively, the design of the equipment and its reliable operation according to published schedules that fundamentally determine service quality in airline travel and virtually all other forms of public transport.

Most public transport relies for its quality upon skillful operations management. Aircraft and oceangoing ships, however, also demand an exceptionally high level of technical skill in their operation. Pilots and captains are certified and licensed in their professions. This is principally to assure the security and safety of passengers. It only rarely adds a noticeable increment of quality to the service offered. Variation in quality of transport service is dominantly a function of operations management skill.

Libraries and schools are highly system dependent for the quality of the service offered. Libraries might also be looked upon as using books as a basic tool of the service. More fundamentally, though, it is the system that brings the needed information or learning opportunity to the individual. A degree of know-how and skill is essential to the quality of these services and there may sometimes be requirement for licensing or certification in the profession. The political environment in which these services are often delivered can limit both the quality of the system—rendering it overly bureaucratic and rigid—and constrain the individual teacher's or librarian's opportunity to apply know-how and skill adaptively. Quality of service suffers proportionately.

Other tax-supported services like police and fire protection or refuse removal can be similarly limited in quality by conflicting political pressures. They are, also, quality sensitive to the availability of special tools and systems. Police are dependent on firearms, radio communication of critical information, restraint systems and identification systems to carry out their jobs. Good systems support and service supplier skill can offset other limitations like public hostility or political meddling in the department. Fire fighting equipment is potentially elaborate and systems complex. Skill can vary widely among police and firemen, and the public is generally dependent on the system to allocate the available level of skill where it will do the most good. The quality of service in these fields is unusually dependent on the blend of individual skill with system design effectiveness. Even refuse removal requires specially designed heavy equipment for efficiency's sake and employs highly engineered refuse handling or disposal systems. Skill and know-how in their use can heavily influence service quality.

Personal convenience and recreational services such as those supplied by restaurants, hotels and motels, health clubs, golf courses, racquet clubs and similar offerings all tend to be highly equipment- or facility-oriented. They must also usually be supported by service supplier know-how. The quality of the service can be either a function of the care taken in equipment and facility investment or of the know-how of the service supplier. In some instances, something approaching skill may be involved with the service giver—for example, where "club pros" are central to service quality.

Finally, there is the category of wholly social service supplied by churches, lodges, fraternities, social or service clubs, singles' clubs and similar systems for socially mixing people. This style of service is largely dependent on a system of social structure and member obligation blended with a measure of organizational know-how supplied by experienced members. The object is the provision of useful social contacts and opportunities for fellowship on the part of members. There are other outcomes, of course, such as spiritual enlightenment in church or business contacts in the service club, but the service outcome from these organizations is, nonetheless, dominantly that of enhanced social contact and support. Opportunity to share values, aspirations, personal concerns and know-how with one another is at the core of system success here.

Maintenance services offer know-how in the troubleshooting of malfunctioning equipment. It is a service that often must respond to the customer's immediate need in timely fashion to offer the expected level of quality.

This by no means exhausts service categories. Some businesses like retail sales, freight handling or home remodeling may have enough service content to be good candidates for analyses along lines applied above. They are, though, centrally focused on delivery of a physical product that introduces an entirely separate and distinct quality dimension. For the sake of purity and simplicity of argument, the present discussion focuses on service quality in industries with limited or no tangible product, where service is clearly the principal stock in trade. The dimensions of service that are used in the present analysis can readily enough be generalized to most product-oriented service situations as long as it is understood that service quality in such settings will often be severely intermixed and muddled with quality of the physical product. High-quality service in support of a low-quality product can only be an exercise in frustration for customer and service supplier alike.

To review and summarize the contributions of specialization to service quality, then, we may say that specialization and specialties contribute in some degree to the quality of service in many industries. Specialized tools, equipment and facilities contribute to quality in medicine and the professions generally. They play a major role in the quality of communications, entertainment, public transport and personal service offerings. Know-how is an element of quality in the professions, in communications services, in counseling, public transport, personal services and social contact services. Skill plays a selective role in level of quality found in most of the professions, in some counseling settings, in entertainment, at libraries or schools and with police and fire protection. Licensing assures certain minimum levels of service quality in some professions—for airline pilots, ship captains, landscapers, realtors, barbers and beauticians—but may contribute little otherwise and even raise prices by serving as a barrier to entry in these fields. Stockbrokers, physicians, lawyers, advertising personnel and professional recruiters control specialized access to resources not readily accessible to the public. Access to those resources is typically fundamental to quality of the service offering. Finally, the system by which service is produced and delivered can also represent a unique specialization that shapes the overall quality of the service offering.

Where they are significant to service quality, tools and equipment are useful indicators of the quality of service available to the customer. These are the tangibles of service quality. The influence on service quality of dimensions like know-how, skill, and access to resources must be inferred through licensing or reputation of the firm. The contribution of the system to service quality can be central and major but obscured by other factors. The role of system design in service quality is sufficiently complex and significant to merit further discussion in the next chapter.

SERVICES THAT SATISFY FUNDAMENTAL, COMMON HUMAN NEED

The second and perhaps most common source of service quality from those offered in Exhibit 10–1 is that which describes the most common dimension of service: service that satisfies our basic human wants and needs. This is the sense of service that is rooted in the Latin term *servus*, referencing slavery.

In ancient times before indoor plumbing and running water were engineered, the functions of food preparation, personal hygiene and sanitation occupied the larger part of a day's activity. Social and professional pursuits were impossible without the aid of a servant. In its original form, slavery was as much a matter of task specialization as it was of subjugation. Slaves saw to the physical basics of their masters' lives while the masters attended to politics, professions and social amenities. At the highest levels of social and economic order, slaves served in professional roles to kings and potentates. As much as anything, slavery defined continuing work obligations of specialists who supported a stable social order. Contradictory as it may seem, it is likely that Athenian democracy could never have come to flower without the assistance of slaves.

Slavery in America was distinguished by the clear racial lines between slaves and masters, which made mobility out of slavery, an ancient characteristic of the institution, something between difficult and impossible. Coexistence of democracy alongside of slavery in the New World was a contradiction in ideals unless the slave race could be defined as something less than fully human. That was the fundamental pathology of American slavery. Its forms were otherwise faithful to the traditional structures of slavery, which sharply and cleanly specialized the task assignments of masters and slaves to support organized industry.

Modern factories have preserved specialization at a level that is sometimes described as wage slavery—subsistence pay for dreary, unskilled labor and little option outside destitution for those unwilling to accept their role. The consequence of these various institutions of specialized, basic unskilled labor within a hierarchy of private or public power is a tradition of assigning low status to those who serve our basic, menial, personal and economic needs. Basic, indispensable health support services like those of a hospital orderly, rest room caretaker, trash collector, or restaurant dishwasher are dismissed, ignored or scorned as worthy only of low-status citizens, undeserving of our respect, instead of knowing respect and appreciation for the great value of their specialized contribution to society. Service at the base of the economic structure that frees us to pursue our own political, professional and social objectives passes unrecognized for its great value.

Good service, as a result, is often taken for granted. Its absence generates complaint, but its presence merits no special notice. Where it involves professional know-how or skill, it is common for the servant to adopt a superior approach to a client as antidote to loss of status in the servant/master relationship. Personal services in luxury hotels, restaurants, beauty or barber shops, health spas, and so on, are supplied by willing, highly paid personnel who enact the role of servant for the entertainment of the customer. It is not always an easy role to play. In the most luxurious of accommodations where servants are sometimes better paid than masters, it becomes hard at times to know who is heaping the greater volume of scorn—customers on servants or servants on customers. The provision of personal service in these settings easily becomes a contest for status. As a result, the price of personal service is high and continues to escalate.

Cost-effective personal service is almost a contradiction in terms in the current age. It can, though, still be found. Telephone and postal services are still cost-controlled offerings to the public. Libraries and fast-food restaurants supply their offerings at low cost to the public. Police and fire protection, sometimes supplied on a volunteer basis, are a bargain in many communities. Complaints about quality in these services are often tempered by concerns over cost. Services of the Red Cross in disasters and of local medical emergency personnel are often performed at no cost to the recipients. Food and shelter for the poor or indigent are supplied at minimum or no cost through various community agencies, often supported financially by voluntary donations. A variety of fundamental human services continues to be offered on a cost-minimized basis in many corners of the economy.

A tradition of service without profit to one's fellow man continues through churches, service clubs, lodges, fraternities and sororities in every community. The Christian ideal that "the last shall be first and the first shall be last" holds sway in service projects targeted for community benefit. But the deep, gut-level tradition of low status in the role of service-provider continues to dominate. Where it does, the servant/master relationship often looks more like competition for the upper hand.

It is an enigma of current times that much personal service comes at moderate to high cost but that the quality of service given is often low in the sense of the service supplier's respect for the customer. Insurance companies often treat customer claims as if they must start with an assumption of attempted fraud. Banks, hospitals, physicians, dentists, lawyers, credit-reporting companies, public transport, personal service and restaurants too often deal with the customer as a faceless object to be controlled and exploited rather than as a person to be served. The quality of these services is seriously undercut by the double whammy traditions of mass commodity operations methods and assumed low-status conflict of service provider. There is nearly unlimited opportunity in these industries to create and deliver high-quality personal service if only the effort will be made.

Indeed, future competitive success in these industries will most likely depend on cost effective delivery of the highest quality of personal service. High quality at low or reasonable cost is the most consistently successful business strategy known. Applying it, though, requires exceptional management of service operations to assure consistent delivery of courteous, individualized, respectful service to every customer.

ENTERTAINMENT AS SERVICE

The third and concluding dimension of service illustrated by Exhibit 10–1 is that of entertainment. In modern Western culture, entertainment has taken on the character of superficial distraction through passive spectatorship. While that may be one of the dimensions of entertainment, mere passivity is not the true core of its meaning. Entertainment in its most fundamental form requires a bond of basic and vital communication between entertainer and audience. The etymological root of the word is in the French *entretenir* meaning to hold between or bond together in some fundamental way. Passive distraction or interest is certainly encompassed within this meaning. But so also is the most passionate of love affairs. Those who entertain one another reach into the deepest levels of awareness to communicate. It is instructive that the championship football team, consummate actor or riveting comedian who succeed in entertaining us seem to enact our most basic aspirations for high human expression. For those who have lost either the capacity or the opportunity to articulate their most urgent needs, entertainment in the passive sense is life's most compelling involvement.

But entertainment is also discovery, learning, accessing experience we didn't know existed to meet life's opportunities and crises. We may entertain ourselves or we may be entertained. Entertainment from extrinsic sources is an aid to self-discovery and growth. Drawn from intrinsic sources, it is the creation of a higher self. Entertainment as service is on a par with sorcery. It has the power of magic and the uplift of spiritual enlightenment. The linebacker on our favorite football team who breaks up the opposing team's potentially winning pass enacts our own struggle to win against stiff, competitive odds. The actor who plumbs the depths of personal agony in simulated tragedy echoes our own pain. The comedian who amusingly utters the acid truth about the powerful expresses our own unspoken dismay. Were we willing to discipline our own actions to the challenge, we might forsake passivity in favor of our own active expression. But it would require a wholly different approach to expression. We would have to actively entertain life at its source with all the risks and rewards that entails.

Television, movies, theater, even amusement parks and a walk on the city streets can supply passive entertainment. But there is also powerful entertainment in the services of a skilled physician, an experienced lawyer, an inspired teacher or a good local library. Indeed, the highest source of quality in these services may be their power to entertain us. To the extent that the customer insists on discovery over distraction, they may become entertainments that transform.

The quality of an entertainment is, unfortunately, not found in the customer's activity or passivity toward it. Passive entertainment is as powerful in its impact as an active form might be and sometimes more so because it makes lesser demands on us. In some ways, indeed, it is more satisfying in that it requires no great personal discipline or sacrifice to participate passively. The investment to become an active performer could be immense. The physical conditioning and hazard of injury demanded by the play of football, the talent and training required of a successful actor, or the timing and wit needed in the delivery of a comic's laconic lines— none of these need be mastered to attend passively to their performance.

The greater part of quality in entertainment arises from the power to reach deeply into the mind of the audience and find a match of resonance. Entertainment that is tuned to the experiences and aspirations of its target audience connects with a crash of cheering, applause, laughter or stunned silence. The teacher who can evoke new qualities of student awareness and understanding releases a flood of productive energy. An entertainment that creates a bond of clear communication enlightens and educates. Herein lies the measure of an entertainment's quality; it reaches into the heart of its audience and strikes a sympathetic chord. The power to entertain instructs us as to what may be the deepest and most enduring measure of service quality: success in finding the customer in the innermost tabernacle of his or her being. Ultimately, it is probable that we may find the well-spring of service quality in successful entertainment of the customer. To better understand how to do that, we must continue to examine all the factors that have a bearing on service quality.

Chapter 11

Roles, Skill Level and System Design as Foundations of Service Quality

"Service quality is a function of many complex factors."

From the foregoing discussion of dimensions of service quality, it is apparent that varied roles are played out in the provision of service, and that the quality of the role play itself can be a measure of service-provision quality. Quality of service is, at a minimum, a function of the appropriateness of the role played by the service supplier. The six major role sets that may be drawn on by a service supplier are: servant, technician, expert, advisor, protector, and trustee.

Like roles played on the theater stage or movie screen, these roles can be described to and learned by a willing player for the overall benefit of the service offering. Prescription of the appropriate role under the circumstances is an important and often overlooked element of high-quality service. Poor service, in fact, frequently stems from choice of the *wrong* role for the service setting.

The core of a servant's role is the traditional prescription that "the customer is always right." An element of obsequiousness is found in this principle only for the service provider who believes that making someone else "right" necessarily means being "wrong" yourself. In this age of opulent affluence, self-abasement is equated with self-denial, not with self-renewal as it once was.

The religious ideal of selfless service for the benefit of one's fellow man is an important anchor point for the servant role, though the sackcloth and ashes image it currently carries errs on the side of overkill. One does not always need to grovel to be an effective servant. Absolute obeisance to a master is only one of many dimensions found in servanthood. A good servant can also be a protector and a trustee of the customer. Roles can be complex and multidimensional.

There is, indeed, opportunity for conflict between some dimensions of the servant role. Where there is a requirement for application of competent skill on the customer's behalf, especially when the customer misunderstands what is needed for high-quality service, mere slavish carrying out of the customer's demands may be no service at all. Physicians and lawyers may judge the reasoning or demands of clients to be unrealistic nonsense. A bank clerk may know that the customer is ignorant of account structure when he or she requests an impossible transaction. A household repair technician may believe that the temporary repair requested by the customer is unsafe or illegal. These conditions call for either education of the customer or withdrawal from the service assignment. A well-trained service supplier in the servant mode *must* offer explanation or courteously withdraw. A wise service supplier will, further, *not* demand payment for service that cannot be supplied under these circumstances. Requiring the customer to pay for being unrealistic can be the ultimate insult from a servant, especially an expert one.

In the role of servant, the service provider must always go the extra mile to assure at least minimum customer satisfaction. It is easy but inappropriate to shift into the role of technician or expert as a defense against customer demand. Where the servant cannot explain the constraints he or she works under satisfactorily to the customer, it is necessary to admit failure to serve and respectfully withdraw from the service arena. The servant role requires training in avoidance of argument and eschewal of self-justification. Those whose self-esteem demands self-justification in the face of criticism or disagreement are disabled as effective servants and should not be cast in that role.

Technicians as servants typically lack central characteristics essential to high-quality service because they are good, effective, tunnel-visioned technicians. Technicians specialize in efficient, effective troubleshooting of nonworking tools, equipment, systems and social relations. Almost any routine tool or process requires its support technicians on-call when breakdown occurs. The technical skill called for is almost always specific to the tool, equipment, system, process or relationship. Good mechanics can be competent technicians with physical tools, equipment and systems. Good customer relations people or managers can be skilled in diagnosis and repair of ailing social systems or human relations. The technician role does not generalize well to unfamiliar repairs or breakdowns. High competence in one area may be accompanied by utter ignorance in another. The surgeon who performs open-heart surgery can be innocent of knowledge on how to repair an auto carburetor, or quite unable to resolve the slightest personal disagreement among members of the operating room staff. Because of his inherent high status on this specialized team, though, it may be assumed that he should be able to fix a carburetor or smooth over personal animosities. Technicians are seldom this flexible, but because of their technical status they are often still too ready to assume skill in which they have no practice.

Technicians must either be cross-trained in companion specialties or insulated from problems outside their domain. It is a quality of high mechanical technical skill that people highly skilled at dealing with things are often possessed of only the most rudimentary social skills. Specific training in customer contact skills is appropriate for all classes of technicians. Approached as a problem-solving routine that applies known solutions to common problems, human relations training for technicians can contribute markedly to the quality of service offered. But those technicians who are excessively shy or short-tempered must be identified and applied only to the safest customer situations when they perform alone. If exceptionally skilled in their technology but grossly inept in customer contact, it may be necessary to team them with a less-technically-skilled but more-customer-sensitive partner. Otherwise, they can only be used on the repair bench inside the shop where customers never venture.

The expert role is yet more troublesome for the quality of service. Expertise too easily supports self-pretense and even arrogance. At its foundation, expertise is little more than complex or high-level technology that commands high wages. The expert is a supertechnician. The problems that plague technicians also interfere with the effectiveness of experts. The lawyer who grandstands for effect at the client's expense, the narrowly specialized physician who refuses to admit his or her limitations in the practice of medicine, the architect who puts aesthetics ahead of utility in designs, concert musicians who refuse to perform the works of certain composers or compositions, the chef who won't alter a personal recipe to fit the customer's taste, the college professor who can't take the time to clarify a difficult concept for the willing but confused student—all these withhold from their customers the very service they expect to be paid for supplying. Experts, indeed, are often the last people from whom we should expect good personal service. If they offer a standard, highly predictable service under exact contract, it may be viable to use their skill. Absent clear specification of their performance, though, they are potentially erratic and dangerous. And because they so chronically provide poor-quality service, they contribute disproportionately to giving service a bad name.

The expert role in service is an extremely troublesome one. Public criticism of lawyers and physicians for their arrogance toward clients could easily invite a lawsuit for slander, regardless of the critic's justification. The defensiveness of experts in the face of challenge often places a wall of formality between them and their clients. Blended with just a dash of arrogance, the wall becomes an iron curtain. Where they are buffered from competition by extended education and/or licensing, experts may be able to limit choice in selection of an alternate expert. Quality of service chronically suffers at the hands of experts.

As yet there are few if any satisfactory mechanisms in place to evaluate and raise the service quality of society's experts. Word-of-mouth references between customers is the most common device. Most professions are "self-policing" in matters of ethics and service quality, which means that they will respond only to the most intense political or legal pressure from organized client groups. If professions were to establish complaint bureaus empowered to investigate customer grievances, recommend remedies and maintain formal records of complaint dispositions for future legal reference, progress might be made toward improved expert services. It is doubtful, though, that this will ever come about voluntarily in the major professions. Ultimately it will have to be mandated on them by law.

Fortunately, the expert role can serve as a bridge to better and more constructive service provider roles. In preference to the expert as final answer giver, the sounder approach for possessors of expert skill or knowledge are often those of advisor, protector and trustee. Expertise is expected and appreciated on the part of those customers who obtain advice or extend trust. Protectors must be effective without becoming oppressive of their clients. Quality of the service offered is a function of successful advice, faithful trust and assurance of personal security—all functions themselves of the level of expert skill applied on behalf of the client. The quality trap inherent in these roles is the inclination to act on the customer's behalf without informing him or her of the alternative options. Advisors, protectors and trustees must act with their clients' informed consent, not independently, leaving their clients in ignorance. Lawyers must advise their clients of the rights they give up under a contract. Physicians must counsel their patients on the risks of a medical procedure. Police must respect the civil rights of boisterous demonstrators who threaten other citizens' property, persons or rights. Trustees must prudently invest or use money and property entrusted to them.

Those who call on service of these roles will sometimes demand intervention to solve their problems while withholding willingness to understand strategy and purpose of the advisor, protector or trustee. This is the dependency trap. The customer transfers all the accountability for success onto the service provider without necessarily accepting responsibility for the existing problem or its solution. There is great temptation for the expert service supplier to play rescuer in response to the customer's victim role. Ultimately, it is an impossible assignment to carry out successfully. The advisor, protector or trustee sets him- or herself up inevitably to fail. The quality of the service offered is low because there is no consistent way to deliver the implied promise of "leave it to me; I'll take care of everything."

Advisers, protectors and trustees thus frequently find that the quality of their service is judged low either because they satisfy their own standards of service quality without concern for the customer's expectation, or they take on impossible assignments by failing to inform customers realistically of their choices. Provision of sound advice, protection and trusteeship lends strength to the expert role as long as the expert does not exploit the customer's dependence to raise his or her status as expert.

Approaches to managing customer expectation for service quality levels will be reviewed in Chapter 13 and methods for selecting and training service-providers are examined in Chapter 14. Here we are only concerned with recognizing the inherent advantages and traps of the possible roles available to service providers. Clearly, there are many. Each role dimension contributes differently to the quality of service. The advantages and disadvantages of each must, accordingly, be understood.

SERVICE QUALITY AND SERVICE PROVIDER LEVEL OF SKILL

It was proposed in Chapter 5 that the range and variety of skill possessed by each service worker can contribute importantly to the capacity flexibility of a firm. Workers who can be allocated flexibly across current service projects, applying different skills to different jobs, sometimes following a job through from start to finish, will not sit idle while some jobs wait, and they will often make a significant contribution to improved quality. Task variety and continuity of accountability for product quality are available when workers bring a repertoire of relevant skills to the service workplace.

Verified possession of skill in one's repertoire through credentialing or licensing of skill can only assure a minimum threshold of any skill applied in practice. That threshold will vary as a function of supply and demand of qualified service givers. Any pressure of demand is likely to lower the minimum threshold. An excess of supply may serve to concentrate business with the more skilled. Beyond such crude market forces, though, little in today's service economy operates to encourage or reward exceptional service giver skill. Word-of-mouth reports of exceptionally poor or outstandingly good skill may serve as a guide to the better informed customers, but public records of success or failure in the practice of skill will be rare or absent. In professional sports, the record of a major-league pitcher or quarterback is fully open to public knowledge. Entertainers are constantly exposed to public view and criticism. Even politicians must perform regularly in public for the benefit of constituents. But physicians, lawyers, counselors, architects, civil engineers, teachers, locomotive drivers, airline pilots, beauticians, corporate staff specialists and other similar service givers work with customers one or a few at a time, out of the public view for the most part. Only they and their closest colleagues are positioned to judge their professional skill. Their customers cannot safely presume availability of anything more than bare threshold skill in the service sought.

The major result of this obscurity of performance among service suppliers is a general absence of any correspondence between the cost of service and the skill level offered. The service price established in negotiations between service giver and customer is likely to be determined more by the urgency of customer need than by level of service giver skill. The exceptionally skilled surgeon, indeed, may require far less time to complete a surgical procedure, endure less personal stress in its performance and schedule more patients for surgery on the same day. His rates may reflect his efficiency and his patients may obtain the benefits of more skilled treatment at lower cost. The experienced courtroom lawyer who knows the system can handle five routine cases in a day with billed time prorated across all five clients, while a less-skilled colleague commits the entire day to a single case, letting one client bear the full financial burden of the day's work while the lawyer spends more time sitting than working. The skilled airline pilot brings the disabled airplane down with minimum passenger injury, the minimally skilled one crashes. Robert Pirsig in his paean to the quality of life, *Zen and the Art of Motorcycle Maintenance* (1976), recounts in awe the skill of a small-town all-purpose welder who effortlessly repairs an "irreparable" metal part from the author's cycle, bypassing the anticipated need to purchase at high cost a long-delivery-wait replacement. The skill of this artist-in-metal supplies immediate service at greatly reduced cost. Indeed, in each of these cases, the cost to the customer is greatly reduced by the higher level of skill available from the service provider.

Accounting for skill in service giving is of the greatest importance to quality improvement. Professional and expert service providers can often hide their records of service from the public view. With institutional service providers, like banks, insurance companies, public transport, hotels or restaurants, management skill will translate partially into lower price to the consumer. In general, managers, professionals and experts will be more efficient and cost-effective in their performances when their skills are superior. High-skilled service will often be higher quality, lower cost service. The highest cost service is often likely to be of mediocre to low quality. In the absence of public record detailing service giver performance, the service consumer may do well to comparison price shop and then investigate the bases of the price differences found. Wherever skill is licensed or permitted practice on demonstration of threshold ability alone, superior skill is often associated with both lower price and higher quality of service. It is a relationship worth investigating.

WHEN THE SYSTEM IS THE FOUNDATION OF QUALITY

While service system design is certainly an important element of the service specialization as a dimension of quality, it contributes to quality in several unique ways that deserve added examination. A special case of quality is found in those institutions where the system dominates the delivery of service to the customer. The more obvious industries where this condition prevails are libraries, schools and universities under the category of education. Banks, railroads, airlines and buses are representative of mass transport systems, while information data banks, telephone, postal and package delivery are illustrative of communication systems. Systems also play a key role in a variety of proprietary and franchised personal counseling services.

Libraries must control their stock in trade—books in the stacks—yet make them easily available to their customers. Absence of control leads to misplacement or loss, diminishing quality of service, while excessive control restricts availability, again reducing quality. The system that supports both objectives effectively delivers the highest quality of service. A system that permits hands-on access to books and microfilm, which makes copies conveniently and quickly but prevents damage or theft of the core product, provides superior service. One that requires long waits for labor-intensive trial-and-error search and demands extensive record-keeping labor at every step of the process is an inferior one.

Educational systems, public or private, must deliver relevant learning opportunities to their students cost-effectively. Books and lectures pitched at the level of comprehension of the average student are the staple, traditional basis of these systems. The quality of the service delivered, as a result, is likely to be more a function of the student's flexibility of comprehension than of the system's effectiveness. Most students teach themselves using the standard learning opportunities made available to them.

Educational systems are a holdover from mass commodity operations traditions and thinking. They address the great middle plurality of students well, but badly serve fringe student populations, which are sometimes the majority. A major overhaul is required of the traditional classroom system employed to deliver education as service to the populace. Education, unfortunately, has become the universal example of poor-quality service produced largely if not entirely by the faults of the system. Only a fundamental redesign that finds the individual student will cure these ills.

Mass transport systems are redesigned almost daily in the newly competitive world of deregulated airlines and buses. Terminals and aircraft are regularly reconfigured, routes are frequently revised. Railroads, bound to their physical roadbeds and dependent on large centers of population for their efficiency, have less flexibility, few real cost-saving opportunities or chances for improved quality. Their challenge is to deliver their traditional transport service as reliably and cost-effectively as they can. Renewal of the rail transport system awaits business and political leadership of the highest quality.

Communication systems are in continual revolution today. Computers as decision-making switching centers, automated scanners and readers of every sort, satellite transmitters, home terminals and much more make communication the service industry of the coming age. It is the design of the systems and systems technology they are based on that creates cost-effective, high-quality communications services. Systems, as a concept, has erroneously become synonymous with computers. It is a gratuitous association, based largely on the utility of the computer as a tool for systems design and analysis. It illustrates, though, the significance of the electronic system as the foundation of service quality in this highly significant industry. What is missed in such an observation is the fact that the productive power of computers is dependent more on user skill and imagination than on the computer as an electromechanical system.

An important and frequently overlooked contribution to computer systems utility can be found in examining user skill in the use of computers to produce information. Computers are a highly efficient means for storing data, but the mere existence of data in a computer's memory in no way assures that it will be informative to management or customers. Data is only the record of an observed event in the real world. Information, often confused with data, is useful knowledge of how data relate to one's business or personal purposes and objectives. The production of information value out of computer data is a skill in its own right that depends on mastery of research design and statistical analytical skills. Unanalyzed data are likely to be uninformative data. Many data summaries generated by the computer are wholly uninformative. Managers receive voluminous quantities of summarized data from the computer operation, which lacks any relevance to their business needs or purposes. The same happens in many commercial data bases purporting to supply market or customer information.

Data of questionable reliability are marketed as if they were valuable information, immediately applicable to the customer's needs. Until the data stored have been tested and analyzed, they are often useless. Unanalyzed data are never a service bargain until and unless analytical skill has been brought to bear in relating them to the customer's needs and purposes. Thus, the potential for computers as contributors to service systems enhancement is as yet mostly untapped. When the right blend of skill and system power is achieved, the results may be truly awesome, surpassing the wildest imagination of the current day for systems contributions to service quality.

Systems for personal counseling in matters of weight loss, marriage crisis, substance abuse or career counseling are in many instances the service itself. In dieting, it is typically the portion-control and progress-monitoring system that is marketed. Counselors are mere deliverers of the system's message or method. Like education, these are mass commodity offerings targeted at a large enough customer segment to merit franchising and training cost to deliver the standardized end product.

To the extent that counselors are interested in and able to relate to the individual customer, these may become personal services on a level of entertainment at some point. That is not, unfortunately, yet a requirement of the system or a consistent element of service quality. Marriage and career counselors often use a set of standard questionnaire measures to assess the relative perspectives of their clients and offer systems formula solutions to their life dilemmas. The quality of the measurement/assessment system determines the quality of the counseling given. Many substance and alcohol abuse programs employ a strict ritual of constraints and encounters to work their effect on clients with little real focus on the individual client. If the system fits the client's needs, it may work. If not, it is a waste of time.

Psychiatry, the traditional system of personal counseling by professionals, is, despite its rigid requirement for extensive professional training, cut of the same cloth. It is a system of rational explanation for problematic behavior, often delivered with minimal concern for the individual counselee. It almost always excludes nonrational or spiritual issues in its exploration of the client's need. Like other less professional systems of counseling, it is too often a rigidly prepackaged service offering aimed at a large but limited target audience.

Quality in counseling generally is primarily a function of the fit of the system to the customer, secondarily a function of the relationship between counselor and client. It is no wonder that the quality of these offerings is often controversial. But it is the system at base that is at fault. Good counseling that services the client departs substantially from or greatly modifies the standard system of treatment used in the field.

In some service domains, the customer service system is in and of itself often the key to service quality. The automatic teller machine that returns the customer's bank access card after all other transactions are complete results in a much larger proportion of forgotten and lost cards than the one that returns the card and verifies removal before the transaction requested can be carried out. The computer hard disk operating system that routinely displays the current directory graphically as a branching diagram is superior to the one that merely organizes a listing of files and subfiles. The automotive electronics system that contains back-surge protectors against catastrophic failure down-stream leave fewer motorists stranded with a dead engine. The production system that always simply but accurately identifies the source of poor-quality output puts the spotlight on performance in a way that provides incentive for high-quality work. The design of the system that supports service is potentially a key to high quality. As much care must be put into its design and test evaluation as into the product or service itself.

The style and system of management coordination applied to the organization is itself a major systems contribution to the quality of service. Service, indeed, is highly sensitive to good or poor management systems and management skill. The quality of management offered by the team that oversees coordination of service delivery is basic to quality. Poor management tells in service industries quicker than in commodity production. Commodity efficiency is largely a function of the quality of engineering that has gone into the design of the production system. Management has fewer opportunities to misuse the commodity production system than the service delivery system. In those service settings where the supporting system is *not* crucial to service quality, management style and skill—the management system applied—almost inevitably will be the major source of service quality.

SERVICE QUALITY IS COMPLEX!

Given the extended variety of quality bases for service, the uniqueness of quality to the specific service or service provider and the many unresolved problems of service quality control, it is no wonder that understanding service quality is often a puzzlement. Quality is a matter of kind. It is concerned with designs, patterns, features, attributes, traits and characteristics. It can always be evaluated but often cannot be measured, at least not in any of the conventional ways quantity is measured. In these chapters, only the barest beginnings are made toward cataloging the bases of quality. There is much more to come in chapters that follow.

Chapter 12

Objective Dimensions of Service Quality

"So many ways to look at quality. Which is correct?"

In the previous chapters service quality was approached as a question of what goes into producing it. Tools, equipment, specialized know-how, skill, access to resources, ministering to the basic needs of customers, entertainment on any level from passive to peak experience, appropriateness of server role, relative degree of server skill and system design—all these dimensions describe service quality in terms of the sources out of which it is generated. As with production of a tangible merchandise, the elements of which service is created can limit or raise its ultimate quality. Some of these are visible to the customer, most are not.

Alternately, quality of service as delivered can be evaluated in terms of its outwardly observable traits, characteristics and patterning. There are at least a half-dozen dimensions on which service quality can be objectively evaluated, any one of which may dominate a given service, all of which may play a role in some service offerings. The most obvious dimensions are those of cost, service output result, degree of customization, technological superiority, reliability and aesthetic appeal. The potential for such wide variety in the patterning of these objective characteristics raises the question of how to get the best mix of service characteristics. There is opportunity if not need to set strategic priorities that will guide the mix of factors constituting service quality.

THE COST DIMENSION—WHAT IS REASONABLE COST?

Some service providers would prefer their customers to believe that cost is no legitimate consideration in determining the quality of service. "Cost is no object when you want the best" is their motto. This point of view has less to do with quality in service than with pricing. It is an element of the price negotiation process. Service is intangible and its delivery establishes a relationship between customer and service giver. Depending on the quality of the relationship, service may either be pricey or priceless. Just about any price may be established, depending on the view of the principals to the service contract.

Moreover, price has only a minimal linkage with cost. For some the personal cost of rendering service is infinite—the fire fighter killed in the line of duty, for instance. For many the opportunity to serve is fulfilling. We may take notice of political or religious missionaries in this regard. The lawyer who loves the law because it is the foundation of civilized society serves first and thinks about the fee later. Service lends meaning to their lives. Without the opportunity for self-expression in service, there is only emptiness and depression.

For some, alternatively, service is demeaning. The personal service supplier who experiences diminished personal status in delivering service will expect high wage recompense in return for the perceived humiliation that goes with the job. For some, inevitably, service is the quick route to riches. The physician who hates people or the teacher who hates kids, but is in it for the money, will focus on maximizing income. These are not questions of cost; they are matters of price. They are part of the service provider's personal value calculus in establishing the price that will be asked of the customer. Real cost is another matter.

Were we to construct an exact calculus of the cost of service, we would have to begin with the immediate physical costs that the service giver must bear. Supplies, tools, equipment, rent, taxes and payroll expense of assistants would all be accounted for under conventional accounting procedures and then allocated across service clients as equitably as possible. We will, for the moment, overlook the leverage that high-price service givers employ in maximizing these costs to justify the highest possible charge. That will be classified as luxury service designed to satisfy clients who fear they will not get the best service if they do not pay the highest price. These apprehensive and status-sensitive customers, at the least, are likely to get substantially individualized services at maximum price. Whether other dimensions of service will be superior or not is a separate question.

The opportunity to control and minimize cost at a level justified by real service need and client expectation exists in the service setting as much as it does in a mass commodity sale. Exceptional service can be delivered in a spartan setting with just the essential supplies and tools applied to its creation. Where service quality is principally a function of know-how and skill on the service provider's part, the associated physical costs may be entirely incidental and substantially controllable. The service provider who prodigally employs expensive, high-tech tools to deliver a simple basic service may lack either skill, good judgment or ethics. The high cost of service can be a device that distracts the customer from noticing the absence of more significant dimensions of service such as server skill.

Beyond the basics of accounting for the physical, tangible cost of service delivery, the next element in a precise calculus of service would be the service provider's personal investment to develop the skill and know-how required to deliver satisfactory service. For now we will be concerned only with threshold-level service satisfaction. The availability of superior service must be considered independently.

Physicians who may spend a decade in training, professionals or academics who endure years of advanced study, actors, writers and artists who may spend even longer mastering their crafts, researchers who may apply a lifetime to the pursuit of a specific problem solution—all invest heavily of their brief life spans in acquiring the skill, know-how and experience demanded of their trades. What payback should they reasonably expect in return? In strict investment accounting terms, we can calculate the earnings lost because of the time diverted into training and add to that the out-of-pocket cash cost of formal education required to arrive at a monetary value for the investment made. This may be treated as a straightforward problem of return on investment—a standard accounting concern.

The problem with return on investment (ROI) is that there are no exact standards as to what is fair and no real limits on what is acceptable. ROI may vary from negative return (a real loss on the investment) to a positive payback that is many times the original investment per year. For convenience, ROI can be benchmarked approximately against interest rates. These have been volatile in recent times, but they are still much less variable than ROIs published for publicly traded firms. Against a very liberal range of normal interest rates, something between 5% and 25% annual return on investment is likely to be a fair ROI depending on the market and the economic risk involved.

Risk, though, is also a legitimate element of cost in pricing. We cannot ignore it altogether. The third element of calculus in the worth of a service, thus, may be risk of some kind. It may either be the economic risk of premature obsolescence of career skill or the risk to life or health inherent in the occupation. Fire fighters and police can be killed in the conduct of their duties. That is a known and calculable risk. But anyone can be killed on any job. The job mortality rate of farmers, construction workers and truck drivers is higher than that of police officers. The known risk is often more acceptable than the unknown one. Fire fighters and police may feel safer in their trained knowledge of the known risks they face than they would feel in an alternate occupation where the risks are hidden and hard to identify.

Earlier generations of factory laborers were innocently exposed to highly dangerous chemicals and materials, and some have suffered grievously in their ignorance. But others in safer occupations have smoked cigarettes and consumed alcohol to the point of also destroying their health. Those exposed in innocent ignorance may collect damages in the courts. Those who have voluntarily used dangerous nicotine and alcohol typically may not. When and how, then, should risk become a factor in the pricing of service? When is it fair and equitable for the client to pay for the service provider's personal risk exposure?

Where risk is perceived as an element in the cost calculus of service, it can become a factor in establishing the market value of service labor and be reflected as an increment in wage differential. Service provider and buyer may deal with it in their price negotiations. The increment negotiated need never be a large one, since it is only the perceived possibility of risk that is considered. Actual risk of death or injury or job insecurity may be less significant than perceived risk, and cost is incurred only in the event the possibility is realized.

The proper approach to costing risk is through a contingency arrangement that reflects the odds of its occurrence. The technical name for this arrangement is insurance. The real costs of life-threatening risk are dealt with practically through measures like medical and life insurance policies. Indeed, the value of these risks is exactly measured *only* as the cost of adequate insurance to fully satisfy worker concerns about them. Where the risk is unacceptable the worker must stay out of the occupation altogether; no amount of pay increment for risk can compensate adequately. Thus, any pay increment over and above insurance cost is unnecessary and gratuitous except as it is acceptable as an element of price negotiations.

In many cases risk is no more than a useful bargaining chip for obtaining economic benefits that would be harder to gain on their own merit. Long-standing policies of early retirement from careers in the police and military, for instance, are not as much a matter of job-related risk as they are of career burnout. The exceptionally high wages demanded by teachers of inner-city schools have less to do with risk than with career burnout. These are not matters of risk, except as we might conceive of a poor career choice as a risk. They are the direct result of archaic and poorly designed service delivery systems, which put high stress on individual performance without providing support to solve system problems. Sometimes they reflect the marginal value of excess labor demand over and beyond the limited number of job candidates suited to handle the jobs without undue stress. Redesign of the service system or of the system of recruitment and selection of new entrants may be a much less costly solution to the problem.

In the current economic age there is often greater risk in obsolescence of a career than of diminished health or threat to life. These costs are ignored at present in many occupations. Top managers in a risky, volatile industry build in their golden parachutes, arguing that worry about their careers would impair their managerial performance. (They should be summarily fired as managers for even raising such a defense.) But workers on the production line are laid off with two weeks' notice and the prospect of standing in the unemployment claims line. Perhaps public policy should require, under corporate policy, that everyone be insured against risk of career obsolescence equally or that everyone share the risk equally. Risk that is not precisely and rationally costed as a contingency and fairly applied to all members of the firm should have no place in the pricing of service. What's good for an executive is good for a worker.

Only one element of cost remains to be considered: the market value of the service provider's skill and labor. This can be estimated by observing the wage paid to a service provider who is trained under contract, supplied with all equipment required to deliver the service and fully insured for the risks of the job. The physician intern on the hospital staff, the newly graduated military pilot, the retired officer or fireman in a no-benefits job—these and any number of other similar benchmark comparisons can help establish the true base wage.

Service cost then comes down to these factors: basic value of skill and labor in the open market; cost of supplies, equipment and overhead required to deliver service; return on self-financed training/learning investment, and the cost of insurance to cover reasonable job risk. There are no other factors that deserve to be considered in establishing the cost base for a service supplier's labor. The quality of delivered service is thereby predicated on a sound cost basis.

Some clever service providers discover how to manipulate the labor market to their benefit. When we find physicians restricting the market by raising threshold skill requirement excessively high for even the most routine health delivery and then limiting the number of physicians in practice, we must conclude that the market is being manipulated to raise prices. Lawyers manipulate the market in their way, too. They proliferate like rabbits and then increase the complexity of the law through congressional and state legislation to expand the overall market for legal service. They manipulate market mechanisms to assure a steady supply of clients.

Other service professionals, like airline pilots, police and fire fighters, obtain their training largely or wholly at the expense of taxpayers. Their training wage may be modest, but they are nonetheless sustained at a basic living level while they are in training. Through their powerful labor unions, airline pilots have successfully raised wages well above market for their service, especially considering the public tax investment made in training their skill. Police and fire protection are often bargains, except where their unions have negotiated excessively large retirement entitlements and medical coverage that follow foreshortened, twenty- to thirty-year careers. High wages or generous pension perks in these careers may be rationalized on grounds that the occupation carries high personal risk of injury and loss of life, even though many generously remunerated retirees go on to other police or fire fighter jobs in smaller jurisdictions that may lack generous benefits and pensions.

BUT LOW COST IS ASSOCIATED WITH HIGH QUALITY

The foundation of truly high-quality service will consistently be found in high-quality know-how and skill. Where these are high quality, cost is consistently if not automatically low. The independent painter, carpenter or business consultant with exceptional skill delivers better service at lower cost just to stay in competition with their organized business counterparts. By contrast, the minimally skilled, limited-experience service provider laboring within a poorly designed system toils inefficiently, misusing the available time, energy and effort. The minimally skilled entry-level counselor, stockbroker, computer programmer, teacher or accountant spends days accomplishing the same task that skill and long experience accomplish in minutes or hours. The sheer time and energy expended to service an equivalent number of clients will necessarily be anywhere from double to ten and sometimes a hundred times greater than that applied by the highly skilled, experienced service provider. Aspiring to the level of financial success enjoyed by the skilled service provider, the lesser skilled must charge each client many times more in price to bring hourly earnings equivalent to their more skilled counterparts. Even so, these far-less-efficient service providers expect to earn on a par with their vastly more efficient colleagues. A sense of industry equity creates a community of skill owners that fixes prices at a standard for each service so that the auto mechanic, lawyer or physician with limited skill charges the same standard fee on a task-completed basis as one with intensive skill or long experience. By setting the fee at a fair rate for average skill, the lesser skilled can make an acceptable wage for their time and effort, while the highly skilled draw a premium wage for their greater efficiency in skill and time applied. Limited skill thereby inflicts major, immediate cost on the pricing structure by offering low quality at high price.

Perhaps the lesser skilled, inexperienced service provider should price less. Where the market is free and unimpeded by licensing requirements, giant competitors or political power centers, price may be less. If they have the opportunity, customers will seek out only the high-skilled, experienced service provider. That is difficult to do, though, because where licensing, market distortion or restricted competition control the market for service, all skill levels and service delivery tend to look alike. From the customer's perspective, the service result simply does not appear noticeably different from one service provider to another. It may sometimes be only the labor time required to reach service standard that differs, and not the standard of service itself. The only clear cue customers and clients have is the stress the service provider is under and sometimes the lower price charged by the more skilled, experienced service provider with a strong social conscience. These are not easily observed or measured cost variables. Higher skilled, experienced people are not likely to lord it over their lesser colleagues. Only a very competent investigation will uncover the differences here.

The presence in our economy of special interest groups that serve as political power centers has continuing potential to distort market pricing mechanisms, especially so for service. Labor unions, professional associations and industry lobbying groups can, using their political influence, obtain a price advantage through licensing, through legislation that gives market advantage or through threat of reduced service if wages are not increased. Special political advantage seems to be an old and time-honored tradition in American business, but it inevitably distorts pricing and reduces the fairness of economic exchange. It should be scrutinized whenever and wherever it appears.

In some instances, investment by the service provider in high-cost tools and equipment may offset weak skill. The lesser experienced physician with access to a CAT scanner or nuclear magnetic imaging can accurately diagnose a patient's ailment that only a highly skilled colleague could otherwise correctly detect. Equipment can make up for lack of skill and, in exceptional cases, may increase the level of diagnostic skill. Alternatively, equipment may only raise cost and remove incentive to achieve skill. In medicine, overdependence on machines at the expense of skilled diagnosis could lead to lower quality at the same or higher cost. In nearly any custom or short-run job where economies of scale are unavailable, the skilled craftsperson or professional using unspecialized, conventional tools effectively will produce a higher level of quality at lower cost than the unskilled service provider using expensive equipment.

The relationship between service cost and service quality deserves all the emphasis we can give it. The trade-off between cost and quality of service is seldom one where higher cost significantly increases quality. That is likely to be the rarity. High skill and low cost are the expected combination that produces consistent high-service quality. Service skill is seldom visible to the customer, though. Where it is found, its detection requires experience and sharp observation by the customer. Often, only those inside the trade or profession know who the real skill leaders are.

THE SERVICE OUTPUT RESULT

Where service is subject to variation in the output result, the quality of the result will be an important dimension of service quality. There are significant opportunities for variation in the output result in services like hospitals, physicians, stockbrokerage advice, counseling, entertainment and personal services of almost every kind. The reliability of equipment, level of staffing, acceptability of food, sterilization of operating room equipment and comfort of rooms may be subject to variability in a hospital. Physicians are better or lesser skilled, make good referrals and comfort patients in distress with varying levels of personal effectiveness. Stockbrokers advise soundly for the client's profit or advise aggressively to increase their commissions. Counselors are quacks and geniuses. Entertainment connects and illuminates, merely distracts or falls flat. Personal service of basic human need is either appropriate and sensitive or mechanical and off the mark.

The range of possibilities in output result are variable and important. Service supplier skill and design of the service delivery system are the most consistent sources of output result variation. For hospitals and investment houses, sound management that assures an effective system of incentives and controls is fundamental to service quality. Physicians' and stockbrokers' reputations depend on the open record of their success. Counselors should be rated on the improvement of their clients. Pure personal service in the form of beauty shops, realtors, restaurants and police protection can be measured by the satisfaction of their customers. Police are measured by their success at apprehending criminals.

CUSTOMIZATION OF SERVICE

In the context of present-day mass commodity operations thinking, customization does not occur without an increase in operating cost. In the context of project shop operations thinking, there is no reason, given sufficient tools, skill, know-how and system support, why custom service must be uneconomic compared to mass commodity service. It is likely to be more valuable and perhaps more cost-effective too. It is mostly a matter of perspective.

Even where added expense is inevitable, cost increases need not be major. Cost can be graduated and incremental to represent increases in value to the customer generated by customization. Ultimately, as commodities become universally available and constitute the foundation of production and service alike, they serve as the cost-minimized foundation of customized service where it is customization that adds the major value. Mass commodity production is driven to the lowest possible cost with the lowest acceptable profit margin because there is minimal economic risk in it and because anybody with the price of machinery can enter the game. Used machinery becomes widely available at bargain prices, know-how in production is common and anyone with requisite operations management skill can make a good and secure living. All the excitement and high profit potential, however, has migrated into customization. The doctrine that cost control is limited to mass commodity production serves only to prevent discovery of the cost reduction devices that apply to customized production and service.

Standardization must finally give way to customization. Insurance companies today offer customized packages that meet the needs of small companies at a level once available only to megacorporations. Banks differentiate their accounts and services to fit the life-styles of various customer segments. Substance abuse counseling is targeted by age, career path and socioeconomic status. TV and movies seek an ever more varied format with an increasing variety of specific offerings to match the entertainment hot buttons of the widest possible variety of viewers. Churches and social and service clubs become increasingly dissimilar to one another, reflecting the character of their immediate membership more fully, following the standards of their umbrella hierarchy organization less often and less strictly. The custom needs of the individual customer are increasingly the measure of service quality.

The highest good in service is not necessarily always the one-of-a-kind offering. Small, homogeneous groups enhance service in some settings. Service is unique in its use of grouping as a device for customizing offerings incrementally. Marketing of any noncommodity, differentiated product or service relies on a variant of grouping for its success—segmentation of the market. It is customization of service that leads to customer grouping in segments.

Education and counseling are cornerstone illustrations of groups as devices for achieving efficiency in the delivery of service to customers. These services can readily enough be delivered on a strictly individual basis. Learning can be tutored just as counseling can be carried out one-on-one. Both, however, achieve economies of scale and gain effective advantage from the social benefits available in a grouped customer setting. Group counseling, for instance, provides a normative base of comparison—"I'm not alone, other people share my problem"—and the emotional support available from empathic nonprofessional companions. Schooling gains a similar normative comparison, but one of competitive quality where students compare their performance with one another and strive to match the highest standard in their group.

The power of grouping to serve effectively and control cost simultaneously is in the similarity of group needs and interests. If common ground is not easily found, participants may gain little value from listening to one another or find little help in describing their distress. The counseling group must share similar problems and backgrounds that enable its members to relate to one another easily and naturally. The pain of isolation is one of the greatest pathologies of some diseases. Group counseling sometimes enjoys so powerful and unique a learning product in its own right, indeed, that one-on-one counselors find it desirable to apply a blend of individualized and group counseling to their clients. The social benefits of group process are unobtainable anywhere except within a group of people with similar problems and needs.

Education further illustrates the power of sound grouping versus the failure of poor classification of students. It has been public policy since the 1960s to democratize American education by mixing students with diverse kinds of cultural background and educational aptitude in the same classes. The ideal of mass commodity education that delivers the same learning product to every student has dominated education in the United States for fully a generation of students. It has been implemented in public policy through heterogeneous grouping of students designed to maximize the differences in student social background. The result has been increased mediocrity of education as measured by the highly respected Scholastic Aptitude Test (SAT) used by colleges as the measure of aptitude for higher education. A sixty-point average drop nationally in SAT scores has been documented in the span of twenty-five years during which public education has been mass-produced.

In the same term of experience, schools that have carefully classed students by ability and aptitude in each specific subject area have continued to achieve high results in their students' learning scores. Any experienced classroom teacher can tell you why this occurs. Too broad a range of ability makes it impossible to meet the needs of all students in a class. The teacher can either ignore the least able in favor of the best, as was the policy in the first two-thirds of the twentieth century, or ignore the most able in favor of the least. The latter strategy serves the democratic ideal admirably but does so by diluting the standard against which the classroom compares its performance. The worst of all possible worlds in this arrangement is to give every student a *little* help, so that no student has the opportunity to discover his or her true level of ability. Students learn and grow faster if classed with their intellectual and social peers. The greater the similarity of background and learning readiness among members of the group, the closer the service offering can come to customization. Only by giving up the democratic ideal of group diversity can greater customization be achieved in education and counseling.

For services that are inherently individualized like the professional and personal services professions, customization is at the maximum when delivered individually. The potential for individualized customization is at least as vast as the number of living human beings. Assuming that individual tastes are subject to change, it approaches infinity. The present-day fragmentation of personal service in restaurant, beauty shop, real estate, health club, counseling and entertainment industries reflects the demand of customers for personalized, customized service in these arenas. A mass commodity offering in any of them is unstable. McDonald's, for instance, has been forced to differentiate its menu to a length ten times its original, simple hamburger and fries offering. To survive, it must differentiate its product offering and partially customize it to fit the customer, as all of these industries must. Failure to offer personalized service means the demise of a business in these industries.

At its minimum, customization begins with knowing and using a customer's name. Calling the customer by name communicates appreciation of his or her unique individuality. It evokes a reciprocal respect in the form of the presumption that if you care enough to extend individual recognition of identity, the customer at a minimum owes you a hearing for what you have to say. The context in which the customer's name is used is important, though. Cold telemarketing calls to the customer's home that routinely start with use of the customer's name then immediately ask "how are you today?" sound phony and immediately raise a credibility barrier with many. Polite, respectful formality is more often appropriate. Where there is no basis for the service provider to be on a cordial personal basis, that basis must be founded first. It is essential to show respect for the customer's privacy at the outset of a cold contact and to maintain a proper social distance. If common ground for exploration of mutual interest can then be found, the relationship can develop on an individualized basis from there.

Customers are usually ambivalent about offering information in personal domains. A ground of acceptance and trust must be established before sensitive questions are broached. But they also want to be known, accepted and appreciated as individuals, and may even be fearful of being lost in the crowd. A skilled service provider will be alert to the small cues that indicate issues of personal commitment or interest. She or he will make good inferences and sound guesses about the customer's background and his or her areas of strong personal concern. Beginning from knowledge about subject areas of strong personal involvement, the skilled service provider can encourage the customer to volunteer large quantities of significant personal information.

A good service provider must be a skilled listener when the customer unloads with volumes of background information. Key facts must be grasped quickly and accurately. Details may have to be reconfirmed later, but the basic story must be heard and understood as it unfolds. There may be no second chance. In some circumstances it will be appropriate to take notes while the information flows. In others, it will appear overly formal and inappropriate to take notes. The service provider must judge appropriately when to write down information supplied as it is given and when to wait until later to make a record of the conversation. Sensitive, interested encouragements, signs of warm approval in response to personally sensitive revelations, questions and comments that reflect listening and understanding will all help develop the relationship and yield information about the customer. An informal setting such as a coffee break or customer reception can be effective in creating a climate for casual conversation and broad information exchange. Beyond using the customer's name respectfully and appropriately, listening intently, attending to the customer's story, demonstrating interest in and attentiveness to that story are the next important steps to discovering how to customize the service offering appropriately. The service provider who really doesn't care about fitting the service to the customer reveals it at this stage of service delivery by not listening.

When the customer is a real, unique individual to the service provider, it is time to examine the opportunities for meeting the customer's unique personal needs. It is not necessary to go to elaborate lengths. A customized detail here and there will often be enough to start. That will provide foundation for specific direct questioning about customer preference. But it is a serious mistake to become the expert and leap to categorical conclusions about what the customer wants and needs just on the basis of the information gathered to this point. True, accurate customization includes the customer's inputs in the service design process. The service provider asks what aspects of the service are right as they now stand, which need change, what is the preferred pattern in the whole. Then after it has been tried out as designed, is the service what the customer expected? Are there unexpected aspects that need reconsideration? At this point, customization becomes an ongoing dialogue in which information is continually being exchanged about service expectations and preferences. As the exchange progresses, the cost implications of customization, along with any emerging customer needs and related opportunities for service, can be explored.

The quality of service customization is a function of the skill of the service provider in developing the service relationship to this level of mutual trust and communication. Product customization can sometimes be handled as a branching decision process where preferences at successive stages of product design are chosen. Service does not lend to mechanical choice of preferences. Quality is a direct function of the communicative relationship established between service provider and customer. The service skills that lend to development and maintenance of that relationship must be developed by the effective customizer of quality service. Ultimately, it is the quality of the service relationship that assures maximum useful customization of the offering to the individual customer.

LEADERSHIP IN TECHNOLOGY DEVELOPMENT

Some services are sought out simply because they utilize the leading edge of technology. In part, this is the result of the customer's interest in novelty or innovation. The accelerated pace of technological change is one of the more exciting events of the current age. In no more than a single life span, many now living have seen the dawn of personal autos, nuclear energy, television, electronic computers, jet-powered aircraft and space travel to the moon. It has been a dizzying ride that shows no signs of slowing. The twentieth century was ushered in at the great Chicago World's Fair as a century of progress for mankind. Be it viewed as progress or not, there has been dramatic and massive technological advance in this brief span of human history. Following new developments in technology is a major form of entertainment for many.

There are practical reasons, also, for seeking out products and services on the cutting edge of progress. Progress has reduced the quantity of human labor required to secure the basics of life and, in doing so, has greatly increased our comfort and leisure. As a labor saver, technology has revolutionized life and business competition. The computer alone made possible the multinational megacorporation. The sheer cost of controlling the finances of a major corporation at the conclusion of World War II to meet Securities and Exchange Commission standards was an absolute barrier to further growth. Veritable armies of clerks were employed to process financial documentation and accumulate the required records. Months of time were required to turn out an annual profit and loss statement. The computer replaced most of the clerks and shrank the time from transaction to financial report to the time required for data entry into the system. Bar codes and computers in the workplace have subsequently reduced that time lag to minimum. One manager connected to the computer in a remote office anywhere in the world can follow, minute by minute, the transactions of an entire multi-billion-dollar corporation with a touch of the finger to a button. Banks, insurance companies, hospitals, communications systems, TV and cable, transport companies, architects, engineers, libraries and a host of other service industries today cannot function cost-effectively without computer support in handling data.

Technology applied to the instrumentation of science and medicine represents an ongoing tidal wave of technological innovation. New instruments, new materials, new methods are introduced monthly that reduce labor, increase measurement accuracy, speed discovery. Ultrasound and nuclear magnetic imaging were unknown at mid-twentieth century. Today they are indispensable to the practice of medicine. The only electronics in the physician's office of 1930 were in the telephone. Today they are everywhere.

Communication and entertainment have participated fully in the revolution of technology. Photographic film has in many cases given way to magnetic videotape. Voice and data signals bounce off satellites to remote parts of the earth. Special effects create animated images automatically with minimal assistance from the human artist. Performers are amplified to reach the ears of tens of thousands in a vast stadium or open field.

Transport systems are continuously being improved as new problem-identifying and problem-solving technology are applied. Train tracks are electronically tested for weakness. Automatic collision warning systems are installed into commercial aircraft. The weather around an airport is continually monitored by radar and computer models for emerging hazard. The new and technologically advanced in transport is assumed by all to be safer, better, more comfortable by nearly all its customers.

Police departments demand the newest weaponry and communications electronics. Advanced systems for identifying suspects and stolen autos speed action to preserve public safety. Fire fighters employ the newest safety gear and methods to permit more effective, less hazardous performance of their job. The military, a grand example of security service, unveils an aircraft invisible to radar and a spectacularly successful anti-missile missile in its prosecution of the Gulf War. More than twenty military personnel far from the battlefront are killed when a glitch in the antimissile software control system fails to stop an incoming enemy missile, thereby tragically underscoring our dependence on sound technological innovation for our present safety.

Even in health and recreation services, new, more cost-effective, more health-efficient equipment is introduced each year. Better materials for surfacing the racquetball court, improved steam room temperature control, a new whirlpool bath system, better weight training equipment, electronically monitored exercise machines that tone upper and lower body muscles simultaneously—the list is endless.

For better or worse, technology is part of this new way of life. Much new technology has the potential to reduce cost and/or improve the quality of service offerings directly. Adequate testing of new technology is sometimes lacking before it is widely introduced into the market, but eventually the test is obtained in use if in no other way. The quality of service may sometimes be reduced by advanced technology but, more often, it will be enhanced. The presumption continues to be in favor of technological advance, even when there are some risks. Each realm of service must measure the utility and added quality of each new technological advance for its industry and customers.

SERVICE RELIABILITY

Reliability of service is a relatively straightforward dimension of service quality. For most it is a simple matter of counting the frequency of failures and mistakes made in the process of delivering service. Insurance companies, banks, accountants, stockbrokers and hospitals can and should be measured against the number of mistakes made per standard number of transactions or customers. Communications and entertainment delivery systems are reliable to the extent that they are working or inoperative. Police, fire fighters and emergency personnel are reliable to the extent of the promptness of their response to call. Personnel service providers are reliable if they listen carefully and successfully identify the customer's wishes. Hotels and restaurants are reliable when they honor reservations consistently. Professionals are reliable if they keep their contracts and commitments to their clients.

While there are varied shades of reliability in different corners of service, most failures can be classified in terms of whether they represent either insufficient capacity, limited skill or poorly designed support systems. The computer systems that support vital records for insurance companies, banks, accountants, stockbrokers and hospitals can be designed with built-in checks and audits that improve the system. Data that are heavily used and/or quickly fed back to suppliers are subject to continuous audit. Performance quality that is continuously audited is improved. Errors that are tolerated multiply. System design is critical to service quality.

Reliability of communications systems and electronically transmitted entertainments are partially a systems issue, partially a capacity issue. The system must usually be redesigned to use excess or backup capacity that will take over in the event of breakdown in the primary system element. The on-board backup computer that delays a space shuttle launch, for instance, is a commonly reported phenomenon of our age. Redundancy of systems design that builds in excess capacity increases reliability and overcomes the hazard of breakdown in substantial degree. The local cable TV service may also have a backup computer to assure continuity of service.

Reliable promptness of response on the part of police, fire fighters and emergency personnel is simultaneously a problem of systems support and service capacity. The undermanned police department will respond less quickly to emergency. But the police department with a personnel allocation system that can instantly identify an officer who should be diverted from low-priority to high-priority assignment may offset its capacity limitations in some degree. Where excess fire or emergency personnel at the scene of one call can be instantly identified and reallocated to a new emergency, service capacity limitations can be overcome.

Consistent availability of hotel or restaurant reservations is always a function of capacity for service, but can be significantly improved by implementation of a well-designed system for monitoring capacity availability and reservations. The same is true of airline reservations. Competent forecasting, careful assessment of the probabilities and a generous built-in margin for error (excess capacity) can all improve service.

All of these services can expand capacity further by increasing the skill of service suppliers and system operators. This is particularly true of personal service suppliers. The skilled beautician, waitress or repair technician can increase his or her customer load in busy times without personal strain or loss in quality of service.

Reliability as an element of high-quality service is improved through attention to support system design, available capacity utilization and service supplier skill and by appreciating that these three quality sources have the potential to enhance and offset one another when skillfully managed as a quality nexus. Each must be considered and evaluated in the context of the other two to achieve the highest level of quality.

AESTHETIC APPEAL

Is quality in the eye of the beholder? Well, maybe not entirely so, but the first impact is often visual and aesthetic. Where it is unattractive, there may not be a second look. Insurance companies and banks, otherwise mundane and unexciting businesses, strive for recognition through distinctively attractive logos and impressive looking structures in which to house their operations. An image of stability and trustworthiness is basic to attracting customers. The offices of professionals may be furnished and decorated to convey the image of quiet dignity and comfort, of up-to-date modernity or of exceptional power and success. The professional's wardrobe may be chosen for the style and image statement desired.

Hotels and restaurants depend heavily on the ambiance of the building and its aesthetic appeal to attract customers. Once inside, the aesthetics of table appointments, server uniforms, food presentation, room decor and overall cleanliness will have their impact on customers' sense of service quality. Transport systems decorate their equipment to suggest comfort, stability or excitement in the provision transport. Amtrak attempts to evoke national pride in its passenger rail system through red, white and blue colors on shining stainless steel cars.

The aesthetics of entertainment often dazzle and overawe its customers. Costumes, props, colors and textures are used in abundance to capture the senses and create an impression. Music is sometimes the background, sometimes the foreground of entertainment aesthetics. Extravagant sounds and sights that assault and capture the senses are standard fare.

Indeed, much of the character of entertainment is found in its aesthetics. Like the aesthetics of professions and institutions that are the bait that lures the customer to the substance of the service, entertainment strives first to capture the attention of the customer so that the story message it conveys will be apprehended. Aesthetics focus and hold the customer's attention. They permit the service of entertainment to be delivered quickly, efficiently and painlessly. Sometimes the aesthetics are more interesting than the substance of the entertainment. When that happens, the aesthetics themselves can lower the quality of service. Aesthetics are a powerful attention-capturing and -focusing device that, in the absence of underlying substance or in the presence of poor substance, may become the entertainment itself. In this form it is more accurately termed a distraction or diversion.

Aesthetics have the power to set a mood or emotional tone to any given situation. Within the context of mood, many messages take on added emphasis. The mood alone can lend to self-generated reveries and day-dreams. Abstract art and music are especially useful in this respect. Pure distraction, on the other hand, can shut out everything else. When it is sufficiently riveting of consciousness, it diverts from contemplation, it prevents and impedes understanding, replacing these with an almost primitive mass consciousness ready to follow any compelling command to action. The event sometimes takes on the character of mass hypnosis or an intense religious experience. The quality of the service offering may now be debated as a question of aesthetics and service ethics.

Judging the quality of aesthetics as a contribution to service provision is a complex matter. Where it focuses the senses to enable connection with the customer's experience, it supports communication. But the product is not the aesthetics, it is the message carried on the aesthetically tuned signal. It is easy to confuse the medium with the message and conclude, as did Marshall McLuhan, that the medium is the message (or "the medium is the massage," as he once punned). The quality of entertainment is more properly found in the intensity of communicative connection effected with the customer. The aesthetics that package the message are the wrapping, not the product. When the aesthetics themselves become the central service offering, the service is some form of distraction or diversion. The utility of diversion may be debated and questioned. Its quality is simply found either in its success as a liberator from the immediate and mundane pursuits of life or in the power of the message the entertainment sends.

PRIORITIES OF SERVICE QUALITY

The ultimate quality of service is a function of many ongoing factors and forces. Cost, performance output, customization, technological innovation, reliability and aesthetic appeal are the outward manifestations of quality for most service offerings. It is in the final blend of these characteristics that the summary quality of each will be, in some part, determined. The same category of service can emphasize many different dimensions of quality, including these and others from earlier chapters. A hotel can offer high customized service and limited aesthetic attraction or be aesthetically dazzling and limited in service personalization. The former may fit the quality requirements of one customer, the latter those of another. Taxi drivers may specialize in finding the quickest route to the destination or offering informative conversation. The priorities of service quality will often describe market niches in which service providers can best implement their special skill and know-how.

Competition in service, though, must eventually press service institutions and service providers to encompass increasing dimensions of quality in each service offering. Quality is many different things, some occasionally competing with one another, others merely difficult to combine, some even enhancing of one another. Thought and care must be given to the pattern of service offered to assure the highest possible quality. The competition for quality excellence in service can only escalate. It will inevitably demand more skill, energy and examination. May the best competitors succeed!

Chapter 13

Measuring Service Quality

"Hard specs are awkward and satisfaction is an elastic gauge, but where there is a will, there is a way to measure."

It is rare today to find clear specifications for service. There is, for instance, a characteristic unwillingness to establish clear specifications for service and commit to meeting them in the professions. Because of the price, many patients today demand clear specifications for medical procedures from their physicians. But doctors know better than to make any promises that could be interpreted as a commitment to full success. The lawyer disclaims any certainty of winning the case. Stockbrokers and realtors carefully avoid any clear statements that could be taken as certain commitments. The typical professional avoids commitment to specifics in the outcome for fear of falling short of expectations established and thereby becoming subject to malpractice suits or other retaliation. As we will see in the discussion of customer satisfaction that concludes this chapter, the safe strategy, if the service provider can get away with it, is to promise only the absolute minimum service result to the customer.

The absence of specifications in service is not necessarily the result of inability to establish them. It is often more the result of avoiding their establishment so that low to average quality is defined as an acceptable outcome. The service supplier who sets specifications establishes a standard against which the customer can measure service. Establishing explicit and measurable levels of service quality means that customers will know what they are getting and will be better positioned to negotiate price or demand higher quality. That makes the job of the service provider much tougher and may sometimes reduce his or her status with the customer. That could tarnish one's reputation for expertise. It is just easier to avoid explicit service standards until after service is rendered. This approach, unfortunately, lets the customer judge the quality of service for him- or herself, discourages excellence of service quality on the part of the service provider and leaves service quality generally languishing in a state of limbo.

ESTABLISHING SERVICE SPECIFICATIONS

Specifications that support sound measurements can be established for virtually any service offering. The major barrier to setting specifications is the presumed advantage of having *none*. In the absence of any standard of service quality, quality is either in the eye of the customer and/or whatever the service provider says it is. Setting specifications for the customer to see in advance invites negotiation from the customer that might lower price and/or raise quality specifications. Whether this is the fair and equitable thing to do or not is an independent issue. Clear service quality specifications put the service provider on record. Going public with clear specifications is inconvenient to the service provider and limits his or her flexibility. The rational thing to do from the service provider's perspective is to avoid setting specs. Encounter with this line of reasoning is, perhaps, the surest measure of poor service quality in its own right. Overcoming it to improve service quality will not be easy.

The great variety of specifications and measures that are possible represents a central barrier to clear setting and measurement of service specifications. At best, a broad smorgasbord of specifications and options can be offered, many specific to a service or industry. Confronted with confusion and uncertainty, however, a little brainstorming can go a long way toward defining viable options. By category of service industry, here are some ideas.

Financial Institutions

Numerous opportunities exist to set service specifications in advance as standards of performance and as a competitive strategy in tough financial service markets. Banks, for instance, could set standards for customer waiting time in line for teller service or audience with an officer. Standards for consistency of use of the customer's name in personal or phone contacts, cheerful, smiling greetings and partings or full explanations for delays are often lacking. Banks spend many hours and dollars training personnel to cross-sell services but put very little investment in customer contact skills. Customer surveys or, simpler yet, sampling observations using the already-in-place video-cam security system would be simple, viable methods for measuring customer relations standards.

Insurance companies might measure customer perception of premium rate and claims handling fairness. Few claims departments use any systematic approach to measuring the skill and fairness with which third-party claims are adjusted, yet quality here often determines whether the claimant seeks out legal counsel or not and can color the public image of company fairness for better or worse. Speed of claims payment, quickness of policy delivery and ease with which changes in coverage are effected are all important indicators of quality. Errors in issuing policies, of course, are a basic quality measure. They should always be tracked with care.

Hospitals

Hospitals are easy targets for customer criticism. Both high cost and poor treatment are the basis of patient complaint. The major source of poor quality in a hospital arises out of the basic system through which medical service is delivered. Many doctors who practice in a hospital are not employees of the hospital. They function, nonetheless, as central decision makers in the patient's care. A physician who does not grasp the nuances of the hospital's service delivery system can easily make poor decisions that cannot be implemented, that are misunderstood in the context, or that are inappropriate at a later time when the doctor is no longer available. The patient who is awakened from a sound sleep to take a sleeping sedative is the victim of a doctor's too literally carried out, oversimplistic order. It might have read "only as needed" had the physician taken the time to consider possibilities and the temper of nurses on the floor. The broader quality measurement issue, of course, resides in whether high-quality medical care is measured by exact conformance to orders or by patient comfort and recovery rate. Present quality measures are fitted to the existing system and ignore much of the patients' perspective on quality. Until the system is restructured, there is little chance of constructive improvement in hospital service quality.

Food service in hospitals is typically centralized and overcontrolled to assure that physician-prescribed diets are strictly observed. The system, though, is often slow and ponderous to an inflexible fault. It is not uncommon for a change in the menu to require twenty-four-hours' notice. Patient preferences, once the physician has prescribed, are overridden on grounds of medical requirements, regardless of any real medical need. The systems employed are rigid. They are physician- or hospital-employee-oriented rather than patient-oriented. A hospital with genuine concern for quality of patient service must revolutionize the system. In the absence of willingness to invest in so large a change, the system and its outmoded measures of treatment remain a major barrier to improved service and the most common excuse for failing to provide genuine patient service. The most direct and rational change would be to permit patients, in all but the most critical of situations, to override doctors' orders and obtain immediate, direct, personal response from the system. Challenging the presumed omnipotence of the doctor and returning freedom of choice to patients would, unfortunately, represent heresy of sorts to the current practice of medicine.

Legislation may be required to overcome these barriers to change so as to permit customer service to come first in medicine. The average physician is capable only of prescribing the preferred or standard treatment and has no final powers of medical omniscience. Patients often know better about their own conditions and needs. If they don't, it is still their life and their choice. The traditional hospital system assures poor customer service by treating the patient as an irresponsible foreign object in its midst. It is a wonder that patients put up with this at all. A comprehensive national measure of patient satisfaction with hospital and physician care would undoubtedly disclose a devastating gap between current standards of medical quality and patient satisfaction with treatment.

There are a multitude of other dimensions on which hospitals can be measured if they are willing to focus on quality. Waiting lines for admission can be shortened and the admission process speeded. Discharge can be simplified. The rates of postoperative complications of *all* kinds can be recorded and studied using powerful statistical designs. Analysis of causes and establishment of quality goals can flow from those records. Administration of the wrong medicine can be rigorously investigated by a team of experts, and systems for prevention of these errors can be established out of the team's findings.

Hospitals are already top-heavy with administrative and record-keeping practices. Attention to systems design from a quality perspective is too often still lacking, though. Too much administration is focused on defensive control, too little on quality. The patient is the adversary of the system, not its customer. This is hardly the recipe for high-quality service.

Professionals

Professionals often use the cloak of expert knowledge to obfuscate the quality of the service they deliver. A central measure of professional quality service is truth and admission of ignorance. Real professional service is offered simply, directly, effectively. The physician who cannot say "I don't know" or "I'm stumped by your condition" is potentially dangerous. Professionals are too readily willing and eager to foster the belief that they have all the answers. Patients or clients often, foolishly but innocently, demand exact answers from doctors, lawyers and other professionals when only speculation is possible. Professionals who supply inappropriately exact answers may temporarily comfort the client's anxieties but fail to resolve their problems. Professionals certainly do not deliver quality service when they pretend to have all the answers.

Honesty and scope of experience are critical measures of professional service quality. Honesty begins with the professional's admission of limited expertise when the case is out of their domain of experience, which gives the customer the choice of accepting the service as offered, or of finding an alternative professional service giver. A pattern of dishonesty on the part of any professional *must* become public record for all customers to see. Theft, embezzlement, misrepresentation and malpractice by licensed professionals must be on the public record and made openly available to the public. Protecting the professional's reputation when the evidence is clear is the poorest quality of service a profession offers.

Specialists like surgeons and lawyers should be required to publish the record of their principal professional actions. The number of cases of a specific medical type handled, the frequency of success against an established, objective medical standard, the number of lawsuits won in front of a jury, the proportion of practice devoted to criminal cases, corporate law or real estate contracts, and so on, should be publicly available for potential customers to inspect. Dentists should publish a count of root canals performed or major bridgework done. Architects should be required to reveal the number and value of projects personally handled. Civil engineers might publish the proportion of time spent in land surveys, commercial structures, residential buildings, and the like. Pharmacists routinely take special measures to avoid mistakes in preparing prescription orders and some still make mistakes. Even flawless pharmaceutical performance can be measured against care in assuring that customer preferences for generic substitutions or childproof containers are obtained and matched. Those errors must be put on the public record.

Professionals devoted to high-quality service should certainly consider contracting with a public-relations firm or hiring an assistant who can survey clients to assess level of customer satisfaction with services rendered. In a dominantly service economy, competition may eventually require measures such as these as the basis of pricing. Honestly represented professional experience is the beginning of quality professional service.

The advertising industry competes for ad design awards that establish the quality of the largest agencies. Competition is sometimes extended downward to regional and local market levels where smaller firms can enter and demonstrate their creative talent. Many forms of advertising are measured in terms of orders by ad format and source. Phone-order customers are asked where they learned of the offering, order blanks contain ad codes, and some ads contain coupons surrendered by the customer to obtain a special price. These are available for count. Random sampling surveys to assess brand recognition follows up some ad campaigns. Advertising is in the beginning stages of becoming a quality measured service industry. Other industries could well model after it.

Stockbrokers seldom dwell on their bad recommendations. Their essential service, though, resides in providing information to their clients about the financial markets and recommending sound investments to them. The opportunity to document recommendations made and score their success is present. Investment newsletters invite just such comparison and are often priced to reflect the track record of success in predicting market events. Clearly, the value of investment advice is found in its accuracy and timeliness. Measurement is feasible and can support pricing decisions. Customers, though, are too often left to construct their own personal score sheet on brokers and brokerage firms. There is opportunity to substantially increase quality measurement here.

Personnel search and placement firms vary widely in the type and quality of skill brought to the task. Some prescreen intensively to assure quality of credentials and likelihood of job fit. Others merely send a large number of potentially qualified candidates through to the client to raise the odds that one or more will connect. They specialize, thus, either as good evaluators or good social directors. Customers must identify which service is offered. Sending large numbers of candidates expands choice but requires doing the job of evaluation in-house. Sending a select few simplifies the decision but insulates the firm from the broader job market potential. The service offered must be measured against the service delivered. Ultimately, the success of the service is measured by the success of the placement. Few placements are tracked beyond the first six to twelve months. That much, at least, is a good beginning on measuring the quality of this service but more should be attempted.

Organizational (i.e., corporate) staff are easily overlooked service providers in the broader economy. They are, nonetheless, important contributors to the service industry equation. The nature of the service they provide is frequently professional or quasi-professional in quality. A strong corporate staff, for instance, represents the highest levels available internally of those skills central to the organization's effectiveness. They are often the ultimate experts in their fields for their company's purposes and the final judges of its quality. In this role they are well-positioned to evaluate the quality of skill applied in their field by others in the organization and for coaching or training others to apply it better. Too often, though, they take over decision making in their area of knowledge, inappropriately usurping the decision-making opportunity and responsibility of those properly responsible for the decision on the premise that others are not qualified to make the highest quality decisions. This is a short-sighted view of quality that undercuts organizational accountability and often results in lower quality management decisions as well. Staff tends to envy the decision-making power of line managers and aspires to have its own domain of decision accountability. Conflicts with other domains of expertise that should be reconciled by the accountable decision maker can be quashed politically by the overly powerful experts to the detriment of organizational decision-making quality. The extent to which this is allowed to happen is a measure of the corruption of corporate decision-making processes.

Staff experts are staff experts because they look at only a very limited part of the total problem. The decision that is highest quality from the narrow perspective of the expert is often low quality for the organization. For the organization, the highest quality decision will be the one for which all possibly relevant expert points of view have been identified and included and where conflicts of value or perspective between expert positions have been reconciled. Even then, there may be need for competent managerial refereeing between mutually opposing expert positions where the call is close and experts will not yield their points. The quality of expert decision must not be judged on the limited basis of the experts' problem-solving methods.

The quality of most organizational systems and decisions is a direct function of the range of skill brought to their design and evaluation. It is the product of different points of view carefully blended and reconciled against the broader purposes of the organization. Missing a necessary expert input, permitting one staff expert's point of view or a limited coalition of staff expert points of view to dominate the end result, avoiding differences by compromising to block or bypass argument, all can result in low-quality decision outcome. The role of top management, indeed, is often properly *not* that of decision maker so much as it is that of referee to the organization's decision-making teams. The strongest measure of quality is likely to be the frequency of strong disagreement that is effectively resolved within those teams. Organizations and corporations particularly should track decision making and system design projects closely to measure the frequency (or infrequency) with which critical conflicts are handled openly, fairly, fully and conclusively.

Counselors

Personal counselors, like professionals, tend to avoid setting specifications on or even goals for their services, thereby preventing measurement of quality. Weight-loss counseling points to a few dramatic successes as evidence of success. The real measure, though, should be average success across all customers over a standard term of time and percentage of permanent stable weight loss. Success with addiction counseling is measured similarly, employing freedom from substance abuse over a standard period of time as the criterion of success.

Marriage counselors may have some difficulty deciding whether success is found in keeping the marriage together or assisting with a minimally destructive dissolution of the dysfunctional union. Some marriages should not persist. The harm to one or both parties as well as to children is greater in continued relations than in a clean break. Where both parties want reconciliation, success should be measured by the stability of a reconciliation. Where either is clearly opposed to reunion, success is a matter of a clean, equitable and minimally vindictive split. Ability to catalyze clear recognition of one or the other of these two states is an even more fundamental measure of professional quality.

Career planning counselors can measure success in terms of ease of placement in the desired career and correctness of diagnostic job fit prescribed. The best counseling services provide access to simulated or actual experience in the career field as a test of realism for the counselee's aspirations. Long-term measures of success in the field are difficult to obtain but should be pursued. Quality here is sometimes found more in the customer's satisfaction with career information and expanded experience with career opportunities than in merely entering the profession.

Pastoral and psychiatric counseling may be measured in a variety of ways. Classical psychotherapists may insist that the only correct measure of quality is in full discovery and description of the underlying psychological dynamics that drive the client's problem. This is on a par with keeping score of the number of cases solved by the detectives in a police department. If psychotherapists kept such score, and if there were some clear criterion of success in solving their cases, it could certainly be worthwhile to publish the result for patients to see and compare with the records of other therapists. Many psychiatric cases, unfortunately, are not solved, merely palliated. The measure of quality of service in those instances may be the degree of reduction of discomfort or distress, the elimination of inconvenient or antisocial symptoms and the client's overall satisfaction with the result obtained for the cost incurred. They should all be measured and made public.

Pastoral counseling is sometimes indistinguishable from a confessional to ease the conscience. Just the opportunity to unburden one's mind can be a significant service. There is ample precedent for definition of sound counseling as provision of a confidential, friendly and sympathetic ear. Pastors who operate in this role depend on free-will offerings and pledges to sustain their churches and salaries. The success of their counseling can best be measured in the financial success of their church. More specifically, the frequency with which those who come for counseling become members or become more active, generously giving members should be measured.

Communications

Communications like phone, postal delivery or MIS-based information systems are measurable for quality in terms of time and accuracy. Telephone service capacity is strictly established in terms of the waiting time for connection. Waiting for a phone dial tone is almost unknown in the United States. Where connection on the other end is to a computer or fax machine, service is measured in terms of the quickness of answer and connection in response to the call. Postal delivery is measured by the time lapse between mailing and receipt. Service time can often be measured and recorded exactly for these services. Where the system itself does not lend to direct measurement through the system, sampling of service time can be accomplished. System downtime is another dimension of service quality. Downtime is often a variation on waiting time. Systems design that avoids or offsets downtime can contribute measurably to improved service quality. Clear specifications for service and measures of results in all these terms should be routine for information services.

Accuracy of communication services is measured in terms of misconnections, misdeliveries and misinformation. Passing the job of establishing the connection on to the customer, as in phone dialing, does not wholly absolve the phone company of responsibility for accuracy. Even where it is the wrong key punched rather than a crossed wire, it is mostly system design that determines ease of use and likelihood of inaccuracy. Equipment must be simple and reliable. Measures of frequency of misdialing can be obtained by offering instant account credit for misdialed toll calls or by systematically surveying samples of customers to obtain data on misconnections or wrong numbers. Human factors research to establish the perceptual and hand-eye motor failures that lead to errors will improve system design. Sampling surveys can be used to determine the frequency of misdelivery of mail. Audits of MIS systems on a sample basis can establish the frequency of data errors in the system. These are all necessary and useful measures of communications service quality. All should be carried out.

Entertainment

The quality of entertainment services is most directly measured by the financial success of the entertainment offering. The message and its underlying experience either reaches the audience or it doesn't. Sales in one form or other measure the result. Whether it is the attractive/distractive power of the entertainment or its message that drives sales may not always be clear, though. The underlying quality of entertainment depends on which of these entertainment dimensions dominates the offering. The power of entertainment to inform, instruct and influence may be somewhat increased or attenuated by the popularity of the offering. The ability of entertainment to reach its audience heightens or mutes its message. The message itself may be constructive or destructive of social value quite independently of its attraction. Entertainment that lacks a message may be attractive solely in its ability to amuse and distract the audience, yielding no lesson at all. It is appropriate, then, to judge the quality of entertainment in terms of its redeeming social value as well as on the basis of its commercial success.

Critics and the media generally offer up qualitative evaluations of many entertainment offerings that may be useful in measuring its quality. Often, though, they are part of the entertainment industry, meshed in the industry nexus, swayed by its mystique and attuned to its commercial payoffs. Some limited help may be offered by published assessments of entertainment quality, but it may still be difficult to accurately assess the social value of the entertainment message. Industry ratings attached to movies warn of violence or explicit sexual themes. The result often is a careful balancing of the entertainment content so that it titillates sufficiently to attract but does not go so far as to offend grossly.

Totalitarian societies characteristically attempt to censor entertainment to fit social values and goals of its leaders. To some extent, the effort to shape the messages of entertainment with heavy-handed government controls does work. Inevitably, though, the oppressed message goes underground to partially evade control. Art is impossible to judge from a single standard. Censors are too often moral and intellectual mediocrities. Censorship too easily reveals the bad taste or poor judgment of the censors. It is a crude and overly narrow device for improving the quality of entertainment.

A major unmet need exists for qualitative evaluation of popular entertainment in the form of rock music, movies and television that does not depend on either censorship or industry prejudice. The educational system currently ignores the influence of these media on students unless it grudgingly employs them as adjuncts to standard subject matter presentations. Entertainment as applied cultural anthropology, revealing the values and yearnings of its audience, has yet to be adequately addressed by formal research and schooling at any level of learning, much less as an accepted academic discipline. The literature and the imagery of entertainment media are a mirror of current society into which we may look to see ourselves caricatured. Education must begin to address this opportunity for self-inspection if the quality of entertainment is to be made explicit, evaluated and improved. Entertainment is the single greatest adjunct and competitor to formal education. Neither can ignore the other. The impact of entertainment on education and the study of entertainment as a social force are worthy of our concern as major social issues. We must discover how to measure them.

Education

Public education has changed very little over 150 years of U.S. history. The major revolution was a radical deemphasis on traditional academics that began in the 1960s. Concern for subjective feelings was substituted for intellectual grasp of fact and concept in a large part of the public school system. It was a revolution born out of awareness of the lack of emphasis given intuitive human understanding by traditional academic learning processes. Students were sometimes described as educated only from the neck up in the former, traditional, academically orthodox systems of teaching. The new emphasis on subjective feelings, unfortunately, is subject to criticism on grounds it educates only from the neck down. Students have become more aware and sensitive to one another and to their differences as people. But they have become less knowledgeable of history and less skilled in the tools of intellect that allow them to understand a complex world or to make exacting choices. It is tragic because there is no need to sacrifice one for the other. Both objects can be sought and obtained in a sound educational system. Indeed, the fullest quality of education can never be achieved until both are integrated completely into the educational system and both are measured on their quality.

Unfortunately, the compromise that is made between intuitive sensitivity and intellectual depth in the new era of education fails to address adequately either the problems of society or the personal benefits of intellectual discipline. Tensions in the form of ethnic or racial conflict that widely characterize America's school systems today offer a measure of the system's inadequacy. Social awareness and human tolerance as taught in schools fail the critical quality test of application in the streets. English is often poor, oral and written expression are weak, logic-solving problems are limited among today's school graduates.

On almost any terms, the quality of education delivered is deficient, especially so when the cash cost paid by taxpayers is calculated. The academic quality of education is best measured by standardized tests like the Scholastic Aptitude Test or California Achievement Test. But the measures themselves are under attack. Testing is suspect in an educational system dedicated to human equality because it tends to differentiate students by class rather than level them as social equals. The possibility that both objectives could be sought in a sound educational system seems to be overlooked. Quality of education has fallen in measured, academic terms, certainly so as measured by instruments like the SAT. But a broad social parity among students has not been successfully produced to take its place when measured by prevailing social tension. The nation is denied quality of education on both counts. There is no reason why that result has to be accepted. The measures of educational failure are clear; we need only resolve to act upon them.

When it comes to getting along with one's fellows, for instance, sound methods for teaching teamwork and improving interpersonal interaction exist but are not applied in the learning process early or intensively enough. The technology available in social psychology for lessening intergroup tension is well-documented and widely available. It is not part of most current education systems because those systems have not been redesigned to include it. The structure of education that was designed nearly a century ago to support orthodox academic learning is misapplied to social learning needs with attendant poor results.

In education, it is the system that produces consistent low quality. There is still need to measure academic achievement in the traditional ways with standardized achievement tests. There is also urgent need to measure social attitudes and achievement with the methods and instruments that can be applied. A regular score sheet on the incidence of ethnic or racial conflict must be kept in every school and community. Without measures in place the failure of the system is not apparent. Pressure must be kept on the system for early, radical redesign that supports academic and social objectives with equal effectiveness.

Transport

Quality in public transit is measured by on-time performance, cleanliness of the vehicle, reliability of equipment, safe operation and courtesy of operators or support personnel. Nothing quite punctuates poor quality like consistently late arrivals due to unforeseen delays. Delays are unavoidable in public transport. They can be ignored or managed. Most delays have a common cause. Airlines must deal with heavy traffic or bad weather. Heavy traffic is often the result of inadequate capacity—too many small aircraft with small passenger loads using limited runway space. Weather delay can be overcome by investing in the right navigational equipment. Quality is, again, largely a function of the design of equipment and systems. The system must be measured for its adequacy and performance.

Railroads, buses, taxis and limos can be subjected to preventive maintenance, or, as often is preferred today, maintained only when they break down (failure maintenance). The customer is always inconvenienced first and most by the breakdowns. The pressure to meet customer demand by spreading available equipment capacity too thin, then having no-fall back equipment, leads to disastrous service. The rental of a competitor's equipment or capacity is sometimes the only viable solution to the breakdown. As with every form of service dependent on physical plant or equipment, care must be taken to assure that there is ample excess capacity available at all times. Maximizing capacity use of plant and equipment is inevitably the route to poor service quality. Otherwise, service must be on time, rendered according to commitment and courteous. It is measured by frequency of adherence to schedule, speed of response to customer call, cleanliness, infrequency of breakdowns and customer comfort.

Personal Service

Measurement of personal service quality necessarily begins with the level of availability of skilled or experienced personnel who deliver the desired service. Capacity for service is fundamental to quality of service. Barbers and beauticians can work on either an appointment or a walk-in basis. Appointments are required by those service providers who are in heavy demand. An appointment system permits the service provider to utilize his or her labor time efficiently or near fully. Any personal service that typically exceeds 75% demand on scheduled service time probably needs to work on an appointment basis. Even here, though, there will be gaps in the schedule that could optionally be filled with walk-in demand. From the customer's point of view, greater convenience is offered if it is possible to drop in for service on impulse, unless the waiting queue on arrival is lengthy and delay for service long. The quality of service offered is greatly influenced by the quality of operating decisions made regarding capacity availability and use of appointments. Attempts to fill service capacity to as near 100% as possible with customers will inevitably create delays and inconvenience for customers. Scheduling to provide on-demand service without waiting typically requires 50% or more excess service capacity above demand. Balancing the countervailing forces of customer demand verus excess service capacity demands high-quality operations management judgment, regularly tested against customer satisfaction.

Realtors typically operate at a very high level of excess capacity for customer service. The absence of a service provider in the realty industry almost certainly means that the customer will go elsewhere. Realtor waiting time is filled with odd jobs and personal study. The realtor waits patiently for the customer. The customer arrives in his own good time. There are few appointments here and service is almost always available on demand. Quality of service in realty will more often be measured by the quality of client referrals for technical or financing assistance and the resolution of differences between buyer and seller.

Tailors and seamstresses are advantaged in that the largest part of their time is production independent of their customers' presence. They need only divert briefly to attend to the fitting when the customer arrives. There is seldom a wait or a need for an appointment. Ample time is available for customer service, though too many customers can still stress capacity toward the maximum and result in slow delivery of the finished item.

Health clubs, recreation facilities, hotels and motels all require extensive physical plant capacity to serve their customers. It is limitation on this capacity that constrains service capability most severely. Good operations management requires that physical capacity be as near maximum anticipated demand as possible. If it is not, competition is invited to fill the unmet demand of customers. At maximum capacity demand, customers experience some inconvenience or diminishment in service, but they are, nonetheless, still served. Reservations systems are employed to handle maximum demand situations fairly and smoothly. At demand below maximum, walk-ins without reservations are welcomed and served easily. It is then essential that service labor be scheduled efficiently to meet customer demand without needlessly raising variable operating cost. Fixed costs for maintenance of the physical plant also must be kept low in support of a competitive break-even point for operations. We are again faced with a capacity trade-off situation where the quality of management judgment in establishing and adjusting capacity for service is critical to cost and to service quality. The measure of quality service is in its availability at a competitive or attractive cost.

The easy way out with personal services of every kind is to offer capacity at a level of excess that virtually assures instant service on the customer's demand, and to cover the cost with premium pricing. Combined with a few touches of luxury to help justify the high price, this service attracts the customer to whom cost is little concern but who expects instant attention upon arrival. When delays occur, the customer is distracted by entertainment of some appropriate sort. The personal service process itself is often converted into an entertainment where the customer plays the role of "star." The core service offering itself may be of high to below-average quality. The provision of a luxury offering conveys the impression of quality and sometimes masks low quality. Price is seldom a reliable measure of high-quality personal service. The same service offering at considerably lower price will often be superior in quality from alternative suppliers. Cost/capacity trade-offs are fundamental to high-quality personal service and require industrywide study and standards for measurement of quality to be improved. The best personal service is quick, moderately priced and highly customized.

Restaurants are a variant on personal service that demand the right customer capacity decisions and must also offer a high-quality, perishable commodity in the form of wholesome, nutritious food. All the dimensions of personal service plus a few added ones are represented in food service. Measurement of quality is complicated to the maximum here. Customer waiting time for service must be minimized. Waits may sometimes be made easier with entertainment, including self-entertainment in the bar or lounge. Capacity is critical, especially at peak demand times. Personalized attention is expected and central to food service. Many orders are customized to the customer's exact requirements. The food itself must be attractive, tasty and healthy. Putting it all together is a major operations management feat. Restaurants that do it well are successful. Those that do it poorly are quickly out of business. There is little way to avoid measurement of quality in this industry.

Capacity for service is the foundation of price and pace of food service. Fast-food is served at minimum price almost instantly. Family diners serve up the order in minutes, while high-cost tray-service restaurants specialize in extended, leisurely dining. Price is heavily influenced by the service capacity levels demanded by each type of service. The fast-food attendant can serve hundreds of customers per hour, the diner waitress handles several score per hour, the tray service restaurant waiter may handle five to fifteen per hour. The difference in capacity utilization is amply reflected in the price, and the quality of service is more properly measured by the appropriateness of the service offered.

Menus will also vary by level of service but will be matched to the tastes of customers all the same. When customers demand a change of menu, the restaurant, be it fast-food or luxury service, will accommodate them. Quality of food served can be as high or higher in the fast-food offering as in tray service. The care that goes into selection and preparation methods for food in McDonald's, Wendy's or Kentucky Fried Chicken is often equal to that found in the finest French restaurant. The quality of the food itself is basic to competitive success at all levels and in all styles of food service. Style of food service differentiates the social level of function of the restaurant. Clever management of capacity is the largest factor in differentiating pricing between them.

Public Service

Public service agencies in the form of police or security services, fire fighters, refuse handlers and others perform the dangerous and difficult services demanded by civilized society. Police in the larger cities once operated as personal service providers, accepting fees and gratuities for special attention, directly intervening on an informal level to resolve disputes within communities or neighborhoods. Quality of service was then measured in personal service terms. Abuses in this service that favored the police's good, paying customers led to rules that restrain police to act in a more bureaucratically formal manner in our current age. Quality of police service is now measured by the extent to which the community's problems are effectively handled within the rules. On many occasions, the rules effectively prevent any service other than putting a report on file. Personalized service is limited to offering sympathy to the upset or the injured victim.

Police service, stripped of its personalized qualities, is more equitable and just to all concerned, but it provides far less protection and satisfaction to the average citizen. Rigorous pursuit of justice for the underclass has greatly reduced the safety of the average citizen. It is, in fact, highly efficient for police to assume that any poorly dressed, suspicious-acting young male, especially one from the underclasses of society, spells trouble for the community. It is reasonable to assume that anyone without a visible economic role in society is more likely to turn to crime. When officers of the law could freely play these odds and act on their independent judgment as to the hazard they represented to public safety, there was noticeably more control and safety within the community. In terms of public safety, police service was much higher in quality. In terms of justice and equity to all, though, it was much lower. Society today is torn by the choice that is offered in competing forms of police service quality. Which offers the greater quality of service: equality under the law or public safety with increased police discretion and presence?

Society is radically split on this question. This conflict between antagonistic objectives reduces the quality of police service at the outset. But in strict quality terms, neither is an acceptable measure of police service quality. It is the conflict itself that measures the poor quality of police service. Until a solution to this conflict is found and implemented, there can never be high-quality police service in our communities.

Fire fighters, by contrast, have a clear public service mission. The effectiveness of fire fighting service is readily measured. It is mostly a matter of speed of response and skill in handling the conflagration. Continuous training fits nicely around the on-call scheduled nature of this profession, and it is fundamental to quality fire fighting service. The average response time from alarm to arrival on site still can be measured, and postmortems of every fire that identify successes and mistakes can be regularly conducted.

Regrettably, the legal contentiousness of many present-day citizens may discourage honest, thorough documentation of both police and fire fighter performance in some communities, impairing accurate measurement of service. Police and fire fighters should be exempted from legal challenge for action in the line of duty unless guilty of gross misconduct. Society does not benefit from casual harassment heaped on its public servants, even though that harassment may well be a measure of the public's dissatisfaction with quality of service delivered.

Trash collectors, street cleaners, road repair personnel and other public service providers can and should be measured in terms of their productivity. Pounds of refuse moved, miles of streets cleaned, number of repairs effected and quickness of response to public emergencies are all suitable measures of service quality. Cost-effectiveness of service delivery is also an appropriate measure of quality. The policy of gathering and publishing these measures need only be established and enforced to raise service quality in all these areas.

Service Agencies

Finally, the realm of pure service as provided by churches, lodges, fraternities, social organizations and service clubs deserves to be addressed. The quality of these services is measured in two ways. First is the number of paying members who are active in the organization's service, and the rate of member turnover. Second is the hours of service performed on behalf of the community and the objective record of results from this service time.

The record of hours and results need only be kept and documented. Membership and membership turnover is a measure of the quality of organization and operations management. It is closely analogous to number of customers and rate of customer turnover in profit-making businesses.

IMPROVED MEASUREMENT METHODS FOR SERVICE

Turnover is regularly measured among paid employees of commercially oriented organizations. It is seldom measured in voluntary organizations. It is only infrequently measured for general customer populations. For some services it is possible to maintain exact records of customers. Professionals, counselors, personal services, business services, communications services, insurance companies, banks and hospitals *know* who their customers are. It is feasible to track their use of the service over time with precision. Customers who disappear for extended periods can be contacted by phone or mail to determine if there has been a problem with service quality. Most businesses find that it is many times more expensive to develop new customers than to keep old ones. Special efforts to preserve the customer base and measure change in it are sound investments. Pure service organizations with voluntary memberships should follow the same policy of working harder to keep existing members than trying to find new ones. Churches with high turnover, for instance, usually have someone of importance, often the pastor or priest, whose interpersonal abilities are seriously deficient. It is worth taking note of who may be chasing members away.

Other businesses that do not identify customers by name can survey random samples of probable customers to measure customer loyalty and service quality perceptions. Restaurants, entertainment media, and public transport are subject to this manner of service quality measurement. Even government at municipal, state and national levels can be measured in this fashion. Public opinion regarding national and state policy is often gathered by professional pollsters on behalf of TV news or newspapers. Municipal surveys are more rare. The rather crude index of quality supplied by periodic elections adds something to measurement of government service quality, but much more is possible. Phone sampling of neighborhoods from which customers are likely to come, mail or phone contact with lists generated from "specials" coupons or prize drawings, and on-the-spot interviews with customers seeking service or exiting after receiving it are all sound approaches for directly measuring customer satisfaction. They should be undertaken with great care, though, because this type of contact, especially by phone or in person, can affect customer estimates of the quality of the service. Customer surveys require the maximum of service skill on the part of the survey taker. Customers can be gained or lost in the conduct of the survey. A poorly conducted survey that lacks genuine customer respect and a sound service orientation can alienate current or prospective customers. Indeed, the ability of a business to successfully conduct a customer survey with in-house personnel is one measure of the quality of available service-provision skill.

Every service should deliver a measure of personal attention and show personal interest in the customer. Respectfully addressing the customer by name; remembering occupation, interests, past conversations as a basis for discussion on a personal level; maintaining sensitivity to reactions that tacitly say "do" or "don't" are all fundamental measures of high-quality personal service. Large personal service firms may employ a computer data base with capacity for customer data in file for ready reference. Customer history and preferences can be recorded for quick, accurate recall. The service system is thereby upgraded and elaborated to support the personalized dimension of service quality.

Customer evaluation of personal and professional services might be greatly improved through systematic attention to data gathering on a local level. Personal services could be measured by a local consumer services association, perhaps one sponsored by the local newspaper. A panel of anonymous customers could rate local services on specifics of skill and personal service supplied. Alternately, customers could be surveyed by phone or mail. To avoid excessive active resistance on the part of those measured, the results would be summarized on a strictly normative basis of cost and service outcome result. With no names named, it could then be published so that customers *and* competitors might compare their experience against a normative base of data.

The great advantage of a normative approach to evaluation is that there is no need to identify individual service givers or firms. Indeed, they would benefit from the data directly themselves. A large base of normative data that describes what is expected and what is possible from various service offerings would provide guidelines for improved service by personal service firms and service providers. Until there are objective and quantitatively descriptive reports on medicine, investment, counseling and personal services that are as good as the professional quality of current consumer reports on toasters and autos, there can be no real incentive for service suppliers to look for ways to increase their service outcome result quality.

This tentative summary of potential measures of service suggests the variety of approaches that may be possible and appropriate to various service industries and businesses. Measures of service quality come in many forms. They apply unevenly to the broad mix of service industries, sometimes fitting, sometimes not. There are *always* ways to measure quality of service. The greater problem is the unwillingness to invest time and/or money to do it. "It isn't worth it" as an excuse for not measuring quality is always an indication of inferior quality. Unless it is measured, unless there are quality goals, quality is always questionable. High quality welcomes measurement. It is often an important marketing and sales tool. A little study will reveal many ways in which quality measurement can easily and cost-effectively be carried out for any business. There is no excuse for failing to measure it if quality is a genuine, central goal of the business.

KEEPING CUSTOMERS SATISFIED

As observed at the start of this chapter, the prevailing practice in service measurement is to avoid published, explicit standards and specifications for service. The rationale for this practice is that the absence of any clear commitment for service makes any level of delivered service acceptable. Thus, whatever service is offered must be "satisfactory," since there are no standards or specifications to disappoint. It is a legally conservative if marginally sleazy position in that the absence of legally binding commitment or contract means that anything offered in the way of service is defensible under the loose terms of the contract. The customer must take what he or she can get.

The customer's best defense is to demand specification of service standards in advance of delivery. The cynically clever service provider then strives to negotiate the lowest standards possible, insisting on maximum price if the customer demands excellence. Many customers accept what they are given rather than court the aggravation of extended argument. At a minimum, this is an indicator of marginal service ethics. Making the customer fight for a definition of service standards is poor service in its own way. Customers do well to assume that the absence of clear and explicit service standards is a precursor of poor service as well as a form of inferior service itself. The game of "hide the standards" is part of a foundation philosophy of service that defines the customer as enemy or adversary. The customer who is denied explicit service standards is not an honored and valued friend to the service giver, he is an inconvenience, if not a threat, who deserves to be defeated by a variety of clever defenses. The customer, in turn, defends him- or herself in whatever manner possible, often by refusing to be satisfied.

Avoidance of explicit standards does not change the customer's satisfaction other than to make dissatisfaction more likely. Customers arrive at the place of service with expectations and experience about the service they seek. They have their own standards already in mind. Where those standards are met, there will likely be satisfaction. Where they are disappointed, dissatisfaction is the probable result. If the service provider takes advantage of the customer's immediate need for service to make an easy, "you've got no complaints" type of sale, the dissatisfied customer will probably go away never to return again. Until the service provider sets service specifications and asks what the customer expects, customer satisfaction is totally beyond his or her knowledge and control.

The ultimate measure of service quality is customer acceptance and satisfaction. We may ask the customer, "are you satisfied with the service you have received?" We can request that the customer rate service on a scale from good to bad, from excellent to horrible. It is possible, of course, to phrase our question in such a manner that the expected or desired answer is encouraged. A simple leading assertion like "I trust the service was everything you could ask, sir!" conveys the expectation that only a positive answer could possibly be forthcoming. A scale of service quality that extends from "excellent" to "good" and then ends at "fair" clearly indicates there is no tolerance for a message of poor service. Few officers of service businesses are yet willing to invite customers to say that their service is wretched. But unless they are willing to ask the question in the starkest of terms they may never discover the truth.

Satisfaction is alternatively expressed in the actions and behaviors of customers. The mere fact that they are on premises purchasing the service bespeaks some degree of acceptance and satisfaction. Referring friends is a clear indication of a satisfied customer. Ordinary social exchanges at a level of pleasantry exhibit comfort and acceptance of the service situation. The customer's body language—relaxation, tension, acceptance, rejection—all bespeak the message of satisfaction as clearly as anything could.

Satisfaction can be measured with reasonable reliability given a minimum of discipline on the questioner/observer's part and a readiness to hear and see what is there. Measurement of any subjective or attitude variable, of course, is never precise and may sometimes be relatively unreliable. The problem with reliability, though, is that satisfaction is not necessarily the same thing from one time to another. Satisfaction is fluid, changing and malleable. Customers in a good mood are easily satisfied, while those in an angry one are impossible to please.

Some customers may be difficult or impossible to satisfy because they choose to use their dissatisfaction as a competitive weapon to manipulate and control the service supplier. One who can never be satisfied never ceases to demand higher standards of service. Perfectionism can sometimes be made to pay off. Customer satisfaction, alternatively, may be manipulated and managed by the service provider by raising or lowering the customer's level of expectations. The key to customer satisfaction is, perhaps, not so much in the reliability of its measurement as in understanding how it is formed and changed.

Withholding or expressing satisfaction can be a personal strategy in relationships. People can elect to be satisfied or dissatisfied as a matter of personal policy. Nice people elect to be easily satisfied. Tough ones may refuse to be satisfied by anything. Expression of satisfaction is used as an olive branch of peace or a whip for superior performance depending on personal style. Whether to be satisfied or dissatisfied is a personal choice in some instances, employed as a tool of social interchange.

But satisfaction is also a function of individual expectation and experience. It is a comparative process. No one is dissatisfied if they cannot travel from New York to Paris in ten minutes, but almost anyone is dissatisfied if it takes ten minutes for a phone call to go through from New York to Paris. The former is clearly known to be impossible, the latter a departure from expected service norms. One may dream of instant transport across vast physical distances and imagine it in science fiction, but the reality of current-day physical travel technology rules out any such possibility in fact. A century or so ago before the continent was connected by rails, the expected and satisfactory travel time from New York to San Francisco was measured in months. Today, satisfactory surface travel is calculated in days, while transcontinental air travel is measured in hours. Satisfaction changes as a function of the feasibilities.

Mere dissatisfaction alone sometimes may not result in immediate loss of the customer because of delay in seeking out another source of service. Thus it may be easy for service-givers to exploit the customer's need for immediate service, or to take advantage of the added time and cost to the customer of seeking out an alternative service. Customers may also be embarrassed at the prospect of walking out on the service provider if satisfactory standards or price won't be promised in advance. At the point of service sale, there are barriers that thwart easy switching by the customer to an alternative service provider. The competitive instinct that characterizes much of U.S. business automatically fills the gap and maximum advantage is seized by the service-provider. Where the customer is not wholly put off by being taken advantage of, and where the customer's expectation for service is met by the service as delivered, the sale may lead to repeat business. If offense is taken by the customer at being squeezed or if service falls short of expectation, this is the first and last opportunity to build a customer relationship that the service giver will have. Unfortunately, the entire transaction is nearly always carried out on a level of habit and vague impression that blocks awareness as to why the exchange has failed. No one ever grasps fully what has gone wrong, only that it has, indeed, not worked out. The importance of customer satisfaction is ignored.

Explicit definition of service standards when blended with open, competitive pricing offers greater control over the transaction to both parties and greater potential for avoiding costly customer dissatisfaction. Where the customer expects a lower-than-posted price but has limited experience with standards of service offered, a one-time introductory discount can be proposed to ease uncertainty. Where standards are not stringent enough for the customer's taste, it is fair and appropriate to discuss a revision in price structure to support a higher level of service standard. If that is not possible, the service provider can offer genuine service by recommending an alternative source of the sought service. The service provider must not attempt to do what cannot be done. That is extremely poor service and a certain route to customer dissatisfaction. Where the customer's expectations for service standards or price are excessive or unrealistic, only shopping around and testing the market will correct the unreasonable view. These are all approaches that offer the customer respect and opportunity for satisfaction in some measure, thereby assuring that as and when the customer is ready, satisfactory service can be delivered.

In setting service standards there are principles that can be applied for maximizing customer satisfaction. The greatest customer satisfaction comes when expectations are modest and service results noticeably exceed them. The severest customer dissatisfaction arises when standards are high and service clearly fails to meet them. The actual level of service delivered can sometimes be identical in both circumstances. It is expectation level that drives the resulting satisfaction.

Whenever standards are not met, failure must be openly acknowledged and compensated through price reduction or rerun of the service performance. Very high standards that are just barely met can be a disappointment to some customers, because expectations may have been raised to an exceptional level that makes mere performance at that level an anticlimax. High customer expectations are typically capable of generating only threshold satisfaction. Great satisfaction seems to arise out of modest expectations that are unexpectedly surpassed. It often depends on an element of comparative surprise.

The secret to customer satisfaction, thus, is in managing the customer's level of expectations for quality of service. Setting high expectations may get the customer's signature on a contract but may also guarantee limited or low satisfaction. Extravagant promises that raise high expectations merely escalate the height service must reach to satisfy the customer. Modest expectations that are far exceeded generate exhilaration and excitement, but, then, what do you do for an encore? Attempting to manipulate low expectations to make satisfaction easy, especially when the service specifications are below market standards for similar service, may only create doubt in the customer's mind about the service giver's integrity and competence. A mix of specifications, most of which have high probability of being met, in combination with one or two that are high and important to the customer, probably is the best strategy for achieving satisfaction. Expectations then are moderately high going in to the service relationship, some dimensions of service quality can likely be exceeded, and effort to assure meeting or exceeding the critical high specs can be focused for maximum effect.

When service specifications are clearly and explicitly published, the customer's level of expectation is usually influenced significantly by those specifications. It is only necessary to perform to specs and occasionally exceed them with a little bit of a flourish to keep customers excited and satisfied with the service offering. That is the soundest strategy for achieving consistent customer satisfaction.

Chapter 14

Building a Service Culture: Selecting and Training Service Givers

"Quality service must become a deeply scored habit."

Western culture is schizophrenic; humane service is its ideal, but competitive triumph is its purpose. These are not necessarily incompatible goals but they do require clarity of purpose and high skill if they are to be pursued jointly. Rotary International, the worldwide service club, sets as its guiding principle, "service above self; he profits most who serves best." It is no accident that an organization made up of the leading businesspeople in a community finds it appropriate and necessary to continually remind its members of the service imperative. Nor is it surprising that good service is causally linked to high profit in this lofty statement of principle. Competitive instincts of good business managers are deep and strong. The quick, easy route to profit is by way of ruthless exploitation. Among people who must live and work together on a continuing basis in a community of shared value, raw economic exchange is disruptive and inefficient. Only a bond of mutual service will suffice as a foundation for profitable business relations.

Rising to meet the competition comes naturally for successful businesspersons. Offering service, on the other hand, must often be learned and practiced. At least, that is the typical case in Western culture. Some individuals do possess the instincts of good service giving, though often at the expense of their competitive instincts. It is easy to follow either the path of competitiveness or of service, but difficult to join them. Good service providers usually need to become effective businesspersons. Service that brings no near-term profit is sometimes martyr-like in quality. But cutthroat, immediate profit derived from others' fears and hardships is limited and bittersweet. Strong competitors need to be taught the lesson of good service and its contribution to high profit. "He profits most who serves best."

Businesses that offer limited or no real service survive on nonrepeat sales as best they can. Dealing with the customer at arm's length on a competitive, adversarial basis does nothing to build a stable, loyal customer base. Eventually, these firms must either come to terms with the service imperative or go out of business. A service culture that makes a profit must be planned and cultivated. It is not likely to come into being by itself. It may be developed out of the hard lessons of economic give and take, but this is the slow and expensive way to bring it about. The direct route is to select and train personnel to fill the organization's service roles, taking care to build a strong, stable service culture that effectively meets the economic and personal needs of the customer.

SELECTION IS AN ART AND A SCIENCE

The core of excellent service is a genuine respect and liking for people. By contrast, raw competitiveness is self-centered and wary of others. There is a basic quality of mutual exclusion between these qualities. Many people develop along one or the other of these two paths without ever combining them. Several major institutions of Western society tend to support this separation of behavioral paths.

The social milieu in which young people develop, for instance, can be warm and supportive or cold and distant. Family, friends, church and school all may offer opportunity for closeness to others or discourage interpersonal exchange by meeting congeniality with hostility and derision. For better or for worse, parents who are preoccupied with their own success and survival may leave a child to fend on it's own. The well-defined processes of group dynamics then swing into operation and the developing person finds him- or herself either included or excluded from the natural groups available. Inclusion offers the reward and practice of warmth and friendship in social relations. Exclusion teaches the hard and sometimes painful lessons of independence and competitive self-sufficiency. Inclusion and social outgoingness may either be generalized to those outside the group or restricted to an ethnic or religious in-group, thereby training social skills exclusively to a particular social setting. Ability to express warmth and outgoingness toward strangers depends on opportunity as a young person to encounter a variety of communities or ethnic cultures.

Individuals who frequently change residences or schools as young people either adapt socially or learn how to function as chronic social isolates. Genuine, generalized social skill with people of all kinds and backgrounds is, to some extent, a matter of experience and luck.

Of those exposed to the opportunity for social inclusion, some are able to connect quickly and happily with strangers. Many are capable of developing friendships under favorable circumstances. Of those excluded, some become social recluses. A rare few develop sociopathic charm as a defense or a weapon, unable or unwilling to trust or establish an authentic social relation. This is the fund of natural talent from which service givers are to be selected. In others, it must be trained and developed from scratch.

Public schools further process people along lines of either social or independent preferences. Deemphasis of academic standards in favor of students' social development that overtook public school systems in the 1960s was in large part a reaction to the social isolation in which many young people were previously shaped by formal, competitive schooling. The inability to tolerate and work with different ethnic cultures from those central and familiar ones of school and home formerly stunted the social skills of people throughout society, often to the detriment of the quality of social life. Public schools, with their emphasis on rational learning, contributed by placing highest value on mastery of technical skill over social skill. Academics is primarily a left-cortex function that appears to develop independently and in isolation of social judgment. The hemispheric specialization of the human cerebral cortex seems to foster narrow development of intellectual skill at the expense of social skill and commonsense judgment when the school system focuses too strictly on intellectual growth. Emphasis in public school education on independent, competitive achievement further reduces opportunity for collaborative, cooperative experience in learning and problem solving. Practice with social skills is an incidental and unplanned by-product of the traditional, academically focused educational system that has always favored independent, self-centered accomplishment.

As a result, people come to service jobs with differing practice and predisposition toward social aptitude and skill. A few are socially adept. Many are socially handicapped. At the entry stage of selection, candidates for service jobs can be evaluated for their existing, natural social competence. A standard preemployment interview serves well to measure the ease with which a person deals with unfamiliar individuals and situations. The interviewer, of course, must have high-level social skills to conduct an interview that uncovers and measures social aptitude and skill. Interviewing requires easy confidence and comfortable, open exchange with first-time acquaintances. It demands comfort with extended eye contact, ability to put others at ease in discussion and unusually good listening skills. The interviewer who possesses these skills will readily recognize them in the interviewee's behavior.

On occasion, the interviewee/candidate will take charge of the exchange and guide it to his or her own purpose. This may or may not be appropriate to the requirements of the service offering. It generally reflects a tendency to control and manipulate social situations. This kind of person cannot be supervised or directed by the passively retiring boss. It takes an equally aggressive manager to handle take-charge social skills. If the interviewer cannot achieve his or her objectives in the interview for technical or background information because the candidate has too much control over the process, it may alternatively be an indication that the interviewer needs to strengthen his or her social and interviewing skills. Outside help may be needed to carry through the completed candidate evaluation.

The most desirable response pattern in service provider candidates is when the candidate approaches the interview confidently, answers questions fully and straightforwardly, smiles when smiled at as well as at other appropriate times throughout the interview. The impression conveyed by this person is pleasant and confident. There are a minimum of semantic misunderstandings in the interview and a sense of efficient information exchange lingers when it is finished. It has been noted that in earlier days, McDonald's hamburger stands selected only self-confident, chronic smilers to serve as counter personnel. Fast-food as a commodity service offering leaves very little service content other than at the point of purchase. A customer who experiences warm, pleasant service at the point of purchase goes away feeling good about the speed of service, the low price of the food and the social rewards of congenial service. McDonald's created an international empire of fast-food outlets on this basic foundation, using selection for social skill as a key to service quality.

With explosive growth in size and scope of its franchising operations, McDonald's was forced to dig deeper into the available labor pool to find its counter personnel. Chronic smilers are increasingly in short supply with the expanded demand for pleasant purchase-point personnel. The next best natural pattern of service characteristics is the individual who, though generally expressionless, is quick and accurate in filling the order or otherwise serving the customer. There are a far greater number of people in the general labor market who are efficient and meticulous in their performance than there are those who are efficient, meticulous *and* chronic smilers. It is notable, however, how greatly enhanced the service experience can be when the smile is added to quickness and accuracy. Applying this complete package of personal qualities at the point of service delivery is a remarkably powerful and effective customer service device.

We might ask why efficient, accurate service providers who don't habitually smile can't simply be told to smile more. The answer is deceptively straightforward; smiling to facilitate social exchange is a deeply set habit in those who possess it. Telling someone who is chronically expressionless to smile usually elicits a weak and unconvincing effort. The smile thus obtained looks contrived. A natural smile seems to require a genuine liking for people and for the attendant social interchange. Many people learn to mask their feelings as a defense against emotional manipulation. Good poker players carefully train themselves to maintain a perfectly expressionless "poker face" to avoid giving their hand away. Nonsmilers are likely to have extensive natural training in how to avoid smiling.

That great tide of humanity that exists in chronic personal misery or fear finds it necessary to hide emotional expression so as to avoid exploitation. It is a habit that may be impossible to alter. Some people can be trained to smile, but the time and cost required to achieve success can be high. For now, McDonald's may find it cost-ineffective to train counter personnel to smile. Eventually, though, it will probably become a competitive necessity. Service without a smile seems a contradiction. The coldly efficient waitress who deftly fends off personal overtures may earn the respect of her customers, but the one with the engaging smile earns the tips.

SKILLS AND APTITUDES THAT ARE BASIC TO GOOD SERVICE

Before turning to training methods for service providers, there are other elements of selection that deserve examination. Service is not just pleasant, quick efficiency in service delivery, though these qualities are certainly a grand start, especially so at the point of customer contact. Service is also cost control, sound operating methods, quality control, responsibility, honesty and an understanding of the individual customer. These are significant service provider selection objectives in their own right.

Assessing a specific aptitude or ability on the very first contact with a job candidate (or anyone else) is exceptionally difficult. There are, inevitably, many mistakes. It is a probabilistic process that, like predicting the weather, requires willingness to improve the percentages of success without any expectation of error-free performance. The interviewer/screener looks for cues or signs and checks past history of performance as closely as possible for whatever corroborative information they may offer. There are many useful cues to service-relevant personal qualities.

Some happy, friendly individuals seem to have no sense at all of thrift or sound money management. They behave as if money is no object and physical resources are inexhaustible. Lip service is easily given to the need for fiscal accountability, but behavior leads to prodigal spending. A person's personal credit history is sometimes a good indicator of attitudes about money management. It is not so much a matter of how much debt an individual has run up as what it is spent for. Young people who take on large debt to own a home or finance advanced schooling demonstrate investment mindedness. Large debt for vacations, leisure and related consumer spending, on the other hand, reveals unconcern for the hazards of living beyond one's means. Debt in the service of personal advancement and ambition is often a wise investment and certainly no disgrace. Debt to enjoy the good life before it is earned is irresponsible. The candidate who exhibits responsibility in personal finances will more likely appreciate the importance of fiscal accountability in business.

Work experience sometimes provides encounter with cost-cutting or cost-reduction programs. Attitudes about such programs and especially personal contribution to their success can be informative about cost attitudes. Service suppliers who have inadequate or no sense of cost/price equity cannot appreciate the customer's concern for value. They are too ready to run up expenses and otherwise exploit the customer to the longer term detriment of the business. Where the business offers the temptation to run up the bill, and especially where service suppliers are on a percentage commission, quality of service will often be measured by the readiness of the service provider to recommend choices that are in the customer's interest *instead of* in the service provider's benefit. Where opportunity arises in the usual course of selection, candidates should be asked to describe how they would handle the conflicts of interest when they present themselves. A "what if" hypothetical question in the interview based on real, known business conflict of interest is sometimes the simplest way to address this concern.

Does the service supplier appreciate the necessity of continually and critically evaluating the operating methods used to deliver service to assure value and quality for the customer? Describe a method that would improve service if it were implemented and contrast it with one that would not. Does the candidate see the difference? What is his or her preference based on? Ask about suggestions, formal or informal, the candidate has offered in previous jobs to improve work efficiency. Were there any? Were they realistic or were they self-serving? Does the candidate know anything about or have experience with inventory or work flow practices from past work? How does the applicant view the need to set and maintain high work standards for the job? Does his or her past experience reflect resentment of methods and standards changes, or appreciation of their necessity?

What is the interviewee's personal attitude about quality of service? How would he or she evaluate service quality from the customer's side of the transaction? What response would likely be forthcoming if a supervisor criticized his or her quality of service delivery? What response would he or she offer to a customer's criticism of the quality of service offered? Is there appreciation of the quality imperative and ability to emphathize with the customer's point of view regarding quality?

Does the prospective employee take responsibility for his or her actions and life situation? Here it is appropriate to test for readiness to blame others for problems. Why was the poor grade in school assigned? Any auto accidents? Who was at fault? Why? What issues are worth arguing over? When and with whom was the last argument over that matter? What were his or her arguments and counterarguments? What were the adversary's arguments and counterarguments? Who's to blame for high taxes? Who's at fault for high unemployment? Who causes high prices for service? The intensity and persuasiveness of the arguments are incidental, except as indexes of energy and aggressiveness under intense conditions of inter-personal exchange. The candidate who finds little or no opportunity to focus on his or her own actions as a significant input to solving these problems probably evades personal, individual responsibility as a matter of habit. Service givers who blame their poor service entirely on the institution, its systems or, worst of all, on the customer, are almost certainly going to be poor quality service providers.

Honesty is an extremely difficult quality to identify in the absence of opportunity to observe actual behavior under circumstances of temptation. Where honesty is critical to service, structured, observed temptation should be offered to see how it is handled. A confederate, for instance, can enter the interviewer's office to ask help in a momentary crisis. As he leaves, the confederate "accidentally" drops a ten-dollar bill while removing something from his pocket. Another confederate or a hidden video camera records the candidate's handling of the opportunity.

Some care must be taken in judging such events. Honesty is situationally specific. Open, aggressive competition tends to justify dishonesty. Winston Churchill openly praised the "bodyguard of lies" carefully planted around Britain's wartime operations to deceive the German high command. It is perfectly acceptable for a fielder in a baseball game to deceive a base runner by appearing to throw a hit ball which, in fact, has not yet been retrieved. But deception is a tit-for-tat matter. Perceived unfairness or inequity in an exchange is sometimes offset with dishonesty. The customer who feels overcharged fails to correct a billing error that would raise the price. The cashier who suffers insult from a customer short-changes him or her. In the competitive give-and-take of commodity operations, taking advantage of a mistake made in one's favor sometimes seems natural. Dishonesty can be a straightforward social exchange. Good service suppliers may need to be trained to substitute honest service for competitive advantage-taking.

In service operations it is important to establish a climate of mutual self-interest that defines a fair price and high quality as being mutually beneficial to service giver and customer. Honesty on the customer's part in pointing out an error should be rewarded by offering to let the mistake in his or her favor stand as a special discount. Errors that are in the service giver's favor would best be amended with immediate correction *and* a discount in equivalent amount, just as expression of apology. These are policies that should be handled through management directives and careful training. Service providers can in some situations be given authority to correct their own or the system's errors as expressions of appreciation. The restaurant that permits employees to pick up the check or offer a free bottle of wine when gravy is spilled on the customer will create customer goodwill in measure far beyond the small cost entailed. The physician who zeros out the billing of the patient whose appointment was forgotten by his secretary earns ample appreciation and loyalty in return. The hallmark of true service is willingness to put service above profit. Any and every opportunity where this fundamental principle can be demonstrated and acted out by service givers enhances the service climate by enhancing both the qualities of responsibility and honesty that characterize it.

Standards of honesty should of course be explored with service provider candidates in the interview. The interviewer can describe several typical situations where dishonesty by customers or employees is conventionally encountered and ask for a personal evaluation of that kind of dishonesty. The candidate can be asked if he or she ever encountered a similar situation. The question can be put "under what conditions is it better for the business to deceive a customer"? Long delay in response is usually a sign that the candidate's recognition faces a difficult moral dilemma in responding. The scrupulously honest person will usually answer instantly, "never." But the intellectually quick social operator will probably offer the "right" answer just as quickly. It is worthwhile investigating the personal rationale and philosophy behind the answer when it is

Exhibit 14-1
Qualities of a Good Service Provider

```
                  Social Grace
                 Responsibility
                    Honesty
                    Empathy
          Cost and Quality Sensitivity
```

"right." Scrupulous honesty is usually supported by adherence to high moral principle and strict personal discipline. But social manipulation may underlie glib answers and gratuitous agreement with issues related to honesty in the interview. There are no easy paths to assessment of honesty because there is so often personal conflict of interest in being honest. Service, however, is not bona fide service without honesty. It is important to assess honesty as a quality of service givers (see Exhibit 14–1).

Empathy for the needs and interests of the customer is a rare and valued skill. Like smiling, it may either be a deeply ingrained habit or, under the right conditions, it may sometimes be cultivated with experience and training. The habit of empathy for the concerns and needs of others develops out of personal trial and agony in the company of others facing similar travail. Nonempathic individuals fail to notice or appreciate the vast differences in life perspective and individual values that exist around them. They attribute and generalize their own feelings and values to everything and everyone around, overlooking obvious differences of action and purpose. There seems to be a failure of imagination when it comes to appreciating the potential for human variety of experience in nonempathic individuals.

In an affluent society where many problems are typically "solved" by spending more money on them, it is easy to ignore the travail of others. "Streetwise" is a colloquial term used to describe those who must be sensitive to the differences in the actions of people around because those differences signal the major opportunities and hazards inherent in a marginal economic existence on the "street." Empathy comes out of being kicked around by the circumstances of life. It arises out of tragedy, either personal or that which strikes a loved one. Privilege, high social status, security and tranquility are the nemeses of empathy. As society becomes wealthier and more civilized, the store of human sensitivity and empathy diminishes unless it is actively cultivated.

Empathic persons can often accurately identify the feelings, values and point of view of others merely from observing their circumstances. They personally feel the fear expressed in the eyes of the confused, lost child. They know in their own heart the helpless anger of the mugging victim.

They respond with concern to the expression of sadness in an old woman's face. Show them a picture that portrays emotional expression of any kind and they will develop an elaborate explanatory scenario to go with it, becoming emotional in the process. When the same picture is presented to a nonempathic individual, especially where the central characters are of different age or sex, the description will be emotionally flat and factually superficial.

Empathy either is or isn't there. Lack of empathy can be partially offset by a vivid imagination. Imagination can sometimes improve in the face of crisis or challenge. The challenge of getting the job may improve the empathic quality of candidate responses. Limited empathy can be partially overcome by an active imagination. At a minimum, a vivid imagination signals potential to learn and improve empathic judgment through training.

But empathy can often be trained even where imagination is lacking. Where empathy isn't there and a person's native imagination is weak, its discovery can come about through real or simulated travail. This can be an arduous experience that requires high commitment to self-discovery and tolerance for stressful challenge. The overprivileged, self-indulgent, nonempathic individuals with limited imagination have a long way to go to become empathic and will typically defend themselves from such pain of learning. These people are also poor candidates as service providers. Good service demands that the service giver seek out and comprehend the customer's point of view. Without empathy, that's not going to occur. The candidate must either have it or be trainable. Empathy is fundamental to meeting the service imperative. Without it, service can never rise above its commodity competitive past.

The limited supply of smilers and empathizers in the labor market can only be overcome by training candidates with the aptitude or commitment to achieve mastery of these skills. It is a make-or-buy situation where it often will be impossible to buy as much as is needed. Each business must develop its own service-provision skills in its workers. Provision of sound training for service will be fundamental to competitive business success throughout service industries.

TRAINING SERVICE PROVIDERS

Training is a service too. Most training, like most education, is delivered as a mass commodity product. The most popular of the current-day mass quality trainings, Philip Crosby Associates, is strictly standardized even to exact translations of the training script into alternative languages. Trainers follow the script with disciplined care that rivals the engineering precision of a high-tech electronic product. What customization there is in it represents careful differentiation by major market segments. This is an efficient way to shape the trainee's standardized verbal behavior, but it is likely to have limited effect on basic attitudes and little or none on overt behaviors.

The approach adopted for delivery of training service sets the fundamental tone of the student's learning experience. A mass commodity approach clearly conveys the expectation of ritualistic uniformity in trainee performance. But a mass commodity approach to service training is a contradiction in terms. Each trainee comes to the experience with a unique set of values and perspectives, as well as with his or her own level of empathic response. Finding the trainee's special, personal starting point on which to build new attitudes and skills is central to the customization process. If the training fails to address the trainee as an individual, how then can it train him to address the customer as an individual? Where there is contradiction between the process and the content of the training, how does the trainee know which is the *real* message?

The subject issues of service training may be of any sort or variety. Some proportion of skill or technology must be trained. Policies regarding work and quality standards must be clearly communicated. Models of effective and ineffective service delivery must be clearly portrayed. But the individual student must never be forgotten even though training may partly be in a mass communication mode for the sake of efficiency. Each trainee must be identified and appreciated for his or her special and unique characteristics.

Good service training starts when the teacher knows and uses every student's name. Where the instructor feels the need to be close to students, first names should be used. That suggests a quality of personal intimacy between teacher and student. Maintaining a modest but respectful distance calls for the teacher to address students by their last names. Use of first name by one in an official or elevated position emphasizes the status difference and can be interpreted as a put-down. Use of last name between close friends may suggest the onset of formality and coolness in the relationship. Generally and in the classroom, trainees should be addressed by their last names when addressed as members of the class to reflect the appropriate formality of the situation. In face-to-face conversation, though, their first names can be used.

These same principles of name usage carry over to the customer contact. Service suppliers must be trained to use customer names but to use them appropriately. It is difficult to remember names until one practices doing it. It is also hard to know the proper form of address when using a customer's name. There is potential embarrassment in both forgetting the customer's name and in using it improperly. Honesty and caringness in the early stages of any relationship, though, are well-expressed through readiness of the service provider to ask to be reminded of the customer's name or to simply ask, "how would you prefer to be addressed?" "Call me Bob" means that a first-name basis is preferred. "It doesn't matter" or "whatever you prefer" cues the use of a little more formality until the relationship has advanced to a more comfortable, informal level. "You may address me as Mr. Smith" indicates keep your distance and address me formally. The rules are slightly different for addressing the service provider. One who offers first name as basis of address withholds his or her full identity and thereby maintains social distance from the customer. Offering full name, first and last, suggests openness to a personal and formal service provision relation. Understanding these principles is foundation training for every service provider. Use of the customer's name defines a fundamental difference between service and commodity offerings. The customer is a person to the service provider. He or she is only a sale to the commodity seller.

Service training begins with discovery of the trainee's name. It must not end there, though. The qualities that make each person unique must also be discovered. Indeed, it becomes increasingly easier to remember another's name as the shape and quality of his or her personality begins to emerge. The person's name now stands for the package of values, skills, preferences and behaviors that is unique to the individual. These qualities emerge when the trainee is given opportunity to participate actively in the learning process. The structure of training must allow ample time for each trainee to express his or her individuality in both group situations and face-to-face with the trainer. Training that permits the trainee to sit passively without ever once speaking up or otherwise responding to the trainer is the purest imaginable form of commodity.

Where training formality is high and structure tight, trainees may need to be encouraged to behave as individuals. If no more than check-marks on a background survey form are obtained from each training participant, the beginnings of a personal exchange are made. Written tests or projects, personal inventory forms, and structured performance activity add a wealth of information about the person. Question and answer exchanges (in either direction) in the training setting, personal conversations outside the formal training activity, with appropriate background and records checks of trainees, will further augment the trainer's appreciation of each trainee as a unique person.

A simple test of a trainee's (or instructor's, or anyone else's) openness to unique individuality is to ask: How long does it take you to "size up" a person when you first meet them? and What categories do you use to classify different types of persons? This is a trick test because habitual use of categories *at all* reveals an unreadiness to accept people as individuals. Giving less than thirty minutes to discovery of the other person is hopelessly superficial. Over a quarter-century of in-depth interviewing practice and experience has shown me that forty-five to ninety minutes is typically the minimum just to construct a basic personality pattern that permits me to judge fit against an established, specific job and organizational situation. Knowing someone as an individual in the broader framework of life requires vastly more time. Some husbands and wives discover tragically late they have never known their spouse or children fully. Few people ever bother to look closely at the behavior of another and then to ask good questions about it. These reflect chronic bad habits of self-centeredness. Those bad habits do not support good service. As a start, service provision demands close attention to the actions of others and careful questioning to understand it better.

Many training approaches can be applied to increasing service provider trainees' openness to varieties of individuality. Personality or values inventories administered to the entire training group, then shared, can reveal wide variations among trainees as people. Students can also use self-description instruments to identify similarities of view that will serve as the basis of common agreement. Videotapes of little-known public personalities can be shown and students asked to predict values and behaviors outside those disclosed. Predictions are then compared with actual public behavior. Most predictions will turn out to be wild guesses. Guest "customers" can come to class to be interviewed by the group. The object is to discover customer personal needs and preferences in the context of the service. The training class provides an excellent learning setting for exploration of human variety because it is a natural social setting. Dealing with people in a group requires that differences be revealed and appreciated when the object of group performance is custom service.

Deeply set self-centeredness and insensitivity may be intractable. When too stubbornly set, these are major liabilities that must be identified and avoided in the service setting. The indicators of these qualities are several. Continuous talk about oneself and interests that does not stop to connect with the interests of others is a strong sign. Poor listening that dismisses most of what others have to say is an important signal. One who cannot generate any interest in a subject or issue they are not already aware of is lacking in empathic aptitude. It is usually a waste of time to try to get through with new and other-oriented information. One who seems to know everything that is worth knowing is likely to be empathyless. The world is a closed and finished system to the nonempathic individual.

Under the right circumstances, however, empathy can be trained. The foundation of empathy training is commitment by the trainee to discovery. It requires an appreciation that the universe is continually unfolding around us with new possibilities and with previously unrealized truths. It asks for an imagination that can construct new and untried visions. Becoming genuinely empathic never ends, never offers final answers. There are always more new mysteries to be solved. W. Edwards Demming's foundation principle of "never ending improvement" echoes these qualities.

The simplest structure for creating empathic awareness of the needs and perspectives of others is to place two equally insensitive persons into competition with one another for scarce resources and fairly referee the contest sufficiently to prevent physical injury. The natural form of this experience is among children in a large family or among small business competitors in a fragmented industry. In a family, older siblings may attempt use of physical force to have their way, but younger ones quickly discover how to call in the parental cavalry. The values, preferences and skills of each family member are identified and accommodated in these circumstances. An occasional isolate refuses to join the competition, ascetically accepting whatever is left over to avoid involvement in the confusion. If they watch closely, they will discover empathy. If not, they may become self-centered isolates. Almost the same description applies to small business competitors.

A number of sensitivity training methods are available as commercial training offerings. National Training Laboratories of Alexandria, Virgina, is the original source of empathy training. For businesses, the work structure simulated by Managerial Grid Training offered by Scientific Methods, Inc. of Houston, Texas, can be a useful way to discover how to reach out and make contact with new members of task groups.

Activities like these are sometimes called encounter groups or T-Groups. They enjoy a mixed reputation that arises out of the stress and confusion that many participants experience from them. The challenge of interpersonal discovery is never easy. Fragile, preneurotic personalities sometimes unravel under the pressure of empathy training. Discovering that one is not the center and ruler of the universe can be a severe shock. Empathy does not come without sweat and pain. Presuming to teach empathy to another human being has the quality of playing God. Those who are forced into empathy training, however, will readily discover how to defend themselves from it. Without free choice and full commitment to its challenges, empathy training is a waste of time. The least empathic are sometimes those who edict others into empathy training.

Responsibility can also be trained, but only up to a point. Self-development activities of various kinds such as Dale Carnegie seminars can sometimes help. The key to discovery of capacity for responsibility is in realization that those of this world who are chronically irresponsible have given up control of their own destinies. When one perceives the universe as having total control over their lives, it becomes necessary to blame all events on outside forces and deny one's own power and opportunity for choice. Responsibility means taking responsibility for one's choice even when the meaning of the choice is not clear. Irresponsible individuals set themselves adrift in a raft on the sea of life. Responsible persons are on the same raft, paddling as well as they can and looking for subtle currents that may carry them to their goals.

Irresponsibility has been described as a free-floating umbilical cord looking for reattachment that will provide permanent comfort and safety. Commodity-oriented business organizations are more than willing to exploit irresponsibility of this kind to build a cadre of loyal, passive workers who follow orders, or loyal, passive customers who do not question the value of the product. Commodity-oriented operations methods provide ample points of attachment for emotional umbilical cords. Service operations require people who can think and adapt to the actively demanding customer. The effective service supplier discovers the customer and takes responsibility for meeting his or her expectations. Irresponsibility is a severe liability in a soundly managed service company.

To develop responsibility in service providers, the demonstration of responsibility must be consistently recognized and rewarded. Commodity production ignores irresponsibility. It tacitly sanctions unconcern for quality or operations problems among workers. The worker who tries to solve a production problem without higher authorization may be disciplined or ostracized for his trouble. Good judgment in creating and maintaining customer relations must be recognized and encouraged among responsible service suppliers. Some organizations—Avis, for instance—seek to develop responsible attitudes through employee ownership. If the system does not support responsibility, though, ownership is a lost investment. A sense of personal ownership of problems and opportunity can help improve responsible behavior, but only when one is not knocked down for the attempt.

Ultimately there are also important operations methods and cost improvement techniques that service providers should be trained to apply. All of the basic operations analysis methods outlined in the early chapters of this book deserve mastery by service suppliers. Capacity issues are especially critical in assuring high-quality service. Labor flexibility and excess equipment capacity are fundamental to good service. Pareto decision guidelines, the ability to recognize bottlenecks and effectively manage work flow through them, management of set-up requirements and costs with sensitivity to cost trade-offs are all relevant and significant operations management methods deserving of the investment in training for service suppliers.

Cost improvement in commodity operations is often short-sighted. The cost that is saved in one area is lost in another because no one looked at the broader consequences of the new management policy or a system design change. Change for the sake of reduced cost must be tested against the priorities and goals of the entire organization. This may seem bureaucratic and inefficient to some. But it is a principle that cannot be compromised without risk. Every cost improvement change must be reviewed as widely as it is possible and practical to communicate it. Then it must be subjected to temporary trial implementation before becoming fixed in policy. The most significant product of a soundly administered cost improvement program is often the greatly increased awareness of internal organizational interdependence it generates. The early investment of getting everyone better informed about the priorities of other parts of the business is an essential and productive one.

Certainly, cost improvements that diminish customer service or limit service flexibility to fit customer need must be avoided. Commodity habits of thinking typically do not look beyond the immediate cost of operations. Service operations strategy looks first and last at the impact of system change on the customer.

The opportunities for further training in operations methods and skills for service providers will depend on the business and the service. All service training must be tested against the general principles outlined in this chapter. It must be appropriate to the customer's expectation and support a strong service culture. Reciprocally, culture must also support training. Culture must be designed, evaluated and maintained to support the service imperative.

DESIGNING AND MAINTAINING THE SERVICE CULTURE

A sound service culture is known by its central values. Exhibit 14-2 catalogs many of them. It is customer-responsive and cost-sensitive. It achieves high quality at any level of business volume. It focuses on people as unique individuals placing appropriate emphasis on market segments.

Exhibit 14-2
Qualities of a Strong Service Culture

```
            Responsive to Customers
          Cost and Quality Sensitive
              Volume Insensitive
                  Ethical
      Attuned to In-House Heros as Models
            Energetic, Enthusiastic
          Open to Experiment and Change
              Goal/Results Focused
            Errors Cannot be Hidden
         Skill - not Capital - Intensive
            Invests Heavily in Training
      Sound Service Operations Methods Applied
```

It holds responsibility and honesty in high esteem but also sets high goals for competitive success. These are grand, even utopian, ideals for a profit-making business. Nevertheless, they are the ground on which the coming rounds of business competition in service industries will take place. The customer will accept nothing less. They are not merely high standards; they are our customers' emerging expectations.

Preparation for a service-dominated economy will require redesign of organizations to fit the emerging norm. The strongest competitors will likely be those that design or retrofit organization structure and culture to fit emerging service standards. The challenge to build and maintain a service culture will become a major management preoccupation as competition recenters on the individual customer. The core around which it will be built will often be the entrepreneurial and natural service temperaments.

The seed of culture change is often the individual who personifies those values demanded by and sought in the new marketplace. The entrepreneur who successfully brings up a new product or service offering necessarily embodies the central values of the new culture. He seldom needs to resort to something so artificial as a market survey because he is the living essence of that market. What he feels the market feels, what he needs the market needs. The current high-tech computer age of product competition is driven by those men and women who intuitively and accurately know in their hearts and guts what excites and attracts their customers. They *are* the customer in heart and mind. What they create and offer to the customer will spark the customer's imagination and desire.

An emerging service culture requires a generous portion of people with a natural service temperament. This temperament is relatively easy to describe and identify. The reflexively quick, accurate, smiling, happy, customer-loving person who relates comfortably to a wide variety of people and empathizes easily is the natural seed of service culture. That alone is not enough for a success. There must also be cost and quality consciousness, a strong goal orientation and operations management competence. The right temperament alone is the seed that needs congenial soil.

An effective business culture is *always* characterized by high energy and enthusiasm, openness to experiment, tough goals, focus on tangible results and willingness to admit error. The major difference between a sound service culture and the mass commodity sales culture is in a recentralizing of priorities around human qualities with a corresponding deemphasis of short-term financial goals. The key investment is no longer in physical plant and equipment that banks and investors anxiously (sometimes greedily) monitor for satisfactory payoff. The critical investments in service are in breadth of skill for its labor force combined with greater depth of knowledge and understanding for its customers. A service economy will be less concerned with the scarcity of physical resources than scarcity of days in a lifetime to find human fulfillment. Success will be measured less in a steady profit growth, quarter by quarter, which sustains and increases stock prices. It will be measured more by long-term stability of cooperative customer relationships that command a mutually acceptable fair price for service than by a day-to-day adversarial relationship based on price competition alone. Customer loyalty was once routinely available to the highly reputed market share leader who delivered fair quality at moderate price by exploiting massive economies of scale. No more! Expectations and the price of customer loyalty have risen. Service is the new imperative. Only a soundly conceived and managed service culture will satisfy newly escalated levels of expectation.

A service culture is characterized by deep respect for the customer rather than by that low-grade competitive contempt of the customer that marks a commodity-dominated economy. A service culture adheres to the spirit of the service contract rather than hiding defensively behind ambiguous legalisms that seem to guarantee quality but cleverly withhold any real commitment. Weasel-worded enticements intended to deceive or entrap have no place in this culture. Service makes sound commitments and scrupulously keeps them. There are no loopholes built into the contract that permit safe, easy exit when the arrangement becomes inconvenient to the seller. People who trust one another don't need lawyers to regulate their exchanges or protect their interests. If the relation doesn't work they will disengage by mutual agreement and without acrimony.

Training is a major and central investment in service culture. Many workers in service industries must be trained how to smile and empathize with the customer. Personal development to overcome anxiety and defensiveness in customer contacts will be common. Coaching in the arts of accepting responsibility and exercising honesty in relationships will be a central activity of supervisors and managers. But basic business training will be of equal importance. Operations methods that support high quality and rigorous cost control are indispensable to maintenance of a sound cost structure and a fair price. Competition will not disappear in the service economy. It will be more intense than ever. Poor business practices now become the equivalent of low-quality service. A sound service culture is not the polite, conflict-free country club atmosphere that characterized some former commodity market share champions. Arrogance or complacency are clear liabilities in service culture. Basic business disciplines such as cash and inventory management, sound records maintenance, efficient scheduling of scarce resources and clear communications procedures must all be mastered and applied. Service operations must be competently managed if a high-quality, fairly priced service offering is to be delivered. That is the service imperative.

Building and maintaining the service culture requires an entirely new pattern of organizing and managing the firm. The transition to service from commodity habits of thinking will be difficult. The test of its effectiveness is in the quality of service. Rotary International has articulated that the payoff is: "he profits most who serves best."

Chapter 15

The Economics of Service Pricing

"Haggling is hard enough, but after the sale?"

The bases on which service value can be established are limited. There are basically three: cost, conformity with specifications and customer satisfaction. Cost, it was argued in Chapter 12, is a counterintuitive factor; high cost is associated with less than the best quality of service because the high skill that enhances quality also reduces cost by increasing efficiency of service delivery. Nevertheless, long-standing mass commodity economy habits of expecting greater value with increased cost persist. Some service providers take advantage of this expectation. They produce the illusion of high value by charging a high price and intimidating their customers with the appearance of great expertise. It is a device that creates an aura of exclusivity but otherwise contributes little to the value of the service.

SERVICE VALUE IS INHERENTLY INFINITE

The inherent value of service can easily become infinite. The firm hand of a school crossing guard that restrains an energetic child from running out into traffic is poorly compensated by the modest hourly wage paid. The teacher who brings to blossom the hidden talent; the story of struggle and self-discipline that inspires grand, new accomplishment; the counselor who helps dispel life-long fears—all contribute immeasurably to the welfare of their customers. An important element of the service giver's reward is necessarily found in knowing the great value in the service rendered. Unlike a physical product—a barrel of oil, a pallet of bricks, a box of computer chips or a bag of potatoes, each of which are value constrained by the uses to which they can be put and the substitutes available—service can be and often is priceless.

The various economic models that guide pricing and value in the markets for physical product thus do not apply to the customized world of personal service. The values of human labor and human help are beyond calculation. It is not simply a matter of the marginal value added by customization; nor is there price elasticity in honesty, commitment or depth of understanding. The ownership of capital wealth represented in the tools of production, once the dominant foundation of productive capacity, is a secondary or tertiary factor in an economic system founded on skilled service. In an emerging service economy the critical capital is the skill and self-discipline of the capable service provider. As service offerings come to dominate the broader economy, the food and product commodities necessary to life are supplied by a tiny fraction of the total population—10% or less. The prices of both are driven to a minimum by their commodity nature. Because they are relatively risk-free, produced with standard, widely available equipment, itself a commodity, and are manned by that tiny fraction of the labor force best qualified by temperament and talent to produce them, commodities are price constrained at the maximum. The tools of production are increasingly owned by their users. Where not so owned, production tools are held and used in some form of trust agreement by those who put them to productive use. Even in today's economy the majority of productive resources are absentee-owned or -financed, managed by nonowner employees who are left to do as they will as long as an acceptable return on investment is regularly paid out by the business. Commodity production is on a par with government bonds—indispensable, secure, low yield and uninteresting.

Skill in the service economy is potentially abundant. There is no longer heavy demand for labor in agriculture or manufacturing to compete for available skill. Even more significant to increasing the availability of skill, abandonment of narrow specialization in favor of multiple skill acquisition has potential to multiply available labor skill manyfold beyond mere labor body count. In a service economy there is no cause for any skill to be in chronic short supply. Indeed, the prudent course for every service provider is to develop multiple skills that can be applied variably to fit uncertain and variable market demand. It is a career strategy that offers a built-in insurance policy against shifting demand for skill.

In a commodity economy, the narrow specialization demanded by mass output efficiency can be partially limited in its supply by various cartel arrangements. Those with high-status specialties can collectively bring pressure for licensing and legislation to restrict availability of their offering, thereby keeping the price of their labor high. Labor unions for service suppliers flourish where skill is narrow and workers possess limited or no range of alternatives to fall back on. Prices of physical product, by contrast, are constrained by several factors, the most powerful being the interchangeability of machinery or technology for labor. Specialized labor or experience applied to material product output is subject to sudden obsolescence. There are, at minimum, these sources of discipline to check excessive cartel protection of labor in service of commodity production.

When labor skill is solely the foundation of an economic system, as it inevitably is in a service economy, there *is* no alternative. Price is subject to severe distortion whenever supported by cartel arrangement. There is no upper limit to a price that can be asked other than a customer's unwillingness or inability to pay. Price levels rise to near extortionate levels, even as they have at present in some corners of medical and legal practice. When one's life and well being are at stake, no price seems too high. There are already those service suppliers who exploit this pricing opportunity as if it were a demand for ransom.

Present-day medical services illustrate the effect of a cartel on pricing. The highest paid physicians are the most highly specialized. But this very high rate of pay is not fully justified by the incrementally higher investment required for mastery of their specialty. It is made possible and maintained by restricting the supply of the service through a powerful professional association (the American Medical Association) and exploiting the infinite value of their life-giving services to escalate rates to the maximum. Greed easily replaces the high principle of the Hippocratic oath. Physicians, though, are hardly alone in their pursuit of riches.

The greatly valued service of a university education offers another example of rapacious price escalation. Even in a poor economy, the asking price of a college degree escalates annually. The value of the good life that higher education offers is near infinite. Professors and administrators who guard the gateway of success progressively test the limits of value by demanding increasingly higher prices. Higher education in the United States is in crisis today *only* because there is a serious oversupply of educational opportunity left behind in the wake of the baby boom now grown up. But even overcapacity has not yet had an impact on the cost of education. A better demonstration of infinite price potential in service would be hard to find.

The obscenely large payouts demanded and obtained by chief executive officers (CEOs) of major corporations demonstrates another service—management—that escalates its fees infinitely. CEOs, indeed, sometimes are better paid when their company is failing than when it is successful. The price of their service keeps going up even when its value is questionable. Extortionate fee demands succeed regardless of whether the business succeeds or fails, thereby fueling still higher demands. In the manufacturing sector there is ready demonstration of the power of management service to command escalating high wages from the owners of physical plant capacity. This is a harbinger of how the worth and value of service must eventually dominate value in ownership of physical assets.

Society's first and best defense against extortionate service pricing is to prevent the formation of cartels and bar artificial limitation on availability of skill. Professional associations, licensing and labor unions exist primarily to protect the economic interests of their members. Labor unions, for instance, were once outlawed under the legal theory that they improperly and artificially restrained trade. Licensing is a weak and often ineffective way to assure minimum professional skill, but it is always effective in limiting the supply of professionals. Professional associations offer opportunity for expense-paid vacations to exotic locations under the umbrella of enhancing professional skill. They also set prices and lobby for legislation favorable to the profession. The benefits to society of these institutions are typically outweighed by their cost, but they are sustained by the substantial personal and economic services they deliver to their members. Appropriate legislation to offset the excesses of cartel arrangements remains to be discovered and enacted.

OVERSPECIALIZATION EXACTS AN ECONOMIC PRICE

It is, of course, overspecialization that creates economic insecurity. Even in the professions, it is the narrow specialist who feels the greatest vulnerability to economic dislocation. The physician or lawyer in general practice has a steady stream of clients with varied needs. The highly specialized heart surgeon or criminal lawyer has fewer clients with more serious needs. The pressure to charge high fees for overspecialized services is great. Specialization is, indeed, a major enemy of sound pricing. The commodity operations habit of narrow specialization of skill is the root cause of many pricing excesses. Where workers are multiskilled, resort to a cartel arrangement is far less necessary to protect against economic dislocation. Obsolescence of skill, vulnerability to economic cycles, narrowing of interest or perspective and career burnout are all typical of high specialization. They are the bane of the specialist, but not of the generalist. The generalist's work is more interesting and more stable. Often, generalists depend on repeat customers for a large part of their income, whereas the narrow specialist serves each customer only once. Pricing is naturally restrained for the service supplier who works from a base of multiple skill. Career redirection and revival are natural events in the work life of the generalist.

Reliance on narrow skill leaves service industries more vulnerable to economic change. Narrowly skilled employees are a liability to the service firm. The availability of a range of skill from each worker permits flexible allocation of labor hours over the current mix of work to reduce cost in the service firm. The more broadly skilled worker is more valuable and profitable to the firm. The narrowly skilled worker is harder to keep busy, more likely to be idle and a potential source of increased cost. Multiskilled workers are fundamental to a sound service economy in all terms, particularly efficiency, cost control and pricing.

WHAT IS A FAIR PRICE FOR THE SERVICE?

In establishing a fair price for service, the cost elements outlined in Chapter 12 can be rigorously applied. The base value of the service supplier's labor is the foundation. Then appropriate increments are added to account for overhead expense, investment in acquiring skill and occupational risk. This is a rational economic calculus that accounts for the worth of labor for service. Given the extreme variability of cost and price that otherwise can prevail, such a calculus is a reasonable and necessary element of pricing.

But that is often not enough. The quality of service is defined by a set of specifications for the service offered and by the resulting level of customer expectation. The mere availability of specifications, indeed, is an important quality measure in service and an indispensable index of fair pricing. But sound specifications for service are often lacking. As we have seen in earlier discussions, consistent generation and application of good specs for service require that a variety of barriers be identified and overcome. Not the least of those barriers is the unwillingness of many service providers to commit in advance to assured levels of quality and price. It is more profitable to exploit the customer's dependence on service and then bill at least as much—or a little more than—he or she seems able to pay.

From the service provider's perspective, satisfaction with the service is more easily factored into the price after the fact than before it. Full satisfaction with the result invites maximum price. Less than full satisfaction permits creative haggling beginning with the maximum price. Demanding maximum "going" price offers a strong initial bargaining position to the service supplier. The customer faces the potential of being held legally responsible for the full amount. Any lesser amount is a win against that possibility. The service supplier can reduce the price to "settle" with the customer and still obtain a generous return for time and labor. Handled right, the settlement might be made to look like magnanimity on the service supplier's part that creates goodwill with the customer.

Service pricing can be a significant element of the service art in some instances. Priced marginally high to start with, then reduced to a "special" price level, the customer may be convinced of getting a real bargain. It is a subtle and effective element of the service pricing game in which the customer may even learn to take pleasure.

This game is nothing new. Pricing in many domains begins with a "want to get" price, offers special limited discounts, is adjusted downward after a suitable passage of time and keeps dropping until it is a bargain to someone. Unused service capacity is leisure or learning time. Physical product, by contrast, must be held in inventory and represents both sunk opportunity cost and hazard of deterioration. Real pressure exists to move it and start with a fresh offering. Service is intangible. You have it, you sell it and you still have it. Only the time committed to its delivery is lost. Once a base income is established for the service giver, the cost of the time allocated to service delivery is a marginal trade-off against the value of added leisure. High demand for service that cuts into desired leisure time will inevitably command a high price. Where the service giver is sheltered by cartel restriction on service availability, his or her demand for higher price will probably be met by a large enough segment of the market to justify asking it. The upward cycle of price escalation is potentially endless.

Professionals raise their fees to the maximum, rationalizing them as justifiable given their long years of training and high status in the community. Collection agencies dedicated to physicians and medical bills proliferate as patients, desperate for medical help, accept the service, then simply neglect to pay. Lawyers demand high retainer fees, then refuse to file or appear on behalf of the client until more money is forthcoming, thereby delivering poor service and elevating legal blackmail to grand, new heights. Architects and civil engineers lobby for legislation that requires their services, then charge the maximum for routine technical assistance. The public either buys their services or breaks the law.

Counselors play on their clients' vulnerabilities to increase client dependence on counseling or capture client gratitude as grounds to raise their fees. Where the counseling service is likely to be painful or unsuccessful, large up-front fees and contracts are the rule. Personal servers charge the maximum, then expect a gratuity. Police and firemen, represented by aggressive unions, play on the guilt and fear of the public. The devices available for escalating service price are legion. Service suppliers sense that there is no real ceiling on price and look for levers that raise theirs.

Perhaps the quintessential illustration of service pricing that reaches toward the infinite skies is found in the entertainment industry. Actors and actresses, once limited to the basic existence of itinerant road shows, suddenly become international celebrities, able to command obscene fees. Sports heroes, still in the traveling road show mode much of their career, demand equally spectacular fees. Mass commodity entertainment via film, television and videotape supports exorbitant production budgets and princely wages for performers, often tied, commission-style, to earnings. The uncertainty of a fickle public or potential for career foreshortening injury further justify ever higher demands for performance fees. But it is the absence of an effective natural ceiling on all service prices that permits them to rise indefinitely. Even ordinary hellfire-and-damnation preachers who can gain a television following are corrupted by the infinite potential of financial gain in service. Service pricing easily runs wildly out of social control, distorting economic and social values. Eventually, something must be found to constrain these excesses and bring fair pricing to services.

So much potential for gross excess exists in pricing services that it becomes a potential time bomb in the economy. If service industries do not police their own pricing policies for fairness, assuring high quality and a fair price, restrictive legislation will result. Protection from wildly escalating medical costs is already on the national agenda. The product of legislative control over health care will most likely be reduced quality and rationed availability of health care. What is probably needed is not price controls or even more doctors but, rather, better systems for routine medical treatment that can be reliably delivered by paraprofessionals. The presumption that physicians have all the answers to health problems and alone are qualified to judge what medical treatment is required deserves challenge. Birthing could be more humane, less costly and safer if handled by well-trained midwives. Most physicians already rely on laboratory tests done by technicians for accurate diagnosis. Much diagnosis could be programmed and offered as a commodity. More than half of medical care offered today could be approached as an opportunity in skilled operations management where high-quality, price-effective service is made available on a price-competitive basis with minimum or no involvement of a trained physician.

Insurance rates are progressively coming under siege from outraged citizens and legislatures. But any legislation restricting insurance costs that does not limit court-ordered awards and attorney's fees can only restrict coverage and leave the general public inadequately covered for personal liability. That would clearly represent a major diminishment of quality in insurance coverage, delivered at increased cost. But liability insurance is not the only area in which there is threat of poor quality in insurance coverage. All areas of property and general loss are equally vulnerable to diminished quality at higher cost.

A major crisis in medical insurance is on the horizon, borne of the independent pricing problems found in health care delivery and insurance. Taken in tandem, they threaten to amplify the summary result. Insurance insulates the public from the cash cost of the service and encourages maximization of claims, while medicine promises to repair poor health of any kind, even that arising out of an undisciplined and self-destructive life-style. There is little or no incentive for the individual to accept responsibility for problems that, in reality, only he or she can solve. Service suppliers are more than ready to escalate the cost because of customer recklessness, especially when there is no natural price ceiling. Customers demand ever increasing service, then expose themselves to rising risk, placing more demand on the service and pushing up cost still more. The escalation of medical prices may already be out of control.

The economics and related politics of service pricing are worlds apart from those of commodity production. Service is the future of the economy but commodity production is its history. A transition of major proportions is in the offing. Pricing policy is a major and central problem in service. Unwillingness of service suppliers to deal realistically with excessive prices on a voluntary level promises backlash from customers. Indeed, backlash is already visible on numerous service industry horizons. The unwillingness of banks to drop the extreme high rates on credit card accounts; the continued provision of golden parachutes to ineffective executives who summarily lay off employees, expecting them to survive on unemployment compensation as best they can; physicians who leave a critically ill patient waiting long past the appointment time for service, then charge the maximum; politicians who vote themselves generous unfunded retirement benefits and bail out just ahead of public outrage— these are explosive service issues that demand solutions. More are waiting in the wings to stir up the public ire. Something must be done.

Many of these problems are as much the result of very poor service quality as they are of extortionate pricing. Sound economics do not bar high price, even extreme high price. Pricing is best left to free market forces as far as possible. Poor service quality should simply be exposed to customer evaluation and priced for what it's worth. Making the basis of good quality visible to all may first require definition, either by convention or by law. The definition applied will often be specific to the industry it concerns. Insurance and medicine are useful examples to begin with.

THE PRICING DILEMMAS OF INSURANCE AND HEALTH INDUSTRIES

Insurance has escalated in cost for two major reasons. First, the general public treats insurance as a form of lottery, expecting generous payoffs for its "losses." Second is the increasing involvement of lawyers and litigation in the settling of insurance claims. With an increasingly expanding supply of lawyers being trained by the educational system, often at public expense, lawyers become more aggressive at seeking out clients. Legislators, also usually lawyers, pass new laws that increase liability exposure and litigation. The court system becomes clogged with trivial, if not baseless, cases, slowing the settlement of insurance claims down, thereby reducing the quality of service.

The prevalence of claims padding, as well as plain fraud, forces insurance companies into an adversarial mode with their policyholders and third-party claimants alike, pitting the interests of the insurance company against those of their customer. Bypassing interrogation and documented proof of loss to speed up claims-handling service requires acceptance of substantially more questionable or weakly substantiated claims. That too raises the cost of insurance policies.

The higher the cost of the policy, of course, the greater the overhead burden it can carry. Custom, broad-coverage insurance policies, like luxury autos for automakers, increase gross revenue and raise gross profit. In dealing with property lines of coverage, the industry is torn between offering a cost-effective, bare-bones product, which it certainly could easily do, and selling the bloated, lottery-mode policy that is policed by detective-styled claims investigators.

The easy way out is to offer policies that pay full replacement value of lost property, priced at premium to cover the lottery element of loss. The service thereby offered is no longer insurance; it is income redistribution via lottery based on accidental loss or damage to one's physical property. Incentive is created for the policyholder to meet financial stress or replace worn property by inviting loss through neglect or irresponsibility. So-called deductible provisions may discourage small claims, thus reducing service quality in the greater proportion of policyholder losses, but have no effect on the major claims other than to encourage their inflation. If insurance companies were to specify exactly the losses covered, require substantial policyholder participation in the cost of loss and demand specified evidence of policyholder prudence in avoiding loss as a condition of payment, insurance costs for property losses could be reduced greatly. Use of fire detection systems for insured homes, alarm systems for autos, fire- and burglar-proof safes for valuables, intruder alarm systems for businesses, with provision for reduction or denial of payment where not used or maintained, would markedly reduce losses and costs. These are measures that insurance companies can implement directly and immediately. Competition may eventually require it. The major impediment will be the public's unwillingness to give up its insurance lottery system. It may take considerable education to convince the average insurance buyer that low cost and high quality are possible when insurance covers only real loss by accident that is wholly beyond the policyholder's control. Policyholder irresponsibility raises prices and lowers the quality of insurance coverage. Self-help in the form of intelligent participation in preventing loss reduces price and permits higher quality service.

Abuses of third-party liability claims are more difficult to correct since the third-party claimant is not a party to the original insurance contract. Certainly, if liability insurance had not been invented, society would have discovered other methods for dealing with personal loss suffered at the hands of an irresponsible other. The legal basis of liability coverage is the doctrine that when one injures or deprives another through foolish or improper action, one should repair the injury or replace the loss out of one's own resources. Insurance directly contravenes this doctrine by standing in place of the liable party in making restitution for loss. By absolving the wrongdoer of direct, personal responsibility for his or her actions, it encourages irresponsibility. Liability insurance as conceived at present operates largely as a lottery that pays off when another is to blame for one's pain and loss. By undercutting direct personal responsibility for the welfare of our fellows, insurance discourages personal responsibility and diminishes the quality of social life.

Most auto accidents, the more common basis of liability claims, are the result of shared negligence in some degree. Even the classic "rear-ender" can often be prevented by skilled driving in the car ahead. Some drivers seem adept at getting hit from behind. Any negligence at all, though, is likely to be used by attorneys and the courts as excuse to pay off, regardless of whether injury is tangible or subjective. As with medical insurance coverage that covers self-induced injury or disease, neglect of one's personal welfare is made to pay off in the insurance lottery.

Strict adherence to the doctrine of shared or contributory negligence is needed in establishing claims awards for third-party liability. Baring claims for nonmedically demonstrable injury is essential. Pain is not justification for monetary payment. Money doesn't stop pain. If it does, the pain is psychosomatic and the demand for money simply blackmail. Letting lawyers represent accident victims on a contingency basis (a percentage of the award) must be outlawed. The fee must be fixed, reasonable and subject to investigation. It may, if the claim is justifiable, be added to the claimant's expenses. But as long as it is in the attorney's interest to maximize expenses to maximize his or her fee, liability insurance costs will continue to soar.

Accidents do happen, and losses do occur. So-called "no-fault" insurance is intended to bridge the increasing prevalence of gaps where liability insurance is unavailable because of the extreme, chronic irresponsibility of the wrongdoer. As the system now stands, of course, only those with sufficient property at stake to be at risk in a lawsuit for damages are in need of liability insurance. The irresponsible, propertyless drifter is free to inflict injury on anyone, subject only to a term of free room, board and medical treatment while in prison, and only then if the act is criminal and the defense attorney uninterested. The propertyless, irresponsible individual who can claim injury, of course, is free to go for the maximum payoff, even at the cost of enhancing the injury. Liability claims are massive income redistribution schemes that more than "make whole" the losses of the claimant and enrich lawyers many times over for their effort. The system must be radically revised if it is to deliver high-quality insurance coverage at a fair price.

As a start, if insurance is to stand in place of the wrongdoer in an auto accident, there is no rational basis for collecting from the wrongdoer's insurer as long as the act was innocent, a mental lapse, the result of simple negligence. Payment for ordinary unintended damage could as reasonably be made by the damaged individual's own no-fault policy and a common pool funded as part of automobile and drivers' licensing fees. It is reasonable that only those drivers responsible enough to be licensed and purchase insurance should be permitted to collect on their own injuries arising out of simple negligence. Property damage and injury to pedestrians or nonpaying guest passengers could also be paid from a common pool of state-supervised funds in cases of simple negligence.

Irresponsibility on a major scale that injures or deprives another should always be penalized financially. A simple device to achieve this is to require a percentage of coinsurance for any third-party liability claim resulting from gross negligence. A drunk or reckless driver who injures another should personally share in the cost of his or her irresponsibility. As little as a 5% copayment of a liability settlement, which would be the right of the insurance company to collect from its policyholder, would serve as a massive deterrent to irresponsible auto operation, improving the quality of insurance and reducing its price.

Liability insurance for other purposes need not be revised in any major way. Where appropriate, the liability copayment method can be used to enhance responsible action of otherwise ambitious, fast-moving companies and individuals. It is essential, though, that the courts not continue to be misused as referees in the lottery system. The full cost of resort to the court system for damages should be assessed on the losing party at the discretion of the court. That would speed up claims and encourage more disputes into arbitration channels where adjudication costs are lower. All of this requires legislation that requires the assistance of lawyer legislators. Only massive public and political pressure for change is likely to bring about reform in liability insurance. It is much overdue and indispensable to improved pricing and quality of insurance.

The remedy for health insurance costs is to cut hospital costs and set standards for physicians' fees. Hospital costs are best negotiated between hospital and insurance company. Insurance, however, need not routinely cover precautionary admission for observation, doctor's or patient's convenience and other noncritical occasions. Where it is deemed necessary, noncritical care should be an occasion for lower cost hospital care. Bare-bones hospital treatment, once common in country and community hospitals, which assumed that a close friend or member of the family would participate in patient care to reduce cost, should be rediscovered for these and other appropriate occasions. Many hospital patients are victims of unwarranted and unneeded professional care at high cost when all they need is someone to hold their hand and help them when they can't help themselves, keeping skilled professional help close at hand in the event of crisis. Cold professionalism is not an increase in service quality when it is offered at premium price, yet squeezes out common human concern. That is a lesson hospitals need to relearn. Hospitals and physicians are already much too ready to treat patients as if they were merely "pre-cadavers." There is room here to reintroduce cost savings and humaneness of care too.

When medical care is delivered directly by a physician or paramedical technician, it should not be necessary for the patient to guess what the fee will be. The cost of treatment should be stated or published up-front on all occasions. Physician participation or nonparticipation with various insurance carriers should also be clearly stated. The individual patient must have the right under law to require his or her physician in advance to agree to accept the insurance payment, or the insurance payment plus some designated percent, as full payment for services. Negotiation of the fee is then put on proper and competent ground—between physicians and the insurance companies who are better equipped to know what the service is worth. Physicians who depend on repeat customers already follow these measures in many instances. These communications should become routine and be demanded by all patients.

One area of medicine deserves major overhaul for quality and pricing: high-risk, low-success experimental treatment is at present among the most costly of medical services. Physicians experiment on desperate, terminally ill patients with little or no success, other than in enhancing their own professional credentials, usually at maximum cost to the patient. Presumably, it is the large potential for disappointment and a possibility of suit for malpractice after one of the many failures that is the rationale for high cost. It's not always clear whose disappointment is at issue—the patient's because the procedure fails, or the physician's for failing to see results. In any other industry, experiments are carried out at the risk of the experimentee and at the cost of the experimenter. Physicians, armed with their vast personal status and prestige, leave the risk to the patient and also expect high cost to be borne by the patient. Ethically (a term clearly descriptive of high-quality service), experimental treatment should be on a shared-cost or no-cost and no-fault basis. If the medical profession ever gets around to cleaning up its service act, this would be one of the first places where change should occur.

Lawyers often charge exorbitant fees to handle hopeless cases. Clients pay in the false hope that the magnitude of the cost will improve the service (the effort of the lawyer and the odds of winning). The best quality service is still always fairly priced. Hopeless cases are best taken to struggling lawyers who cannot command high fees but who need to win to establish their reputation. Quality here is in the degree of creative problem-solving effort that goes into the case. The experienced attorney who loves and serves the law is rare, but his or her practice is certain to succeed and his or her fees are in line. The attorney who is a hired gun before the bar will drag his or her client through the fires of hell in his or her competitive attempt to win, demand a huge fee for his or her time and effort and deliver a consistently inferior result. High cost and mediocre to low quality consistently go together in service delivery. High price is always an occasion for the customer to stop and reevaluate the service offering. It is also frequently time to look elsewhere for service.

Quality is a central factor in pricing for most other service offerings. The professional who errs in design or execution of the service creates time-consuming rework and potential for lawsuit from the customer. Both, inevitably, end up being added to the price. The ineffective personal counselor benefits by extending counseling services over a longer span of time and running up the fee by doing so. Bad information from a poorly designed MIS system results in the wrong decision, requiring more information service to resolve the question. Poor teaching increases potential for teacher burnout, reduces quality of teaching still further and adds to the cost of health care for the teacher. Ineffective police or fire protection usually results in overmanning of the operations to bring quality up to minimum, thereby directly increasing cost while obtaining only minimum service.

High price for service does not add value. Higher priced services are, indeed, likely to be associated with lower quality. A fair price paid to a competent, high-quality service giver is odds on to be the optimum service result. Quality, thus, is intimately bound up with pricing in services, serving as a likely measure of quality and always enhancing it.

Greed is not only an ugly quality for a service giver, it is a needless excess for making a good living, antithetical to high quality, harmful to customer relations and economically counterproductive in the longer run. It will ultimately be penalized either by the market or by political, legislative restraint. A skilled service-provider generalist who creates a reputation for service quality will always be in demand. Service fees are not subject to impersonal competitive price undercutting as commodity products are. Good service always commands a premium price. It is seldom subject to raw price-cutting competition unless price is seriously out of line or the customer is dissatisfied for some major reason. High quality at a fair price virtually guarantees a lasting niche in the market for service.

A GENERAL MODEL FOR SERVICE PRICING

In an economy based on the intangibles of skill and personal service, there is much less emphasis on the physical tools of production. Commodity production at minimum cost and maximum efficiency provides the base on which other economic value is added. The service supplier's tools are themselves commodities of a sort. Return on investment in training and equipment in support of service is rationally and routinely calculated into the costing of service. Individual service givers cannot serve without their training and equipment. The wisdom of these investments and the need to maintain them as tools of the trade is intuitively obvious. The old rules for commodity pricing must be abandoned

In the early stages of a commodity production economy when investment in the tools of production is proportionately high, severe discipline is required to create the critical mass of plant capacity needed for efficiency. The reward for accepting and enforcing that discipline is, as a result, also disproportionately high. The average citizens will not defer gratification of need to build the needed investment base for efficient mass production. They may participate in the benefits of mass production out of their day wages as workers in the plant. Owners of productive plant and equipment reap disproportionate reward for their self-denial and vision. Workers are better off than they previously were before they enjoyed regular wage-paid work, but lag severely in obtaining their share of the expanded wealth. Wealth accumulates to the owners of productive plant in the form of plant assets and return on investment. Workers often still subsist from day to day.

In a service-dominated economy, these disparities dissipate. Everyone invests in their own training and knowledge, as well as in the tools of service delivery. Mega-investment in the vast new projects of science is more likely to be funded by government through tax monies. The divergence of financial reward between owner and worker closes. The need for that exceptional self-discipline that builds the economic machine diminishes. As it does, we may anticipate a substantial leveling of wage incomes.

The market will still mediate prices and costs, of course, but absentee ownership of productive resources will be less available and less well rewarded. The worker who uses the tools to best economic advantage using skill and meeting customer need is now the source of greatest value in the economic system. The CEO who achieves an acceptable dividend payout and protects the value of assets while the business goes under is a veritable saint to directors and stockholders, but is simultaneously an arch-villain to everyone else and a contributor of net loss to the economy. As the worth of return of physical investment fades, the worth of the CEO's contribution must diminish. The infinite value of high-quality service eventually raises return on skill investment to heights far surpassing those of mere plant and equipment.

Discovery of this new source of value is already changing the economic landscape. Service suppliers are tentatively, sometimes aggressively, testing the upper limits of their service's value to the customer. A massive revolution in the rules and conventions of income distribution is waiting in the wings. Skill, education and experience, once subordinate to physical plant investment, are about to jump out into an undisputed lead over mere physical properties. The scope and impact of this revolution promise to be as far-reaching as was the whole of the industrial revolution. Everything is about to go up for grabs.

The rules for pricing in this revolution will likely be simple. They will begin with the requirement that there be no artificial, political limitation on the supply of any skill or training. To assure that this is the case, it will be necessary for government to supply skill training on a basis of demonstrated talent and capacity for self-discipline to anyone who seeks it. The priority will be on service skill. A "liberal" education that neglects to enhance language and communication skills will be one of the lower priorities in this new scheme of things.

In the new era, it is clearly in the best interests of society to assure an ample supply of service-related skill more than ever. Education and training have been increasingly more important to economic and scientific progress for more than a century. They now achieve status as indispensable for proper operation of the economic system. The services of government in supplying relevant training, particularly technical and vocational training, are absolutely essential to a sound and equitable system of service delivery.

Cartels of every kind must be monitored and limited. Attempts to license service-suppliers or legislate their required use must be sternly resisted. Many will attempt to gain advantage in the race for price advantage. It will be more critical to keep this contest fair than it ever was to prevent unfair concentration of corporate power under antitrust laws. Large industry at least enjoys economies of scale that naturally hold cost down. There are no structural corrections that offset price advantage in service delivery. Full competition is in the best interest of the individual service provider and general public alike.

Labor unions in service industries must be limited in their powers. Strikes in service impact greatest on the customer. In some service industries like communications, public transport and public service, a strike has the potential to deny service to the entire customer base. This approaches the excesses of monopoly. The power to strike could potentially drive prices to extortionate levels. Where the customer has an alternative for obtaining the service, a strike is merely an inconvenience. But strikes by teachers, police, air transport controllers, railroad employees and hospital nurses are attacks on the very foundations of current-day social order. They are price strikes against the customer. To compound the insult to the customer, acquiescence to high wage demands of strikers may be profitable for private management and politically convenient to elected officials. Because they exploit the infinite value of service, there is little defense against them unless they are controlled by broader public policy. If they are not, the public is the major, perhaps the only, loser.

A useful model for service pricing is available in a widely used system for pricing auto repair and similar basic maintenance services. By legislation in many cases, though it could often just as easily enough be voluntary, the repairer is required to supply a written estimate of cost where requested. The hourly rate for labor is openly posted for all to see, and published standards are available for reference that establish the norm for acceptable service repair labor time by type of repair. Service may be guaranteed or not depending on the policy of the service supplier, but availability or nonavailability of that guarantee must be made explicit.

It is not an exact or closed system. Flexibility exists to handle unanticipated repair problems. The posted hourly rate can be adjusted at the choice of the service supplier to fit the going market rate. Professionally developed, published standards assure reasonable, basic equity in pricing. Highly skilled service suppliers are more generously compensated for their high skill, which is also likely to be associated with higher quality service. There is ample incentive to acquire and apply higher than merely average skill in delivering the service. Lesser skilled service givers must work harder and longer for an equivalent wage but are probably adequately compensated at their level of skill. And, assuming that the service result meets specified threshold skill quality requirements (an equivalent of the guarantee on repairs), the result to the customer is satisfactory.

There is still room for abuse in various forms, including diagnosis of repair need that is, in fact, unnecessary, or use of used rather than new materials, supplies or parts. These can easily enough be exposed in audits done by consumer groups or investigative news reporters. On the whole, it is a system that permits give and take between service giver and customer and permits adjustment to their individual and market needs. It is open and explicit, fraud or dishonesty are easily exposed, it allows negotiation before the service is delivered, it permits competitive market rates to be charged and it supports high-quality service. It is a working model that can easily be applied in many areas of personal service.

We may take note that the reason this pricing model exists and works is because there is (in most states at least) no licensing requirement for auto repair. Auto repair mechanics are naturally independent, self-reliant people who need no cartel to seek advantage in the legislatures. Customers can effectively put pressure on mechanics for fair pricing and quality service. Poor-quality service is readily measurable in the performance of the auto, and incompetent repairs are subject to liability suit. The inherent variety and generality of repairs demands broad, varied skill. Unfamiliar repair needs offer opportunity for learning, the benefits of which can offset the added time required to effect the repair. These are ideal conditions for favorable pricing of the service. The service giver can make a good living, and the customer can obtain quality service at a fair price. That is an end result all service would do well to pursue.

This model of service pricing takes into account both the real costs and the intangible qualities of the service offered. Under special circumstances, a service may be available at no cost. The same service may be available at extortionate prices on another occasion and in other circumstances. Ultimately, the price of service is reduced to simple exchange in which price reflects the needs and respective life-style expectations of the service giver and his or her customer. The price can be almost anything from nothing to infinity. The quality of the service should be high at any (or no) price, though it may fall with higher prices as a function of high customer expectation and limited service provider skill.

We may look to a future service economy in which the satisfaction of the customer with the service supplied creates in the customer a need to reward the service giver satisfactorily for the service rendered. Price wars and bargain hunting will pass into the history books. The service exchange could easily transform into a mutual relationship where the service giver rewards the customer with high-quality service while the customer reciprocally and gladly rewards the service giver with a fair price. Once that state has arrived, our economic system can never be the same again.

Chapter 16

Government Reform as Metaphor and Model of the Service Revolution

"Denied real service, taxpayers must inevitably revolt."

A century and more dominated by a commodity manufacturing economy has inevitably imprinted the values of commodity operations onto society's social service sector, government in particular. The watchword has often been "efficiency in all things." Taxation and governmental services have been largely conceived in commodity terms with the result that much service potential is missed in them. The principal services of government beyond the universal basics of police and fire protection are education, quality of life maintenance for the young, weak and poor, and management of large-scale technological R&D. Education and welfare were once services of communities and especially churches. R&D, formerly the exclusive province of the isolated inventor, has outgrown the one-person shop, even outstripped the resources of most major corporations. Only a tax-supported national space agency could take man to the moon. These government services are all under pressure today because of major social changes surrounding them and because, among them, they easily account for two-thirds or more of total government spending.

R&D is the latest arrival under the umbrella of modern government sponsorship. Invention, throughout history, has served military objectives, but never previously has it been pursued on the grand scale of the present age. For half a century or more, R&D has largely been driven by international technomilitary competition. The service of invention to military objectives has been so great, indeed, that fear of nuclear warfare and ecological disruption from runaway technological change has emerged as the pervasive social concern of the age. The collapse of Soviet Russia as a major world power diminishes the fear of war and opens the door to much slowed technological change as well. We may certainly now expect the brakes to be put on technological advance so that social adjustment can catch up with the technological revolutions already in place. So much change has been introduced by technological advance, though, that only government sponsored R&D put into service in support of that catch-up has any real chance of dealing with it. This will require reintroduction of a genuine service orientation into government-supported R&D. In the process, a long tradition of large-scale, efficient production of new science and technology supporting military need will inevitably be relegated to the history books because of its low and often negative service value to the populace.

R&D has too long been a competitive, commodity response to conflict between nations. Warfare, historically used to bleed off internal political tensions while simultaneously establishing political and economic dominance over neighbor nations, has already been replaced by raw economic competition as the major form of international competition. Soviet Russia lost the cold war because its economy could not bear the burden of an unworkable political ideology and the gigantic military establishment needed to support it. The deeply instilled democratic and egalitarian ideals of Russian society foiled those police-state devices necessary to waging war as a solution to internal social and economic tensions. Russia has finally and fully accepted competition on an economic level as the only civilized test of national power. Formal introduction of the age of economic combat without armed military combat is Russia's gift to mankind.

The Japanese, losers in World War II, had already adopted the only alternative form of competition—economic—as the ground for their world comeback, succeeding impressively in the effort. They have achieved higher quality—a critical element of service—in many of their key product offerings. A tradition of close, sometimes intense, collaborative interpersonal and social relationships within their core culture gives the Japanese a headstart in their sense of what it takes to deliver satisfactory service. Commodity mass production is a more recent appearance in Japan's culture. When it arrived it was imposed on an already close-knit, custom-output-habituated society. Major modifications to the institution of commodity output were inevitable in these circumstances. Commodity mass production with a high-quality, low-volume service emphasis has become Japan's competitive weapon in world competition for economic supremacy.

The United States alone now remains as a world class military power capable of substituting military aggression for competitive economic effectiveness. The world watches to see if the United States will use its superior might to maintain political and economic supremacy, or will lead the way to a worldwide system of fair, soundly refereed and humane economic competition between nations. The manner in which R&D is employed will signal the U.S. intent either to revert to a commodity-styled, military-backed society or move to a freely competitive service economy.

The core of this new revolution is the need and preference of the individual customer. On a mass scale, market research is already put to use assessing "market" (though, less often, "customer") preference for various goods and services. Specialists in communications processes work intensively with small, representative sample populations to establish market acceptability of those goods and services. It is a correct start, and one that points the way for coming dominance of one-on-one communication between service giver and customer that establishes the customer's particular, personal needs as the basis for service design.

Computer-based communications with a technology flavor, like electronic mail, are on the wrong track. Massive emphasis on networking of computer systems through instantaneous electronic data flow, for instance, wholly retains the commodity spirit of mass communication. Communicators are buffered from one another by machinery that saves them from the complexity and confusion of dealing with personal singularity and allows them to hide behind anonymity. Communication, unfortunately, is limited to the simplest, most mechanical level when communicators don't have to take the trouble to discover one another's unique personality. Electronic message transmission succeeds at closing the physical distance between communicators but does little to reduce their psychological distance. The on-going debate about computer data bases and loss of personal privacy when personal records are opened to public access is mostly about the superficiality of those records as adequate descriptors of the whole human being they purport to represent. Computer networks encourage people to deal with one another as unidimensional, manipulable objects rather than as individuals to be known and understood.

Computers, nonetheless, have immense potential for expanded social service if government-sponsored R&D is properly applied in that direction. R&D as a basic service of government must be redirected to the solution of human problems on all levels. For instance, real-time electronic monitoring of the location and activity of children, the retarded, the infirm or the mentally ill to protect them from harm or to structure their social activities is close to being practical on a wide scale. Many prisons could be emptied if inmates could be electronically tracked as to location and time of day by a central computer system that restricts each person to an exact, preprogrammed pattern of movement and activity. Many of those for whom unrestrained freedom is an opportunity for crime might be more effectively controlled technologically at far lower cost than with the direct, high-cost physical restraints applied at present. Such a system would reserve stone-wall and steel-bar prisons for those intractable to the discipline of an exact personal routine as monitored and demonstrated by computers. Proof of commission of crime or violation of restraint while being monitored would become mere administrative process, saving society vast sums of money in costs of criminal prosecution.

R&D is urgently needed in the search for solutions to problems of human overcrowding and pollution. Better methods for disposal of all forms of waste, particularly toxic or hazardous waste, are needed. Improved systems for cost-effectively recycling common waste are urgently needed. Solar power generation has been ignored largely because it seems "uneconomic" as long as oil and coal are still cheaply available. It is more efficient costwise to use low-cost, nonrenewable petroleum resources than to shift to higher cost solar power. Low cost pushes out a high-quality solution.

Safe, high-speed long-distance transit needs help. Private corporations are close to the limit of their resources in applying R&D to improvements of air or rail transportation. R&D now in the service of mass destructive weaponry must be diverted to preservation of health and life. Where the private sector is capable of advancing solutions to problems, government should provide encouragement and incentives. Where it cannot, government must manage the project itself as it does at present with large-scale military and space systems. Some government R&D should probably disappear. But broad-based sponsorship of R&D as a service of government has become and will remain a permanent fixture in one form or another. Only government can afford such sponsorship and only democratic political processes can properly guide it. The objectives of that research and development must become the subject of clear, open political debate.

In supplying education as one of its central services, government must soon bring extensive R&D to bear on methods of delivering learning opportunity to *individuals*. Public education as now structured is clearly an example of mass commodity service. Like the cars rolling down the assembly line of an auto manufacturer, educators can only hope that the system works most of the time while knowing that they must tolerate a significant proportion of system failure in the name of cost-efficiency. A class of students in a schoolroom is partly a way to standardize the educational offering, partly a device for engaging competitive spirit in the learning process, partly an opportunity to develop students' social skills, partly an efficient vehicle for applying teacher time and talent. Individuality is ruled out unless it offers a good model of mass educational purposes and values to other students. Class is a leveling device, not one that enhances individual qualities. Public education serves first of all to emplace those minimum social and communication skills required by a mass society, even though educators may claim development of maximum individual potential is their highest value. Education thereby portrays the anomaly of an individual service conceived and produced as a commodity offering.

The primary and secondary education systems, mostly public, offered to the young attempt to do many things that are better accomplished by mass television, mass-produced games and toys, mass entertainment. It comes up a poor second to these competitors, it bores and it fails. The classroom is no longer the window on the wider world it once was for students cloistered in the restricted confines of a conventional small-town family home. The family TV provides a big, broad, individually flexible window that opens the world to a child as nothing before has ever done. Today's classroom is a holding area, a jail to some, a joke to others. A teacher who can identify the gaps of student experience, reach individual students on their individual grounds of interest and reengage student interest can succeed. The conventional classroom structure of the educational system is a barrier, not a help in that pursuit. Increased tax money cannot make it work better. Increased teacher salaries only draw greater numbers of teachers who seek maximum income without concern for the quality of their career lives. In the pursuit of high pay, teachers are themselves victims of the mass commodity system as many accept a misfitted career for high pay. The best students and teachers are lost in a thicket of bureaucratic mediocrity. Public education is a clear and present example of service distorted by commodity operations management models and methods.

If government is to provide a quality educational service to its citizens, it must begin with extensive R&D for restructuring the system into a predominantly service mode. The commodity base of learning, iterated practice and drill at math and grammar must be automated to the maximum. It must be converted into an ongoing contest of skill among constantly shifting groups of competitive coequals, whose knowledge and skill are tested and verified with multiple, efficient, high-reliability automated methods.

Teacher time and talent must be applied to student problems rather than to the routine of drill. Teachers must be qualified in student learning skill diagnostics as well as knowledgeable of a full range of individual differences that come to school. Teaching social skills must become a special and particular objective of every school, with methods and systems of ongoing evaluation that assure it will reach every student. Social skill as incidental, unplanned fallout of the system, which it is at present, is intolerable in a strong service economy. It is no accident that inner-city youths find more relevance in gangs for learning social skill than in their schools. As now approached, social skill is an accidental outcome, not a clear, measured objective of the educational system.

Service in education requires that each student be found *psychologically* where he or she actually is. This requires great tolerance of the considerable variety in individuality and uniqueness that characterizes humankind. Students must continue to be trained up to a minimum level of communications and social skill to permit competent participation in politics and business. But it should not be necessary to settle for this minimum as the standard, basic commodity output of education by the system. Certainly this is the fundamental service supplied by educators to society, one that makes every citizen employable and permits knowledgeable political participation. The fullest potential of each person should be developed over and beyond the limited goal of basic literacy in a service-oriented educational system. At present the system is at cross-purposes with itself. It often is not even achieving the minimum of competent literacy. A service revolution is waiting to erupt in education. Government must lead the way.

If the educational system with its classroom tradition is already an anachronism, public welfare is on a par with crossing the Atlantic Ocean on a raft. Raising the quality of life of the poor is the chronic wasteland of governmental service. The principal reason the welfare system fails is because help is impersonally conceived as a matter of providing money. In mass commodity terms, the money paid out must be efficient, even optimum, at that level where life is barely maintained. There is never enough to support the achievement of individual independence. As a matter of public policy in the service of efficient distribution of cash money, the poor are forever kept in the dependency limbo of a bare subsistence level of income. In the absence of service that helps overcome dependency and achieve self-sustenance, dependency is permanent.

Welfare officers and welfare recipients play a tough game of "justify the need." The social worker who uncovers fraud so that the wrongful recipient can be prosecuted is as well or better rewarded than the one who finds a way to help get a client self-sufficient and off the welfare rolls.

Caseloads of welfare workers are kept high to reduce costs (efficiency is still primary here too), minimizing personal contact and limiting individualized understanding of the client's needs. The core of this governmental service is simple raw redistribution of income from the haves to the have-nots. The process has gone on long enough to make legitimate the claims of the have-nots on the resources of the haves. Picketing, even rioting, is accepted by society as legitimate counteraction by the poor to reduction in expected cash payout. Encouraging riot seems hardly a constructive service of government, but as long as welfare is conceived as but another mass commodity item of expense, delivered efficiently at low cost, it is probably an unavoidable eventuality.

If raising the quality of life for the poor is the real objective of good government, a commodity-style redistribution of cash money is hardly the answer. It is a cheap conscience insulator for politicians and the economically well-off, but a soul shrinker for the poor. In an earlier time and in a simpler society, the pastor or merchant who was approached for alms saw to the immediate, short-term need for food, clothing and shelter, then looked for a place in the socioeconomic system where the poor could be integrated. At worst, the benefactor exploited the poor, at best he raised them up. Universal public education allowed some of the children of the exploited to break away from dependency. It was a harsh but open system in which opportunity could be seized when it arrived. In modern times when it is administered as a government service, anyone who successfully breaks away from welfare is a major news event.

The poor are viewed, commodity style, as a homogeneous mass, all with the same needs and problems. There are, in fact, two distinct categories of the poor. There are those who cannot get above subsistence level because of prejudice, lack of basic educational skill or absence of sound models for thrift and money management. Models of opulence on TV drive appetites for costly things beyond the means of these poor, keeping them in perpetual poverty. Sickness and social ineptness prevent stable income generation from steady work, pulling the ambitious back into the abyss of poverty, over and over. Money may help in the short run, but only social and economic competence can solve the trap the poor find themselves sinking into. The poor need the services of mentors, counselors, sponsors and life-style models who can show them the way out of their wilderness. They need *some* money but they need service much more. Professionals in government service can perhaps efficiently organize a system of service in support of these needs, and should continue to be responsible for efficient payout of money. Delivery of the service, though, is likely to be more effective if channeled through trained volunteers or part-timers compensated for their successes rather than for their time. The objective must be to break the cycle of poverty among victims in this category of poverty.

The other category of poor are the chronically inept, socially disconnected indigents who can never or will never find a place in the mainstream social system. They are the mentally ill, the chronically unemployed, the physically or addictively impaired, the life drop-outs of society who will likely never be recovered to productive endeavor.

In a marginal subsistence economy, these were once abandoned to the whims of chance and fortune. A society of affluence cannot in good conscience ignore the plight of such as these, however irresponsible they may be. Partly, we cannot escape the responsibility borne of knowing that a complex economic system that supports such affluence may be a cause of the condition of these poor. Partly, we cannot turn our backs on these fellow human beings without diminishing our own humanity. There is, indeed, great wealth at hand. Only a tiny part is needed to sustain these lost souls.

The Salvation Army offers a strong and effective model for assisting the lost and destitute. It is a throwback to the time when church and community handled all forms of welfare. The objective of "Sallies," as they call themselves, is still to uplift the poor by offering salvation for their souls. If there is a rare instance of uplift, it is vindication enough of the attempt. But on the whole, these unreachably lost need a bed and a hot meal to sustain them through another day. The Salvation Army is practical enough to provide the basic essentials that get society's wanderers through today.

Some, like gypsies, follow the sun, sleeping under temporary shelter, begging food or clothing, working briefly for a small cash stake to buy a blanket or bus ticket to the next stop. Others in their pursuit of untrammeled independence refuse help and stake out a park bench or building entrance as home. They are nuisances to the polite and conventional citizen. Thus, they need to be gathered into a quiet corner out of sight where they can live out their peculiar lives without upset to onlookers. The principal service expected of government by the taxpaying citizen is to hide them. The major service to these poor will be the practical provision of public soup kitchens and a place to clean up and sleep. The major need of society in this category is a central, national clearinghouse of information where these wanderers can be identified with their unique personal histories, including characteristic behaviors and even medical problems, described for the record so that government officials anywhere can deal with them appropriately as they enter each new jurisdiction. They are today's orphans of society. We must service them as such.

Protection against natural disaster and social breakdown has always been a central service of government and the community. In an earlier time the church was law and everyone was a volunteer fire fighter. In a mass society, it is efficient to specialize these functions. Fire fighting is an inherent, true service. Where it is not provided by professionals, it must be supplied by volunteers. It is also an economic good because it reduces the cost of property insurance. It goes to the customer, it adapts to present need, it is not subject to efficiencies or cost reduction except as better equipment is created or as full-time, part-time or volunteer fire fighters are found to be the more cost-effective solution to labor need.

Police, on the other hand, are a mixed bag of service providers and law enforcers. In their informal role as maintainers of social order, once the core of police duty, there are many day-to-day services they can provide to keep citizens out of mischief. They can socialize the young, calm the contentious, round up the indigent, frighten off the desperate. They can also become prosecutor, judge and jury in ways that distort their role as public servant into public tyrant. Restrictions on police activity designed to curb abuses of police power and assure civil rights to all have, unfortunately, also curbed those informal social services once offered when they served as referees of common social order. Denied the opportunity to offer skilled service to their clients, police are left with the duty of law enforcement according to the rule book.

Reintroduction of a service element into police work will probably require strict separation of law enforcement as forcible restraint from that part that offers social service in the form of skilled fact-gathering and on-the-spot refereeing of social crises. The paramilitary aspect of law enforcement requires justification in evidence or fact that enforcement is called for. It calls for special risks and tools that permit appropriate force to be applied where needed. Fact-gathering and investigation, on the other hand, are performed in the service of truth-finding. Once the truth is known, society and the courts must have the courage to act on it effectively. A major, positive beginning would be to give law enforcers the freedom to directly restrain known, proven criminals and scofflaws in any suspicious circumstance. Demonstrated criminal proclivity was once and should again be sufficient cause for police to act.

Refereeing of civil dispute to prevent lawlessness is a special art in itself. Some police offers are skilled in this role. But a variety of government officials already serve as quasi-referees in matters of health, zoning, labor and similar regulatory matters. The best of them service their clients by helping solve problems. The poorest merely enforce the letter of the law. Mostly, it would appear to be a matter of mandating genuine referee service and measuring its quality with customers. Good, fair referees in matters under dispute offer valuable service. It is a model of the government service role that should be extended.

Mass commodity habits of analysis and thinking encourage us to live like hermits, wholly within the confines of our private heads and experiences, neglecting and unaware of the variety of life that surrounds us. Present-day delivery of government services typifies that kind of analysis and thinking to a degree that renders it an exemplar of what is wrong with service. A mass commodity frame of thinking makes a mess of any attempt to provide even the most basic services in matters that have nothing to do with protection of life or property, with enforcement of standards or with collection of taxes. A mass commodity approach to provision of humane government services supplies us with the horrible example of what is wrong with service delivery in the current age. Government can lead the way out of this wasteland of nonservice services. That would be the beginning of greatly improved value in government service itself.

The answer to taxpayer discontent in the present age is not necessarily to cut spending and improve efficiency of government. Better systems and methods of service delivery that justify the cost of government are urgently needed. That may mean either higher or lower taxes depending on the public view of the quality of service offered. Police, public school and welfare services are consistently miscast in a commodity operations management mode, and thereby robbed of their service content. R&D is carried out in a commodity mode, defeating democratic debate of its objectives and bypassing urgently needed technological solutions to social problems. When service is restored as the central purpose of government, the value of the offering can offset the pain of high taxes, and perhaps can cure it wholly for many citizens. Government as metaphor of the service revolution offers opportunity to build a service competence and customer orientation into existing, necessary but publicly criticized received services. There is today near unanimity of agreement with the need for change. Putting service and servants back into government can lead the way for private industry. It can be the model that guides the way to our service economy future.

Chapter 17

Conclusion: Now, as We Enter the Service Era

"Without a service emphasis, any business is vulnerable."

The world is in the throes of a great revolution. A tide of democratic spirit has swept over the Soviet Union, shaking it to its very foundations. The globe shrinks as electronics connect each corner to every other in the flash of a microwave bounced off the nearest communications satellite. Marshall McLuhan's vision of a global village daily comes nearer to realization. The United Nations, once little more than a hope of international cooperation, becomes the legitimate forum through which an international law offender, Saddam Hussein, is taken on by an international SWAT team. The Third World waits in the wings for its opportunities to exploit cheap labor and local physical resources to create its own wealth. "Plenty" is no longer sufficient. Quality emerges from this boiling milieu of change as a new imperative of economic life. As the PBS series and the book based on it by Dobyns and Crawford-Mason (1991) put it, it is now a matter of "Quality or Else." Modern people demand the best and want it delivered with a smile at their doors.

The revolution created by these changes is only barely visible as this is written. A great cataclysm of economic change is about to sweep over the landscape. It begins with massive losses in manufacturing employment. The shrinkage of production labor brought on by improved product design and automated production methods has been under way for at least a quarter of a century. As commodity production has diminished toward a 5% or smaller labor base following the earlier lead of agriculture, those gradual adjustments in labor allocation that might otherwise have naturally occurred were hidden by a massive defense budget committed to expanded military production. Suddenly, peace is declared and a production economy artificially inflated by defense output collapses. Wages long inflated by unions and labor shortages give way to competition for nonunion service-sector wages at a much lower level of pay. Service professions in short supply, nurses, computer programmers, CPAs, customer representatives, TV personalities, entertainers and athletes demand and get generous wage packages. A transition of gigantic proportions is under way wherein old skills and capabilities languish unused and run to atrophy while wholly new skills and capabilities rush to the forefront of value. Commodity production, once the certain route to wealth and economic security, becomes a dogfight for share and survival. Service emerges as the arena where the greater opportunity obtains and the major economic action now takes place.

Those who already understand and embrace the new imperative of service stand to win big in this transition. For those who do not, there are many old perspectives, values, habits and skills that must be replaced by new ones. In a dominantly commodity economy, the highest value is cost-efficiency. In a service economy, the once all-embracing principle of efficiency, with its cold, impersonal focus on standardization and volume, is an ugly anachronism. The basic rules of the economic game are thereby transformed.

Service suppliers must know their customers personally and accurately. They must possess highly honed and various skills that permit them to shift service emphasis to fit changing customer need or demand. Anticipation of future customer need is no longer a matter of gross changes in population or number of households. It must now sometimes be accomplished customer by customer, market segment by market segment. Delay because of insufficient physical or skill capacity is likely to be business lost forever. Lead times that build in a large margin of service giver comfort are noncompetitive compared with those that have been shrunk to the bare minimum. Methods for improving work flow must take into account capacity restraints that cannot be wasted and permit flexible allocation of multiple labor skills.

Managing service industry quality is a major exercise in applied management strategy, modern organization design, human resource development, data base management and statistics. The complexities are potentially immense. The variety of systems configurations alone that offer potential in any given industry offers decades of study and experiment as to their quality implications. Cost reduction and containment are no less concerns in a service economy than they were when commodities dominated the scene, but the route to their attainment is wholly different. High, multiple skill with low plant capacity utilization is the imperative for low-cost, high-quality service. Contrast that with the specialized low-skill, high-plant capacity utilization emphasis under commodity production operations and the magnitude of the discontinuity between these two disparate economic domains becomes apparent. The rules for effective operations management have been turned on their head.

Virtually the whole of current Western society and culture will have to be retrofitted to the new demands of service. Faceless masses of undifferentiated humanity will be replaced by unique individuals with specific personal life-styles. Fashion is already subject to such rapid change that it is less the norm of dress and conduct than a smorgasbord of variety to be chosen from as it passes. Even so, the pace of change and introduction of novelty is only just now beginning to quicken.

Rugged individualism that isolates itself from social contact in an ongoing dance with technology is the closest America has come to personal self-expression over the past century and more. Teamwork that accommodates and emphasizes those differences that contribute to enhanced team performance, self-discovery through encounter with human difference and cultural diversity, reveling in awareness of the variety of human experience—all stand in the wings waiting to take full center stage of human economic action. People as unique individuals in a society that is continually reconfigured to fit their talents and needs is the formula of our future. Predictable certainty, standardized social behavior and comfortable conformity will all come under assault as this revolution develops. It is an oncoming tidal wave of change, a social revolution to eclipse all previous experience.

We daily move toward a new economic structure that requires a fresh foundation of attitude and assumption from its players. Competition between bosses and workers for greater autonomy and self-determination will give way to the customer's expectation of full and final say in how the service is configured. Price competition will fade in favor of greatest value in customization of the service offering. Service suppliers will strive to satisfy their customers so fully that competitors cannot even rouse their interest in alternative offerings. Customers will find such satisfaction in the service delivered that they will want the service supplier to receive a fair wage for the effort expended. Customer/service supplier relationships will be long-term, interrupted more often by change in the status of one or the other than by the lure of an alternative service relation. The foundation of antitrust laws and price-fixing prohibition in the American economy is the firm belief that the best interests of the customer are served by open, vigorous competition between product suppliers, which fosters efficiency in the use of resources and drives prices down to a minimum. It is a crude mechanism that works well in a growing, fragmented market, but loses its power as an industry consolidates in its maturity in the pursuit of greater efficiency. Large companies with substantial market share more often do what they please about pricing, constrained more by excess industry capacity than by real competition.

In a service economy, raw, unrestrained competition is inefficient for servicing the unique needs of customers. Service relationships grow and develop around the skills of the service supplier and the expectations of the customer. Some minimal competition may prevail in the earliest stages of the relationship, much like entry competition for a career position now; but once that competition is past, only discovery of a major problem in its fabric or a big change in business circumstances will disrupt it. Customers who get fully satisfactory service will not risk the cost of trying an alternative source unless there is an impelling reason.

At the foundation of this set of changes the attitudes of service suppliers must be revised and reconstituted. Pursuit of raw self-interest by players in the economy, the undisputed tenet of classical economic theory for more than two centuries, will no longer do the job. A service economy requires first and foremost that the interests of the customer be fully served. The service postulate of Rotary International, "he profits most who serves best" has stood as a guidepost for the coming service economy for more than half a century. It has done so in direct contradiction of Adam Smith's doctrine that an invisible hand of self-interest most efficiently serves the greater social and economic good.

The classical, mass commodity economic approach to competition approaches the market as if the greatest value will accrue to the customer only if those who would serve him or her are striving in every way possible to put all their competitors out of business. It is the equivalent of a suitor killing off all his competitors for his lady's hand to assure that only he will win. One may well question whether the lady's interests, beyond the raw strength of her swain, are thus best served.

In reality, constraints on competition have been incrementally added in every major world economy as history has revealed the shortsightedness of unrestrained economic competition. The competition must be kept fair for newcomers. Dominant competitors enjoy too much advantage. We know that advantage begets advantage, which ultimately begets complacency and slothfulness that, finally, only a full-scale revival of competition can cure. But open, dogfight competition is never an assurance that the best interests of the customer will be consistently met.

A service economy requires acceptance of the customer as the final judge and arbiter of value. A "take it or leave it" standardized offering that satisfies some but not all of the customer's expectations is unacceptable unless there are clear and attractive cost advantages that substantially offset the missing qualities. The quality that the customer expects includes custom adaptation of the offering to his or her preferences and needs. The commodity offering, designed to fit 50% of the needs of 50% of the population, has always been a low-quality item, acceptable because of its availability and price, not because it fully satisfied the customer's needs. Requiring the customer to retrofit and adapt to the standardized offering may be efficient in a commodity economy. In a service economy it is little better than arrogant unconcern for the quality demanded by the customer.

Gigantic hurdles stand in the path of adaptation to the coming service economy. The Western path has been by way of competition and individualism in economic enterprise. Japan has bested the United States in world economic competition as much because its economy is founded on cooperation as anything. Some viewing the Japanese economy from a Western perspective would call it "collusion" and "restraint of trade." Whatever the prejudice through which it is seen and judged, it is a high level of coordination, cooperation and adaptation to the marketplace that characterizes the Japanese economic phenomenon. America's smokestack industries were too busy battering one another competitively, then resting on their hard-earned laurels, to see what was happening across the Pacific Ocean. If only at a primitive level and supported by a rigidly hierarchical society, the Japanese understand how to give service. The United States must compete on that same ground to hold share, even in its own markets.

Westerners, inured to civil and world wars on a grand scale, would rather subdue than serve their customer. The customer as adversary is the standard attitude in today's commodity-oriented economic systems. The expert with all the answers, be he doctor, physicist, engineer or counselor, expects the customer to fit the answers, not the answers to fit the customer. We know all about things but little about people. Psychology and psychiatry still offer only limited, highly standardized commodity answers to the problems of their clients. Freud reduced it all to a question of when and how the patient repressed his or her sexual urges. Subsequent schools of psychiatry have progressed little beyond arguing whether it is sex or something else that is buried in the subconscious of man. In this modern era of self-discovery, it sometimes seems more constructive to view mankind's struggle as the battle of a tiny, frightened soul to free itself from the arbitrary limiting constraints of a commodity competitive world so that it can discover its ultimate uniqueness. A few giants in that economic struggle have risen to the top where they could impose a limited worldview on their fellow humans in an orgy of self-indulgence. In a perverse way, they have shown the way to self-fulfillment. The rest of humankind is now crowding forward along the same path.

A service economy cannot be built on a foundation of runaway ego gratification at the competitive expense of others. It must be a reciprocal process where we gratify one another's egos in the acts of service offered. We must discover the certain truths of those principles that point the way. Rotary International's guidepost that "he profits most who serves best" must become a universal axiom of the new service economy. The biblical injunction that "the first shall be last and the last shall be first" must be accepted as a fundamental truth of the new economics. Only in doing so will we surmount the hurdle of blind self-interest, that classical foundation of economic theory for two centuries that at present bars the way to a service economy future.

SELECTED BIBLIOGRAPHY

Bassett, G. A. 1991. *Management Strategies for Today's Project Shop Economy*. Westport, CT: Quorum.

Blake, R. and Mouton, J. 1984. *The Managerial Grid*, 3rd ed. Houston: Gulf.

Chase, R. B. and Aquilano, N. J. 1989. *Production and Operations Management*, 5th ed. Homewood, IL: Irwin.

Crosby, P. B. 1979. *Quality Is Free*. New York: McGraw-Hill.

Dobyns, L. and Crawford-Mason, C. 1991. *Quality or Else: The Revolution in World Business*. Boston: Houghton Mifflin.

Federal Reserve Board of Governors. "Capacity Utilization in Industrial Production, Mining and Utilities." Bulletin G-3402. Washington, DC.

Griffin, W. C. 1978. *Queueing: Basic Theory and Application*. Columbus, OH: Grid.

Love, J. F. 1986. *McDonald's: Behind the Arches*. New York: Bantam.

McLuhan, M. 1967. *The Medium Is the Massage*. New York: Random House.

Pirsig, R. M. 1976. *Zen and the Art of Motorcycle Maintenance*. New York: William Morrow.

Relman, A. S. 1992. "What Market Values Are Doing to Medicine." *The Atlantic*, 269, no. 3, pp. 98–106.

Singal, D. J. 1991. "The Other Crisis in American Education." *The Atlantic*, 268, no. 5, pp. 59–74.

Smith, Adam. 1982. *Wealth of Nations*. New York: Penguin.

Solomon, S. L. 1983. *Simulation of Waiting Lines*. Englewood Cliffs, NJ: Prentice-Hall.

Zeithaml, V. A., Parasuraman, A. and Berry, L. L. 1990. *Delivering Quality Service: Balancing Customer Perceptions and Expectations*. New York: The Free Press.

Index

About the Author

GLENN BASSETT is Professor of Management and Operations at the University of Bridgeport (Connecticut) and a management consultant. Formerly a member of the General Electric corporate staff and a pioneer in human resource computer applications there and elsewhere, he is the author of numerous articles in major media and eight books, including *Management Strategies for Today's Project Shop Economy* (Quorum, 1991).